THE
TRUTH
OF THE
GOSPEL

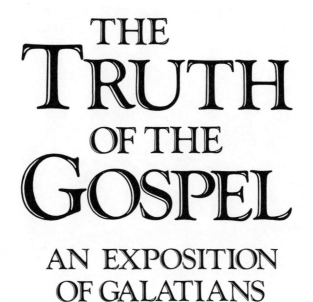

THE
TRUTH
OF THE
GOSPEL
AN EXPOSITION
OF GALATIANS

GERHARD EBELING

TRANSLATED BY
DAVID GREEN

FORTRESS PRESS   **PHILADELPHIA**

Translated from the German *Die Wahrheit des Evangeliums* (Tübingen: J. C. B. Mohr [Paul Siebeck], 1981).

Library of Congress Cataloging in Publication Data

Ebeling, Gerhard, 1912–
  The truth of the Gospel.

  Translation of: Die Wahrheit des Evangeliums.
  Includes indexes.
  1. Bible. N.T. Galatians—Commentaries. I. Title.
BS2685.3.E2313 1985   227'.406   84–47918
ISBN 0–8006–0728–7

K959H84   Printed in the United States of America   1–728

CONTENTS

CONTENTS

FOREWORD
TO THE GERMAN EDITION

"The truth of the gospel"—Paul coined this expression in the Epistle to the Galatians. Only here (2:5, 14) and—with a slight variation—in the Epistle to the Colossians (1:5) does it occur within the New Testament. We find it hard to believe that the claim of truth can be raised for something that is a matter of faith, so that the gospel, the quintessence of joy and peace, must become the subject of fierce contention. Paul was the first to grasp the gospel with the question of truth in all its rigor. His life, therefore, became a struggle on behalf of the truth of the gospel, already under attack from every quarter.

The issue is not identical with the notion of orthodoxy and certainly not with that of orthopraxy, a late substitute and competitor. Each in its own way is important, indeed indispensable, to Christianity: pure doctrine and right action. But each, again in its own way, is fundamentally questionable in the good sense of the word. For neither pure doctrine nor good works—in the medieval or modern sense—must be confused with the gospel itself. They cannot bestow the joy and peace that are the gospel's and that spring only from the gospel. Paul speaks instead of straightforwardly approaching (ὀρθοποδεῖν, Gal. 2:14) the truth of the gospel, that is, of "orthopody," to use an unusual and ugly expression this once for contrast. He means a total orientation with respect to the fundamental truth of life, the place where our life in truth wholly belongs. Therefore, obedience is the appropriate response to the truth of the gospel (Gal. 5:7; cf. Rom. 1:15), not in the sense that the law demands obedience, but in a new way, as confession is the appropriate response to faith. The gospel demands only a full, rich "yes" to grace, without evasion or deviation.

This Pauline phrase "the truth of the gospel" is an appropriate title for an exposition of Galatians. It summarizes the scope of the entire text. And it expresses the untimely topicality of our concern with the Epistle. To approach straightforwardly the truth of the gospel—that is the high calling of the theologian. But it is based on the heavy responsibility of all Christendom, called to be the salt of the earth and the light of the world, just as Galatians is addressed not to theologians but to congregations. This does not, in itself, secure a hearing for this text today, not even among theologians. Other themes than those discussed here are felt to be more urgent for the relevance of Christianity. The Epistle to the Galatians seems irrelevant to ecumenical efforts, or ministry to the Third World, or political controversies. The struggle for the truth of the gospel, waged by Paul and brought to life once more in the Reformation, is commonly considered outdated. Or it is misunderstood even by those who take the field on its behalf, so that the old Adam makes himself right at home in this kind of struggle. There is today a pervasive and exclusive interest in concrete results—changing the world or bringing inner peace. We have all the more reason, therefore, to assign this interest resolutely to its proper place, subordinate to concern for the truth of the gospel.

Apart from the broad horizon suggested by its title, this book belongs in the context of my modest attempt to recognize a general theological responsibility in an academic environment with its specialized disciplines. This responsibility led me in the past to move from the field of church history to systematic theology, although continuing my historical researches. I have long harbored the desire to dedicate myself to a work of biblical exegesis more extensive than the minimum demanded by dogmatic theology, bringing to it the focused interest of the systematic theologian. What was not uncommon in the generation before mine is unfortunately the exception today. My desire was fulfilled with the conclusion of my regular academic career at Zurich during the summer semester of 1979. Invitations to teach as a visiting professor at Tübingen (winter 1979/80) and Göttingen (winter 1980/81) gave me the opportunity to test and correct my conclusions. The relationship between my work in dogmatics and this work of New Testament exegesis, and their common hermeneutical purpose, I have discussed in an article.[1]

The Epistle to the Galatians, it might be thought, has only limited interest to the systematic theologian. In contrast to the related but primarily didactic Epistle to the Romans, and even more than the Epistles to the Corinthians with their constant allusions to specific situations, the Epistle to the Galatians contains an astonishing wealth of explicitly historical statements. It is the major source for the biography of Paul and a priceless document for the history of primitive Christianity. Thus it appears of more concern to the historian than to the systematic theologian. There is a degree of truth in this observation. This very fact nevertheless lends the Epistle to the Galatians enormous importance for systematic theology. The insight it gives us into history, into what was probably the most momentous act of decision within the primitive church, opens our eyes to the explosive force that produced this text, a force which, through this text, can explode again and again. From another perspective, the Epistle to the Romans and the Epistles to the Corinthians far surpass the Epistle to the Galatians, not only in length but in theological abundance. But what gives Galatians its special position is the unusual interpenetration of word and history we find there.

The circumstances surrounding the origin of the Epistle to the Galatians have an analog of major importance in the history of exegesis, which furnished one of my reasons for choosing this text. Of the hundreds of expositions of Galatians that have been written from the time of the early church to the present, Luther's stands out as incontestably unique.[2] The source of its spiritual power is connected with the observation that for Luther the situation from which the Epistle to the Galatians originated corresponded remarkably to the one addressed by the exegesis. The fundamental decision for which Paul fought was repeated, mutatis mutandis, in the struggle of the Reformation for the truth of the gospel. This coincidence gave the text an unusual relevance and luminosity—and not through contrived identifications ignoring the distance of centuries. The theme of Galatians, through a fundamental insight, took on new importance as the theme of the Reformation. The situation from which this text originated was grasped as a situation both illuminating and crucial for the fundamental human situation.

Thus, my work on the history of interpretation and on Luther's hermeneutics had a part in my selection of the Epistle to the Galatians. Here two seemingly contradictory points of view are confirmed. On the one hand, Luther's exegesis cannot be repeated, springing as it does from the immediate situation. The source of its spiritual power cannot be taken on loan. On the other, his exegesis has rarely been equaled and never surpassed in its treatment of the difference between law and gospel and their critical significance at all times for the fundamental situation of all people. This theological meatiness provides an unusual opportunity to practice one's own exegesis. But the systematic theologian can be a successful exegete only by taking the trouble to use all the appropriate philological and historical methods. Here I have learned from many exegetes, past and present,[3] but most of all from my friend Hans Dieter Betz at Chicago, who in the spring of 1979 let me read his outstanding commentary on Galatians in proof. He later read my exposition, so different in form, and provided me with critical notes. For this service I am most grateful to him, while not wishing to make him share responsibility for everything included in or omitted from my exegesis.

The obvious and, by present standards, unforgivable omissions include the almost total absence of bibliographical notes, of historical and philological detail, of references to points where I have followed or agreed with others, as well as to critical definitions of my own position within the broad stream of exegetical endeavors, which flows from many sources. I have deliberately chosen another course than that of a formal commentary. I cannot compete with professional exegetes, nor would I wish to, although it is certainly my hope to suggest to them some new ideas. My attention has been fixed on a broader circle of readers, who might be well served if the focus of biblical exegesis were shifted back to intensive interpretation of content so that they could see something of the general theological process of understanding. Not a few of my listeners were especially receptive to this approach; their number, I am happy to say, always included several nontheologians.

This concentration on the crucial questions of substance raised by the text, the desire to address an audience not made up entirely of specialists, and the determination not to do so at the price of lowering the level of discussion present a dilemma. The task of exegesis cannot be carried out properly without constant reference to the original text. But this requirement puts a roadblock in the way of potential readers. In order to avoid the usual unsatisfactory distinction between an exclusively scholarly commentary and a more popular exegesis for the laity who do not know Greek, I have added transliterations and translations to the Greek words and phrases which are cited with some frequency. This is obviously a makeshift; its more or less consistent application also raises numerous problems requiring discretion. Despite the obvious reservations, I have accepted the consequent inelegance. It is a sober fact that even theologians, students as well as pastors, who have passed their Greek examinations are not uncommonly deficient in their acquaintance with the Greek language, so that even for them the juxtaposition of the Greek and its translation may be welcome and accustom them to the original text. At the same time, I would like to think that I am not wholly wrong in assuming that there are some among the laity so serious about their study of the biblical text that they will accept the need for extraordinary efforts. They will be grateful for this bit of help over the language barrier. It is possible, then, that theologians and nontheologians may join in a common exegetical endeavor.

Among the signs that this is not a commentary in the formal sense is the uneven length of the discussion. Originally occasioned by the requirements of lecturing, this formal deficiency could not be corrected satisfactorily even with revisions. The treatment from its very inception had a certain inner rhythm, an alternation that was not accidental between detailed analysis and brief comment. In the latter part of the Epistle, the interpretation could go more rapidly without skipping essentials than at the beginning or in the middle. I have the impression that at times this succinctness has made certain things clearer. Because of the nature of the work, it would hardly have represented any particular improvement to go into detail, say, in chapters five and six for the sake of balance. On the other hand, abbreviation in the initial chapters would have been even more contrary to the intent of this publication.

Hans Georg and Georg Siebeck have taken their usual care in the publication of this work. Rosmarie Niggli produced the fair copy. Friederike Willenbrock assisted with the proofreading and produced the subject index, while Beatrice Hoffmann prepared the index of biblical passages. My friend and colleague Walter Mostert also read a set of proofs and furnished valuable suggestions. I wish to express my thanks to them and to all the others whose participation encouraged me in the preparation and publication of this work.

Gregory the Great coined a metaphor to summarize what he had learned in converse with the Bible: "Scriptura sacra est fluvius, ut ita dixerim, in quo et agnus ambulet et elephas natet."[4] ("Sacred scripture is as it were a river through which a lamb may wade, but in which an elephant must swim.") The truth of this statement has been confirmed for me many times over in my study of the Epistle to the Galatians.

Zurich, June 1, 1981   GERHARD EBELING

Galatians 1—2
RECOLLECTION

The Apostolic Greeting

1:1–5

1 Paul an apostle—not from men nor even through human mediation, but through Jesus Christ and through God Father, who raised him from the dead—
2 and all the brothers who are with me, to the congregations in Galatia.
3 Grace to you and peace from God our Father and from the Lord Jesus Christ,
4 who sacrificed himself for our sins to deliver us from the present evil age, according to the will of the one who is God and our Father.
5 To him be the glory for ever and ever. Amen.

A letter can be a moving document. How moving it is depends, of course, on both sender and recipient, as well as on its contents, which is contingent on both. But the mere fact of being a letter establishes it as a personal document related to a specific situation. A letter is therefore pervaded by life in a very special way. Letters are said to take the place of oral communication. This is true in the sense that letters are superfluous when the parties are together. It would be fatal if two people were to communicate only in writing when together. Thus, when communication reaches the height of intensity, a desire for personal contact appears in letters. Written contact clearly cannot replace oral exchange between two people in each other's immediate presence. And so we read in Gal. 4:20: "I wish I were present with you now so that I could speak to you with troubled voice, for I am at my wits' end on your account."

But to describe a letter as just a substitute for personal contact does not do the phenomenon justice. A letter does indeed have the full force of a communicative transaction in which one person comes to another in a specific situation, speaks to him and touches him inwardly, shares something with him or comes himself to share the other's concerns. In one way or another, the two parties together represent the nexus of a single comprehensive transaction. A letter has, as such, the nature of an event, not just with reference to the act of composition and the act of receiving, but above all through the transaction that takes place between the two parties by virtue of what is communicated. Whether something is promised or denied, whether desires are expressed or satisfied, whether some message is communicated or the writer in some sense communicates himself—all are mere variations and possibilities, often occurring simultaneously, in an act of communication through which an interpersonal transaction reaches the critical stage.

A letter even has some advantages over direct personal contact. The sender must first of all make himself present to the person addressed from the distance of his absence. As a consequence, aspects of the parties' shared relationships and circumstances, obvious and unnoticed facts, suppressed or repressed particulars, may come to be perceived across the distance and find verbal expression, thanks to the distance and the need to overcome it. Thus a letter can suddenly give utterance to what would otherwise be only vaguely sensed or remain wholly unconscious. In harmony or strident dissonance, notes are sounded that would scarcely be heard in physical presence. A shared love, for instance, can grow in depth or else find its genuineness put to the test when a temporary separation provides the opportunity for letter writing. How much more can sometimes be said in a letter than in oral interchange, which, because of immediate proximity in space and time, can so easily lack the force and breadth that transcend the mere moment.

Even the most extreme deficiency of a letter in the context of a communicative transaction, the silence of the person addressed, points up a unique advantage of a letter. A letter has been called a bisected conversation. The point is well taken. For this reason, scholarly editions of letters always strive to assemble an integrated correspondence in its entirety. But even a single letter cannot be looked upon as an isolated document; it is a letter meant for the addressee and read by his own eyes; it evokes a reaction, which may be mental or may take the form of an answering letter. Thus we are actually dealing with an ongoing conversation, albeit one at times interrupted by extended pauses. The effect can be detrimental but also productive of concentration. And when a letter becomes literary and finds readers beyond its original addressee, its open-endedness is especially valuable.

To illustrate, using Galatians as an example: of course, it is regrettable that—apart from the fact that the letter was preserved and handed down within the Christian community—we cannot find or even infer the slightest trace of any reaction. There is no hint of what effect the letter had or what followed. But in the study of history this very circumstance exerts a special fascination; we can observe a small segment in full illumination but surrounded by utter darkness, as in a Rembrandt. The historian commonly does not give enough weight to the advantage he has, because what was once an unknown future has meanwhile become past and has become a matter of knowledge, at least in part. The structure of the future turned past can be sensed even when the path to observation is blocked.

When the historian has before him a letter whose reception is totally unknown, he is in fact dealing with a torso of communication, a bisected conversation, a mere fragment of a nexus of events. At the same time, however, the epistolary form compels him to realize that here all are addressed in a still open situation. If such a text then speaks through the significance of its subject matter to an unintended reader as an equally involved recipient, the situation addressed by the letter opens, as it were, once more to the future. The modern reader is drawn, to some extent, into what is still an open situation and called upon to commit himself. This is what makes it so attractive to read letters of a different age addressed to different people: the reader comes to share in other situations and other communications and thus expands the horizon of his own experience.

Reference to the potential expansion of a letter's readership introduces another advantage of a letter over oral expression. A letter does not fade into silence in the moment of speaking, echoing at most in the memory; the written form of the letter preserves the communicating word. The recipient can read it again and think about it at leisure. He can also show it to others, share it with them, and ask them their reaction.

Finally, as we have already suggested, a letter can become literary, even if it was not originally so intended. An ordinary private letter, when written by an important figure, can subsequently take on enormous human and historical interest, especially if the author possessed great inner vitality and linguistic power. Of course, private letters are sometimes also written with an eye to their future collection and publication so that they are literary compositions. Or the epistolary form may be chosen as a mere fiction to lend vitality to the presentation of certain ideas or to claim assumed authority through a pseudonym. Besides private letters, there have always been official letters that played an important role and so have been preserved as historical documents.

In contrast to the situation in the Old Testament, letters have outstanding importance in the New Testament. Not a single book of the Old Testament is a letter, but of the twenty-seven documents constituting the New Testament canon, twenty-one have the form of a letter. And two additional documents, the Revelation of John and the Acts of the Apostles, include several letters. In contrast to the pseudonymous and purely literary letters that are also found in the New Testament, the genuinely Pauline letters are also genuine letters addressed by Paul to specific people in specific situations. Even the Epistle to Philemon is not a private letter in the strict sense. Other names appear along with the actual sender and recipient. Even the personal matter of the runaway slave Onesimus does not permit the reader to ignore the status of Paul, who intervenes on his behalf, or the fact that a Christian congregation gathers in the house of Philemon. All the other Pauline letters are official in nature, to the extent that the relationship of the apostle to certain congregations can be called *(cum grano salis)* official.

The only literary form found in the New Testament, apart from the three characteristic forms of gospel, acts, and apocalypse, is that of the letter. This fact is more than outwardly informative with respect to the situation of primitive Christianity. It shows, above all, what genre it was natural for the Christian message to use as soon as any need was felt for written expression. In its original form, the Christian message is an oral message. Only the need to actualize the relationship of the apostle to the various congregations despite spatial separation created the necessity of written expression, which quite naturally took the form of a letter in place of oral expression. The predominance of letters among the New Testament documents may even be due ultimately to the model of the Pauline letter. Because Paul's missionary activity was so uniquely intensive and extensive, the letter came to be an indispensable instrument. And thanks to the unique weight Paul was able to give his letters, the literary form of the letter became a model encouraging imitation.

Because the genuine Pauline letters were, without exception, created by specific circumstances, they are commonly called occasional writings. But this expression needs to be more closely defined. The official character of the Pauline letters undoubtedly secured for them from the very beginning a significance far transcending the historical moment and the congregation addressed. It is reasonable to assume that his letters were immediately copied, circulated, and collected. But the positive element in the notion of an occasional writing also needs to be emphasized. Their connection with specific occasions, circumstances, and conflicts gives to Paul's theological statements an unusual specificity. They reveal how specific problems not only occasioned them but also were dealt with authoritatively by them.

We do not possess the autograph of any Pauline letter. It is not totally fantastic to contemplate such a possibility. Many ancient papyrus letters are preserved in their original form, albeit under certain geographical and climatic conditions and in consequence of certain external circumstances that cannot be assumed for the originals of the Pauline letters. We shall only note in passing that, despite many variants in detail, the textual tradition of these letters is, on the whole, outstanding. The major Pauline letters provide much grist for the mill of literary criticism, but this is not true of Galatians. It is literarily well composed in its markedly situational form; its inward agitation is a seamless whole.

The epistolary form of the ancient world exhibits in its basic structure a schema that also appears in Paul. The *prescript* gives the name of the sender and that of the recipient, and adds a *salutation* formula. Then comes the body of the letter, concluding with a *postscript*. The *postscript* includes another *salutation*, a greeting from others if applicable, and sometimes a date. The date is not part of the regular form and is not found in the Pauline letters, so that we must rely on inference and conjecture for their date and place of composition. Without entering upon the subtle problems of Pauline chronology, I shall content myself with the statement that Galatians was probably written in the year 55 or 56 from Ephesus or (more likely) on the way from Ephesus through Macedonia to Corinth, in other words, during the so-called third missionary journey of the apostle, rather close to the date of the letters to the Corinthians and before Romans. This is the conclusion we arrive at if we rely on the itinerary of Acts for a framework. If, however, we take a more skeptical attitude toward this itinerary, as there is reason to do, we will be more hesitant to locate the origin of Galatians so precisely in terms of place and time. In any case, the letter can probably be dated within the period between 50 and 55.

We must also take into account a further circumstance, which is easily overlooked. We must picture the letter as being brought by Christians from Paul's entourage, even though they are not mentioned explicitly in this letter. Through them the recipients would have received more details about the circumstances under which Paul composed the letter. We may further assume that they brought additional oral messages.

The ancient epistolary form is drawn on in such a way as to give it an unmistakably Christian form. This is visible in all its elements: in the sender's extended description of himself in the *prescript*, in the epithets applied to the addressee, and in an alteration of the *salutation*; likewise in the novel formulation of the concluding blessing and in some other additions in the *postscript*.

The simplest form of a Pauline epistolary *prescript* is found, probably not by accident, in the earliest of Paul's letters that has been preserved—First Thessalonians: "Paul, Silvanus, and Timothy, to the congregation of the Thessalonians, grounded in God the Father and the Lord Jesus Christ. Grace and peace to you." This letter, written from Corinth, is usually dated in the year 50 or 51, only some five years before the traditional date of Galatians. There is no further elaboration of Paul's name; the names of his coworkers and companions Silvanus and Timothy are included, likewise without predication. The congregation of the Thessalonians, however, has its nature described more precisely, beyond what would be conveyed by the mere term ἐκκλησία (*ekklēsia*, congregation): it is the *ekklēsia* that has its origin and existence, its ground of faith and its hope, in God the Father and the Lord Jesus Christ. The *salutation* formula also exhibits a Christian wording: χάρις ὑμῖν καὶ εἰρήνη (*charis hymin kai eirēnē*, grace to you and peace). This is the briefest statement of the formula; in Paul's later letters he always uses a fixed form indicating the source and nature of the promised χάρις (*charis*, grace) and εἰρήνη (*eirēnē*, peace) ἀπὸ θεοῦ πατρὸς ἡμῶν καὶ κυρίου 'Ιησοῦ Χριστοῦ (*apo theou patros hēmōn kai kyriou Iēsou Christou*, from God our Father and from the Lord Jesus Christ). The sender's cordial relationship with the congregation in Thessalonica may account for his omission of his own titles. The short form of the *salutation* may likewise be due to the earlier mention of God the Father and Jesus Christ together in the description of the congregation. It would be reasonable not to repeat this statement of the congregation's origin in the *salutation*. The more likely explanation, however, is that in the *prescript* of the earliest Pauline letter we can observe the development of the Pauline *prescript* form.

The *salutation* formula proper, as we have said, later took on a fixed, invariate form. The other parts of the Pauline *prescript*, however, can vary greatly. This observation suggests that while the *salutation*, as the spiritual center of the *prescript*, takes on liturgical character, nowhere else in the introductions to his letters does Paul use mere routine phrases. In each situation he brings forth appropriate forms of expression with the utmost inner vitality. Therefore, the *prescript* of a Pauline letter by itself constitutes an essential part of the letter's content. His *prescripts* show Paul to be a most gifted and innovative correspondent. Further details will emerge from our interpretation of the *prescript* to Galatians in comparison with the other Pauline letters.

As in all his letters, Paul refers to himself here by his Hellenized Roman name. We know his Jewish name *Sha'ul*, Hellenized to Σαῦλος (*Saulos*), only from Acts. Paul's father may have given this name to his son as a scion of the tribe of Benjamin (Phil. 3:5) in remembrance of its most distinguished representative, King Saul. Paul probably bore both names from the beginning. Acts 13:9 ("Saul, who is also called Paul") has led many to the conclusion that there was a change of name, possibly associated with Paul's conversion, so that Saul turned into Paul. But this is out of the question. The situation here differs from that of Jesus' disciple Simon bar Jonah, to whom the Aramaic name Kepha was given as an honorific—whether by Jesus himself or by the primitive community may be left open. This name was then used in its Hellenized form Κηφᾶς (*Kēphās*) (almost without exception by Paul) or translated into Greek as Πέτρος (*Petros*).

To his personal name Paul adds the title "apostle." As we have already seen, only in 1 Thess. 1:1 is the title omitted. In Phlm. 1:1 (a special case), Paul introduces himself as δέσμιος Χριστπῦ 'Ιησοῦ (*desmios Christou Iēsou*, a prisoner of Christ Jesus). And in Phil. 1:1, Paul and Timothy together are referred to as δοῦλοι Χριστοῦ 'Ιησοῦ (*douloi Christou Iēsou*, servants of Christ Jesus). In the four other letters that are undoubtedly Pauline (Romans, 1 and 2 Corinthians, Galatians), the title "apostle" is used. In the Deutero-Pauline corpus this title is also used everywhere except in the *prescript* of 2 Thessalonians, which has been conformed to the designation of the sender of 1 Thessalonians. In Rom. 1:1, the title "apostle" is preceded by the designation δοῦλος Χριστοῦ 'Ιησοῦ (*doulos Christou Iēsou*, a servant of Christ Jesus); the same usage appears once in the Deutero-Paulines: Titus 1:1, which, however, reads δοῦλος θεοῦ (*doulos theou*, a servant of God).

The absence of any title applied to the sender in 1 Thessalonians raises the question of whether the special relationship between Paul and this congregation is sufficient explanation. In 1 Thess. 2:7, Paul reminds the community explicitly that he did not bring his apostolic authority to bear among them. But it is also worth considering whether at the relatively early date of this letter there was any need to insist explicitly on a claim to apostolic authority in the face of attacks. The question may be left open.

With respect to Paul's use of titles, our observations have so far made two points clear:

1. Paul can sometimes share the self-designation δοῦλος Χριστοῦ 'Ιησοῦ (*doulos Christou Iēsou*, a servant of Christ Jesus) with someone else, although even in such cases his name takes precedence. Even so, the use of this title in apposition with the name of the sender conveys more than just what is true of every Christian. The choice of words may suggest an overtone of humility but no renunciation of authority. This is not necessarily a contradiction. Paul's emphatic designation of himself as δοῦλος Χριστοῦ 'Ιησοῦ associates what is true, in fact, of every Christian with the special office through which Paul exercises his sense of belonging to Jesus Christ. There is an echo here of the Old Testament notion of the servant of God, now applied to Paul's relationship to Jesus Christ. Even in the Old Testament this expression could be used in two ways: it could refer to all those belonging to the people of God or to the people of God as a whole, but it could also refer to one called to special service and therefore occupying an outstanding position among the people of God.

2. Paul claims the title "apostle" above all others. In Galatians, in whose *prescript* the title "apostle" is especially emphasized, only later (v. 10) do

we find the self-designation Χριστοῦ δοῦλος (*Christou doulos*, Christ's servant). But even in Rom. 1:1, where the title "servant" comes first, the primary emphasis is on the title "apostle." He does not share it with any of his fellow workers. He can use the title δοῦλος Χριστοῦ Ἰησοῦ to include himself among them; but when he calls himself an apostle, he is clearly setting himself apart from his companions, although they are intimately associated with him by being called ἀδελφοί (*adelphoi*, brothers: 1 Cor. 1:1; 2 Cor. 1:1; Gal. 1:2).

This is not the place for a detailed discussion of the complex problem of what the title "apostle" means. I will merely set up some guidelines. For the time of Paul it would be wrong to assume that there was a definitively formed notion of an apostle. Quite apart from the controversy over Paul's apostolate, the use of the term was apparently fluid. In Paul's own writings we find alongside his strict interpretation of the title an extended notion of the apostolate, according to which an apostle is the official messenger representing a congregation (e.g., 2 Cor. 8:23; Phil. 2:25; probably also Rom. 16:7). This is the sense in which Paul and Barnabas are termed apostles in Acts 14:4, 14: they are delegates of the congregation at Antioch.

On the other hand, Paul presupposes a strict definition of the apostolate, according to which the apostles constitute a narrowly circumscribed group of those who have been called through an appearance of the risen Lord, a circle to which Paul has been added as its last member (1 Cor. 15:8–9; Gal. 1:17). It is no longer possible to determine who in Paul's view made up this group of apostles in the strict sense, apart from Peter and probably also John. It was certainly not for him coextensive with the Twelve, another group within the primitive community of which he was aware (1 Cor. 15:5; cf. v. 7). Paul had been added to the group as an outsider; he was, furthermore, the first to engage in theological reflection on his own self-understanding. It is, therefore, probably thanks to him that the concept of the apostolate became the subject of theological reflection because it was the occasion of a bitter controversy. More was involved than recognition of Paul's own apostolate. Paul himself rejected the apostolic claims of others as being the claims of false apostles (2 Cor. 11:13) and—speaking ironically—of "superapostles" (2 Cor. 11:5; 12:11).

The Jewish legal institution of the *shaliach*, a plenipotentiary representative, probably stands behind the primitive Christian term "apostle." But various other influences helped shape its content. It is therefore dubious whether the term can, in fact, be derived from a single root.

If we restrict ourselves to the formulations of the Pauline *prescripts*, the following definition is constitutive of an apostle in the strict sense: he has been specially called by the will of God through Jesus Christ to proclaim the gospel, which is Jesus Christ himself. The corresponding formula is κλητὸς ἀπόστολος Χριστοῦ ᾽Ιησοῦ διὰ θελήματος θεοῦ (*klētos apostolos Christou Iēsou dia thelēmatos theou*, called to be an apostle of Christ Jesus through the will of God; 1 Cor. 1:1; without *klētos*, 2 Cor. 1:1; cf. also Eph. 1:1; Col. 1:1; 2 Tim. 1:1). The phrase ἀπόστολος Χριστοῦ ᾽Ιησοῦ (*apostolos Christou Iēsou*, apostle of Christ Jesus) should probably be understood primarily as a genitive of the author in the sense that Jesus Christ is the empowering author and originator of the apostolate. But it already implies the content of the apostle's mission, the nature of his commission and of his authority. This content, the substance of the gospel, is nothing other than Jesus Christ himself. This double aspect, the notion that Jesus Christ is both mandator and mandate, is developed by Paul in Rom. 1:1–5. The focus is on the fact that Jesus Christ is the content of the gospel which Paul has been called through Jesus Christ to preach as an apostle.

In Galatians, too, the apostle's self-introduction is given a further interpretation. It is substantially shorter than in Romans. There is apparently no development at all of the content of the apostolate. Instead, the fundamental formula κλητὸς ἀπόστολος Χριστοῦ ᾽Ιησοῦ διὰ θελήματος θεοῦ (*klētos apostolos Christou Iēsou dia thelēmatos theou*, called to be an apostle through the will of God) receives a polemic interpretation. Even here the basic structure remains clearly recognizable: the apostolate comes through Jesus Christ and God the Father.[5] This can be interpreted on the basis of the self-introduction formula in Corinthians as follows: apostleship comes through the call of Jesus Christ and the will of God, which expresses itself in that call. For the genitive phrase ἀπόστολος Χριστοῦ ᾽Ιησοῦ (*apostolos Christou Iēsou*, apostle of Christ Jesus) and the appended prepositional definition διὰ θελήματος θεοῦ (*dia thelēmatos theou*, through the will of God), Gal. 1:1 substitutes a double prepositional phrase modifying ἀπόστολος: διὰ ᾽Ιησοῦ Χριστοῦ καὶ θεοῦ πατρός (*dia Iēsou Christou kai theou patros*). The change of construction was occasioned by the preceding negative definition. It, too, could have been expressed by means of a genitive: ἀπόστολος οὐκ ἀνθρώπων, ἀλλὰ ᾽Ιησοῦ Χριστοῦ (*apostolos ouk anthrōpōn, alla Iēsou Christou*, not a human apostle, but a Jesus Christ apostle). But the distinction is made clearer when the explanation is given in terms of a preposition like ἀπό (*apo*, from) or διά (*dia*, through) or παρά (*para*, away from) rather than a simple genitive phrase.

The result is twofold. First, the fact that the call of the apostle was an event is expressed more clearly. Paul returns to this point right away in v. 12. The prepositional construction emphasizes the participial sense of ἀπόστολος (*apostolos*, apostle) as derived from ἀποστέλλειν (*apostellein*, send): one who has been sent. The explanation of what makes an apostle an apostle is given by reference to an event that has taken place. Analogous to the calls of the Old Testament prophets, apostleship is established by a call event. Second, use of the prepositional phrase allows more room for exploring various nuances of the antithesis. Instead of the mere statement ἀπόστολος οὐκ ἀνθρώπων (*apostolos ouk anthrōpōn*, not a human apostle), we can have variations: ἀπόστολος οὐκ ἀπ᾽ ἀνθρώπων οὐδὲ δι᾽ ἀνθρώπου (*apostolos ouk ap' anthrōpōn oude di' anthrōpou*, an apostle not from men nor even through human intervention). This form of expression admittedly does not serve the cause of clarity, but rather raises substantial problems of interpretation.

The formulation exhibits a threefold differentiation:[6] first, the change of preposition from ἀπό (*apo*, from) to διά (*dia*, through); second, the change of number from plural to singular; and third, a gradation of the negative through οὐκ (*ouk*, not) and οὐδέ (*oude*, and not, not even), which may express a special emphasis in contrast to an equative neither-nor (οὔτε–οὔτε, *oute–oute*).

These observations are not totally persuasive. In v. 12, the same situation is described by means of a different preposition, παρά (*para*, away from), and by it alone. In addition, v. 12 uses only the singular παρὰ ἀνθρώπου (*para anthrōpou*, from or through the intervention of a human being). And when we turn to the form of negation, although the change has its parallels in the account of the call of Amos, which could also be considered parallel in subject matter, the significance of the parallel is not immediately clear. The LXX text of Amos 7:14 clearly intends no rhetorical emphasis in saying οὐκ ἤμην προφήτης ἐγὼ οὐδὲ υἱὸς προφήτου (*ouk ēmēn prophētēs egō oude hyios prophētou*, I was not a prophet nor was I a son [or disciple] of a prophet)—Amos was in fact a shepherd and a dresser of sycamores; but—and this corresponds to Paul's ἀλλὰ διὰ Ἰησοῦ Χριστοῦ καὶ θεοῦ πατρός (*alla dia Iēsou Christou kai theou patros*, rather through Jesus Christ and through God the Father)—the Lord took Amos from following the flock and commissioned him. The variation in the negative (I was not a prophet, nor even a prophet's disciple) may not be without some substantial distinction, but there is no special importance attached to it. We could accordingly find in Gal. 1:1 nothing more than the rhetorical device of parallelism so that the double expression "not from men nor even through a man" would basically be saying the same thing in two different ways.

Such a weakening and leveling interpretation, however, is itself not convincing. At the beginning of a letter so highly charged in style and content, in an antithetical explication of his own apostolic authority clearly placed so emphatically at the start, Paul can hardly be employing purely stylistic variation. Of the indications of a differentiation mentioned above, the change from plural to singular is most likely to be significant. This is supported by the following observation. Paul may have intended a chiastic construction.[7] The phrase οὐκ ἀπ᾽ ἀνθρώπων (*ouk ap' anthrōpōn*, not from men) would then be the counterpart to διὰ θεοῦ πατρός (*dia theou patros*, through God Father), and οὐδὲ δι᾽ ἀνθρώπου (*oude di' anthrōpou*, nor even through human intervention [lit. through a man]) would be the counterpart to διὰ Ἰησοῦ Χριστοῦ (*dia Iēsou Christou*, through Jesus Christ). In this case we would have a double contrast: the objective antithesis "not from men but from God," and the personal antithesis "not through a man but through Jesus Christ." This corresponds precisely to the pattern of vv. 11–12. The objective contrast between human and divine origin with its implicit contrast between human and divine authority is taken up once more in v. 11 by the statement about the gospel preached by Paul: ὅτι οὐκ ἔστιν κατὰ ἄνθρωπον (*hoti ouk estin kata anthrōpon*, that it is not according to man). The personal antithesis reappears in v. 12 in the form: οὐδὲ . . . παρὰ ἀνθρώπου . . . ἀλλὰ δι᾽ ἀποκαλύψεως Ἰησοῦ Χριστοῦ (*oude . . . para anthrōpou . . . alla di' apokalypseōs Iēsou Christou*, and not . . . from man . . . but through a revelation of Jesus Christ). We note in passing that here, too, the same distinction reappears in the negations: οὐκ – οὐδέ (*ouk – oude*, not, and not).

What may we conclude? The target of these negations has been the object of much puzzlement. The polemical purpose is beyond doubt; the debate concerns the nature of the target. Of course we might have here merely a very general assurance that Paul's concerns—his gospel and his apostolate—are of divine origin and have divine authority. But why should Paul find it necessary to emphasize this so heavily at the beginning of his letter? The obvious reason is the situation in Galatia. If all that were involved were a general questioning of his apostolic authority, a simple assurance would suffice: it comes not from man but from God, and is therefore not human but divine. It is, therefore, reasonable to suppose that the other antithesis, "not through a man, but through Jesus Christ," refers to a specific concrete crisis involving the problem of authority. Two possibilities suggest themselves. According to the first theory, Paul's criticism of his opponents would dominate; according to the second, the opponents' criticism of Paul. In the first case, Paul would be distinguishing himself from his opponents and accusing them of relying on human authority, while he had divine authority on his side. In the second, Paul would be defending himself against the charge that the authority he enjoyed was only human and derivative. The context of the letter makes the second possibility more likely.

Thus, everything centers on the interpretation of the phrase δι' ἀνθρώπου (*di' anthrōpou*, through a man). Let us assume that Paul's apostleship was suspected of being the work of man, a human bauble (ἀπ' ἀνθρώπων: v. 1; κατὰ ἄνθρωπον: v. 11). To what extent could this suspicion be based on a man's having played the decisive role in determining his apostleship (δι' ἀνθρώπου: v. 1; παρὰ ἀνθρώπου: v. 12)? If, however, we are dealing here only with Paul's criticism of his opponents, the interpretation would not be difficult. This would obviously involve people who appealed to a man as their authority and the source of their own credentials. Such a man could be one of the first apostles, or one of the δοκοῦντες (*dokountes*, men of repute) or στῦλοι (*styloi*, pillars), to whom Paul alludes in Gal. 2:2, 6, 9. An interpretation that goes back to the early church sees in οὐδὲ δι' ἀνθρώπου (*oude di' anthrōpou*, nor even through a man) a reference to the earthly Jesus: Paul's opponents boasted of Jesus' personal call, not of course with reference to themselves, but with reference to those within the primitive community to whom they looked for authority.

But what about the other possibility, the insinuation that Paul himself was dependent on human authority? The most immediate interpretation would be that Paul's true apostleship was denied precisely because he had not belonged to Jesus and received his call from him before Easter. By saying, "not through a man but through Jesus Christ," Paul would be answering this charge pointedly: such derivation from the earthly Jesus would amount to deriving apostleship from a man. He, however, had been called by the risen and exalted Lord, just as even those who had been Jesus' disciples during his lifetime had not become apostles in the strict sense until the appearances of the risen Lord. But something like the following is also conceivable: Along with this criticism that he lacked legitimation by the pre-Easter Jesus, Paul was also charged with having received his apostleship second hand. He was dependent on the original apostles and their recognition, or was nothing more than a disciple of those who had initiated him into Christianity at Antioch, or was merely the agent of the Antioch community.

Whether and how we are to decide among these various interpretations depends on further clarification furnished by exegesis of the letter. Possibly a definitive elucidation will turn out to be unattainable. For now, we can say this by way of summary: in his introduction of himself as an apostle, Paul guards against the idea that his office is a human, rather than a divine, concern. The occasion for such a defense is clear: his claim to have been called directly by the risen Lord had run into opposition. He found himself open to the same charge that he, mutatis mutandis, had to make against his opponents: dependence on human authority.

Now the way in which Paul here defends his apostleship includes a kerygmatic element, in the form of a participle that he adds to his mention of God the Father: it is God the Father who raised Jesus Christ from the dead. This is the only time Paul mentions the resurrection of Jesus Christ in the Epistle to the Galatians. This does not mean that the resurrection was considered unimportant but rather that the preaching of the resurrection was not disputed in the Galatian controversy, at least not directly. For this reason it is not introduced here for its own sake with a polemic intent. It has the character of a tradition formula without further addition, such as we find elsewhere in Paul. The passive form, "Christ has been raised from the dead" (Rom. 4:25; 6:4, 9; 7:4; 8:34; 1 Cor. 15 *passim*; 2 Cor. 5:15), does not differ in substance from the active form, which is used here and with roughly equal frequency elsewhere in Paul: "God has raised Christ from the dead" (e.g., Rom. 4:24; 8:11; 10:9; 1 Cor. 6:14; 15:15; 2 Cor. 4:14). The choice of the active was due to syntactic considerations and therefore has no special importance. Resurrection from the dead is, in any case, an event whose effective subject can only be God.

Even when we read in the Bible that some who had died were restored to temporal life by certain individuals, we cannot ignore the fact that this takes place according to God's will and through the power vouchsafed by him. The raising of the dead is not a human matter, certainly not a matter of the dead individuals themselves. Sometimes, it is true, the Bible speaks intransitively of a resurrection of the dead, most often in the noun phrase ἀνάστασις νεκρῶν (*anastasis nekrōn*, resurrection of the dead). But this is clearly meant only as a resurrection effected by God, not as an independent resurrection, an "uprising" of the dead. Above all, when the reference is to the resurrection of the dead in the eschatological sense—and that is the only sense in which the resurrection of Jesus Christ can be spoken of—God is the only possible effective subject, whether mentioned explicitly or not. There is simply no way to speak atheistically of an eschatological resurrection of the dead. For Paul, therefore, the concept of God is linked almost by definition with the expectation that the dead will be raised (cf. Rom. 4:17: God is ὁ ζῳοποιῶν τοὺς νεκρούς *[ho zōopoiōn tous nekrous]*, the one who gives life to the dead). This follows from an understanding of how God and death are related in the Bible. Beyond this general observation, however, there is the concrete instance of our knowledge of what God did in the case of a specific dead man, the crucified Jesus.

The way in which God the Father is here defined more precisely by reference to the eschatological raising of the dead does not compete with his characterization as creator, which is implicit in his being called "Father." Instead, the ideas of creation and new creation are interwoven in the statement that God addresses as existent the things that do not exist, thus giving them life (Rom. 4:17). There is, nevertheless, good reason for Paul not to state that he is an apostle through Jesus Christ and through God the Father, who created heaven and earth. The connection between Jesus Christ and God the Father, who is the creator, is actualized in the raising of Jesus Christ from the dead. Likewise, the connection between Paul's being an apostle and God's being creator is actualized in the event of preaching the gospel, inaugurated by the resurrection of Jesus Christ from the dead. Faith in God the Father is not supplanted but rather incorporated and applied to the concrete situation of sinful existence in this world. The notion of creation is not only preserved but expressed with greater force and clarity.

Such considerations make one thing plain: in this passage we are not dealing with a superfluous addition, a kind of pious window dressing intended to furnish evidence of orthodoxy. That Jesus Christ rose from the dead is a confessional statement that the apostle and his Galatian opponents seem to share undisputedly. In this context, however, it has an important function in the debate that shapes the Epistle to the Galatians from beginning to end. The reference at this point to the resurrection of Jesus Christ is intended to illustrate the connection that exists between the call of Paul to be an apostle and the will of God.

In the basic formula expressing Paul's apostleship, "an apostle of Christ Jesus through the will of God" (1 Cor. 1:1; 2 Cor. 1:1; cf. also Rom. 1:1), the phrase διὰ θελήματος θεοῦ (dia thelēmatos theou, through God's will) is explained most immediately on the basis of the idea of divine election. Paul also refers to this idea in Gal. 1:15. But in v. 1 he sees an even closer bond between his call and the will of God, if it is possible to use a comparative in this context. The two are linked first of all in Paul's own experience, in his historically datable call through Jesus Christ and his eternal election through God. But what is more important, the two elements, the call to be an apostle and the will of God, are linked in God's very act. For what God has done in the person of Jesus Christ and what he has done in the person of Paul go together. This goes beyond merely saying that it is the same God who is the agent of both actions. The emphasis instead lies here: it is the God who raised Jesus Christ from the dead who also called Paul to be an apostle. The God who set the progress of the gospel in motion by raising Jesus Christ from the dead is himself the cause of Paul's being called to this service. The text, in fact, demands a more forceful interpretation: since Paul has been called by the risen Lord, the power of God, who raises from the dead, stands behind his apostleship. The raising of Jesus Christ from the dead is not a mere spark igniting a train of events that runs its course by virtue of other forces. This eschatological event has instead entered into the legitimation of the apostle himself and determined the nature of his apostleship.

It will, therefore, not suffice to conclude, from this appended mention of the raising of Jesus Christ, simply that it was the risen Lord who called Paul. Even if the text touches on the question of what meaning discipleship with the earthly Jesus has for the office of apostle, it would be inappropriate to cite the raising of Jesus as a counterargument. By universal consensus the Easter event is determinative for the preaching of Christ. If any polemical distinction at all is intended, it is a difference in degree: Paul can appeal only to the risen Lord for his call to apostleship, while his opponents bring to bear the earthly companionship with Jesus enjoyed by their authorities as an additional element of legitimation. But according to Paul, the only legitimation that counts is that of the risen Lord. It would therefore constrict Paul's statement to reduce it to the claim that he had been made an apostle through the risen Lord and not through the earthly Jesus. In this case the mention of the resurrection would be relevant only with respect to the time of Paul's call. Instead, the reference to the resurrection stands in a kind of apposition to God the Father; in the chiastic structure, it stands in contrast to ἀπ' ἀνθρώπων and κατὰ ἄνθρωπον (*ap' anthrōpōn . . . kata anthrōpon*, from men . . . in human fashion).

This gives the epithet its full weight as a substantial element in the definition of apostleship. When we compare Gal. 1:1 with the *prescript* of the Epistle to the Romans, we might conclude that the former contains no substantial definition of apostleship; this impression must now be corrected. The apostle's commission does not derive from anything in the realm of human power, but from what God alone in his omnipotence can do and what he has in fact done. And we are dealing with an event that stands in utter contrast to human impotence in its clearest shape, the shape of death, thereby benefiting humanity by bringing life out of death. Thus the fundamental note of the gospel is sounded. True life does not come from what a human being can do, what he achieves, or should achieve. It comes, therefore, not from the law but from the gospel of Jesus Christ.

And so all things that are contained in this name come together. Now, however, we see the situation more clearly. In questions concerning his apostleship, the matters of call and authority are inseparable for Paul from the understanding of the meaning of the gospel. Therefore, the seemingly noncontroversial reference to the resurrection brings to a head the point of contention in the Epistle. A correct understanding of the resurrection of Jesus Christ depends on its relationship to the cross and to the law. The fact that these two primary themes of the Epistle lead to the theme of the resurrection is also proleptically illustrated by the role played in this letter by the idea of freedom.

Beyond the points already discussed, Paul's words in v. 1 raise some additional questions that must not be passed over.

The direct call through Jesus Christ that Paul claims to have received presents a double problem. First, is Paul not deluding himself, ignoring the contribution of tradition even for him? He himself occasionally points this out, sometimes emphatically, especially with respect to the tradition (παράδοσις, *paradosis*) of the Lord's Supper and the resurrection. In both cases the element of transmission is stressed by the correlation of παραλαμβάνειν (*paralambanein*, receive) and παραδιδόναι (*paradidonai*, deliver): 1 Cor. 11:23: . . . παρέλαβον . . . ὃ καὶ παρέδωκα (*parelabon . . . ho kai paredōka*, I received . . . what I also delivered) and 1 Cor. 15:3: παρέδωκα . . . ὃ καὶ παρέλαβον (*paredōka . . . ho kai parelabon*, I delivered . . . what I also received). What is the relationship between the claim of a direct call and the role of tradition? This will be discussed at greater length when we come to 1:12.

Second, whatever Paul's direct experience of his call may involve, does he have criteria by which to determine that he himself has not fallen victim to Satan's deception, that he himself is not what he accuses others of being, a false apostle, who merely pretends to be an apostle of Christ (2 Cor. 11:13–15: "These people are false apostles, deceitful workers, disguising themselves as apostles of Christ")? This question, too, we shall reserve for later.

Let us assume that what Paul says about his office does not strike us in spite of everything as a strange or obscure historical-religious phenomenon, perhaps to be investigated critically. Suppose it permits our assent, our recognition of Paul's claim to have a direct call as being meaningful and true. What would follow? Would it mean that, if not every Christian, at least everyone who proclaims the gospel authentically must be like Paul in being able to point to a direct call from which he can derive his message? Or do we have to be content with the conclusion that this is in fact not the case? Do we have to accept the fact that, because we are dependent on human intermediaries, our own word and office represent nothing more than human words and human agency—a conclusion Paul would have rejected emphatically as contradicting the nature of the gospel and the authority of his office?

In answering this question, we are guided by Paul's distinction between human agency and human mediation, between ἀπ' ἀνθρώπων (*ap' anthrōpōn*, from men: v. 1) or κατὰ ἄνθρωπον (*kata anthrōpon*, after human fashion: v. 11) and δι' ἀνθρώπου (*di' anthrōpou*, through human mediation: v. 1) or παρὰ ἀνθρώπου (*para anthrōpou*, from a man: v. 12). This holds true for all: the gospel is proclaimed only when its proclamation is not in terms of human words and human agency. When someone proclaims the gospel in truth, the message comes from God no less than in the case of Paul: it is God's word and God's agency. Of course this is not determined once and for all, as though God's call could be stored up for future use. It depends on the content of the proclamation. But this content cannot be learned by rote and reproduced. It cannot be separated from the concrete situational message of the gospel. The act of proclamation always involves a risk: is the proclamation in fact gospel?

Now, however, it is not disadvantageous to have received the message to be proclaimed as well as the mandate to proclaim it through the mediation of those who are competent to do so. Such mediation follows inevitably from the historicity of the gospel. Maintaining this historicity is a crucial source of help in preaching the gospel; only the historically mediated contact with the original tradition preserves access to the gospel in its original authenticity. Furthermore, a call and mandate received from others protect against the temptation to carry out the proclamation of the gospel as a personal private project or to flatter oneself that one has a call coming directly from God. Such a vocation through human mediation can be believed in as a divine call; it does not come from men but through men from God. For this reason it can also withstand the temptations growing out of resistance and failure and go hand in hand with a feeling of inadequacy. Here one does not espouse one's own cause but stands in the service of another. Why Paul was not dependent on mediation as we are will be considered later. For now we must be content to note that in the history of Christianity Paul was accorded a special and unique role.

A final question concerning what Paul says in v. 1 arises from the tone he takes, an attitude of almost terrifying sovereignty and assurance. Does it not sound like pride and arrogance? Are modesty and humility not more befitting a Christian? By denying that he has been authorized by any human power, Paul also rejects simultaneously the possibility that he himself might be considered a source of individual authority and authoritarian dominion over others. If a person ascribes to Jesus Christ and God the Father everything that he says and stands for with total certainty, he subjects himself to an authority that excludes all personal power and glory.

This subjection, however, does not rule out, but on the contrary, motivates the apostle to speak in all matters concerning this final authority (and thus the truth of the gospel) with a superiority and candor such as can come only from total dependence and constraint. The utter determination we meet in Paul's first words, as the reference to the resurrection of Jesus Christ would suggest, reveals a paschal liberty in the face of all human powers and constraints as well as in the face of Paul's own life and death.

But this is not something that is limited to Paul alone. Assurance in this way and to such a degree, so inflexible a "No" based on an overwhelming and definitive "Yes," belongs basically to the life of every Christian. And the ministry of proclamation gives constant opportunity to practice such behavior. Sometimes there are extreme occasions requiring one to speak out as resolutely and uncompromisingly as Paul speaks to his addressees in the situation of this letter. At the same time, there is a narrow road here between a self-confidence that pretends to be spiritual but in truth is all too human and secular, and a humility and inward uncertainty that likewise pretend to be devout but in truth deny the liberty of faith in favor of a superstitious resignation in the face of the constraints and powers of the world.

We asked about the relationship between the apostle and other Christians, between a direct call and a mediated call. The difference is resolved in a comprehensive mutuality that is both the basis and the goal of life as a Christian. This is suggested in v. 2, where it is illustrated by the fact that Paul as author of this letter has others with him and behind him, whom he mentions explicitly. Elsewhere in his letters, too, Paul speaks of others alongside him as senders. Only the *prescript* to Romans is an exception, probably because in this letter he is writing to a community that he did not found and is still an unknown quantity, announcing his initial visit. But when it is not a matter of establishing relationships but of cultivating those already existing, Paul is accompanied by associates who represent the reality of Christian fellowship. Usually Paul mentions them by name, thus limiting himself to his closest coworkers. Even if they are not joint authors of the letter, they share responsibility for proclamation of the gospel, a process that continues in the letter.

Here Paul probably does not mention names, contenting himself with the general expression καὶ οἱ σὺν ἐμοὶ πάντες ἀδελφοί (*kai hoi syn emoi pantes adelphoi*, and all the brothers who are with me), because he is expanding the circle of cosenders beyond its usual limits; he does not mention one or two of those closest to him, but surrounds himself with a whole host of brethren. And so clearly the word πάντες (*pantes*, all) makes an important point. A term expressing unbroken totality and solidarity would be inappropriate if only a few were involved, as in the other letters. The indefinite quantitative adjective "all" replaces a list of individuals, which would not make sense here.

But it would seem dubious to seek to extend the circle so wide as to include the whole community amongst whom Paul is presently dwelling. The phrase οἱ σὺν ἐμοὶ πάντες ἀδελφοί (cf. also Phil. 4:21 and Gal. 2:3) seems rather to suggest a group of responsible companions and co-workers. Additional information, transmitted orally, would probably give the expression more concrete meaning for the Galatians. But we can still perceive the most important point. Paul's intent is to show that he is not left alone; all who are with him stand without exception on his side and share his concern for the Galatian congregations. He probably has good reason for citing this consensus beyond the impression it makes. In contrast to the confusion in Galatia, unanimity is to be emphasized as a mark of the true church. This is underlined by the use of the term brethren; its occurrence is natural here, but more detailed examination is necessary to grasp its meaning.

Christians are brothers as the children of the heavenly Father, a status to which they are called and of which they are assured through Jesus Christ. They are not children of the Father by nature but by grace, not by birth but by virtue of rebirth. As belonging to one and the same Lord, they are made each other's equals. None of them is lord over the others. Not even the apostle! Although Paul calls the cosenders "brothers" in contrast to his function as apostle, he is himself their brother and is included among the brethren. They are not brothers as followers of the apostle, as though he were their father or the head of their sect. They are instead equally sons of God as members of the body of Christ, together with all in that body who have an office or are marked by a special charisma.

The use of the title "brother" at this point, superficially so formulaic, takes on a special weight in this letter since Paul does not limit it to those who stand firmly on his side; he uses it repeatedly to address the Galatians, even as he fears and struggles for their very being as Christians (1:11; 3:15; 4:12, 28, 31; 5:11, 13; 6:1, 18). He does not deny them the status of brothers, but rather insists on it. And it is probably not by chance that the last word of the letter is ἀδελφοί (*adelphoi*, brothers), just before the Amen that confirms the final blessing: Ἡ χάρις τοῦ κυρίου ἡμῶν Ἰησοῦ Χριστοῦ μετὰ τοῦ πνεύματος ὑμῶν, ἀδελφοί·ἀμήν (*Hē charis tou kyriou hēmōn Iēsou Christou meta tou pneumatos hymōn, adelphoi; amēn*, The grace of our Lord Jesus Christ be with your spirit, brothers, Amen: 6:18).

Even more noteworthy, however, is the connection between being brothers and being sons or children (cf. 3:26–28; 4:6–7; and especially 4:28, 31): it is as sons that they are brothers. This points to the heart of the gospel, the truth of which is the object of Paul's struggle. And so from the catch-word ἀδελφός (*adelphos*, brother), which appears for the first time in v. 2, hidden threads extend to the single theme that is all-important for Paul.

The fact that the addressees of this letter are saluted as brothers is far from self-evident, as one may sense from the surprisingly terse designation of the recipients: ταῖς ἐκκλησίαις τῆς Γαλατίας (*tais ekklēsiais tēs Galatias*, to the congregations in Galatia). It is limited to the bare minimum, although leaving our historical curiosity quite unsatisfied. This is the only case in which a Pauline letter is addressed to a group of congregations. Even when Paul includes a more extended circle of recipients, like all the Christians in the whole of Achaia in the *prescript* to 2 Corinthians (1:1), he addresses the letter itself to a specific congregation, namely, the one in Corinth. This may indicate that, as the mother congregation, it played a leading role, whether in the Peloponnesus (which might by meant by the geographical term "Achaia") or throughout all of Greece, which was also called Achaia as a Roman province with its capital at Corinth, where the proconsul had his seat.

This ambiguity as to whether a geographical name refers to a region or a province is also present in the case of Galatia. If the address of the Epistle refers to the region of Galatia, it means the high plateau of Anatolia, the center of modern Turkey, the territory around its capital, Ankara. During the third-century B.C., a period of Celtic migration, members of the Indo-European tribe of the Galatians had settled there and given the region their name. "Galatians" is the same word as "Celts." But the process of settlement involved population mixing and total cultural assimilation; it would be wrong to draw conclusions about the Galatians addressed in the letter from any Celtic traits, real or supposed. It would also be wrong to underestimate the level of their Hellenistic education. If, however, the Roman province of Galatia is meant, then the territory around the cities of Iconium, Lystra, and Derbe would have to be considered; this interpretation is therefore called the South Galatian hypothesis. On the whole, however, the North Galatian hypothesis is more likely. The use of Γαλάται (*Galatai*, Galatians) as a personal term of address in 3:1 is a powerful argument in its favor. But the attempt to use the information in Acts (especially 16:6 and 18:23) to decide the question of location and thus also determine when these congregations were founded and even construct a second visit of the apostle to them leads nowhere. It is quite conceivable that some of Paul's individual journeys are not recorded in Acts. Furthermore, we should not expect a solution of these problems of itself to help with the substantial questions of the Epistle to the Galatians. The only other passage that speaks explicitly of congregations in this area also speaks of them as a group of congregations, without more geographical precision. This passage (1 Cor. 16:1) cites directions that Paul had given among the congregations of Galatia concerning the collection being taken for Jerusalem. In this region, therefore, it is clear that no one congregation exercised leadership. There does, however, appear to have been a close bond among them all. For this reason they all were drawn into a crisis by outside forces. It is this crisis in which Paul now intervenes.

It is certainly striking that Paul here avoids all the Christian epithets he normally uses in addressing the congregations he writes to, such as ἐκκλησία τοῦ θεοῦ (*ekklēsia tou theou*, congregation of God), ἀγαπητοὶ θεοῦ (*agapētoi theou*, beloved of God), ἅγιοι ἐν Χριστῷ ᾿Ιησοῦ (*hagioi en Christō Iēsou*, saints in Christ Jesus), κλητοὶ ἅγιοι (*klētoi hagioi*, called saints), ἡγιασμένοι ἐν Χριστῷ ᾿Ιησοῦ (*hēgiasmenoi en Christō Iēsou*, sanctified in Christ Jesus). This may be an expression of the intense irritation that permeates the entire letter. But it would be wrong to draw premature conclusions from parsimony at this point. Paul is not denying that his addressees are Christians. He is not expelling them from the communion of faith and love. It is unlikely that he calls them merely ἐκκλησίαι (*ekklēsiai*, congregations) without further qualification in order to address them pejoratively as a kind of assembly. Without going into details, he thinks of them as congregations whose lives are grounded in God the Father and in the Lord Jesus Christ (cf. 1 Thess. 1:1).

This is underlined by the greeting with which he now addresses them, joining with them in a "we." The *prescript* began as usual by using the third person to designate the sender, changing to the second person when the Galatians are addressed at the beginning of v. 3. Now, however, the greeting shifts to the first person plural, in which Paul and the Galatian Christians are one. A fourfold "our" unmistakably expresses this: our Father (v. 3), our sins, our deliverance, and once again our Father (v. 4). In this they are and will remain united, whatever may otherwise come between them.

Here we find an especially solemn form of greeting. Our own experience of greetings is usually limited to conventional expressions. When we meet someone, we say "Good day" or "Hello"; then we say "Goodbye" or "See you later." Such expressions are accompanied by gestures that are likewise fixed by custom, each having its proper place: we nod or wave, raise our hat, embrace and kiss. When we write letters we choose formulas from a common stock which express appropriate sentiments: truly, sincerely, or cordially. This all seems so insignificant that it doesn't pay to devote much thought to the phenomenon. But even minor changes in what are almost unconscious formulas show that more is involved here than is generally suspected. If we fail to say hello to someone or refuse to respond to a greeting, if we reduce the formulas in a letter to a cold minimum or even make a point of omitting them altogether, we injure others deeply, conveying our disregard. What is there about a greeting that makes its omission so devastating? Or consider feigned and hypocritical forms of greeting, as when we write letters of condolence or congratulations full of sonorous phrases, which are actually hollow because our hearts are not in what we write. We may even feel we should be expressing our feelings in a totally different way, to give our greetings meaning and authenticity. But why is it so hard to get beyond banalities?

The opposite can also happen: we can make our greetings overly familiar or force them into artificiality by ignoring the respectful distance that is often appropriate or the naturalness that is always desirable. Or recall how a greeting can become a statement of political allegiance, an expression of fanaticism, a forced usage offending the conscience and demeaning those who use it. What positive aspects of a greeting are ignored when it takes on such inhuman features?

A greeting is a highly informative interpersonal transaction. If we do not neglect formulas of politeness even in purely business letters, this reminds us that purely objective contacts cannot afford to ignore the personal element. When I address someone, I owe him more than just attention to his immediate purpose or mine. A greeting suggests the authentically human dimension that cannot be neglected even in the most mundane business. When people enter or leave a store, unless it is an impersonal self-service operation, they usually exchange greetings. When a doctor approaches a sickbed, he will certainly greet the patient before treating him. It is beneficial to establish human contact: one does not come directly to the point and set about the job but shows respect for the humanity of the other. When one person addresses another, a sphere of confiding is established that inspires confidence. This is the original meaning of the accompanying gestures: the open right hand, in which no weapon is held; the tip of the hat that recalls the removal of a protective helmet; the bow that renders one defenseless. It all goes to say: I am not your enemy, nor do I suspect you of being my enemy. I will treat you kindly and expect kindness from you.

But when people address each other in this manner, more is involved than a mutual assurance of good will. Each says to the other something in the form of a wish. Greeting and wishing are so closely related, implicitly or explicitly, that many languages use a single word for both. And even what is wished for undergoes a remarkable fusion. In a greeting, one does not express one's wishes to the other person—let alone against him!—but rather wishes for him. What is desirable for him I utter as my own wish, putting myself in his place. The more I can identify with him, the more genuine such a wish becomes.

Furthermore, since those who exchange greetings wish each other well instead of uttering threats, they bear witness to a solidarity among those who are threatened and endangered, those whose lives are all too fragile. What may not still be in store for us during the rest of the day or in the coming night! Reason enough to wish someone a good day, or a quiet night. Each and every one.

Therefore, the wish that accompanies our greeting also makes an admission: what one can do for another is severely limited. We are concerned for the other person, to help him sense that he has worth, that he is not nothing, even indicate that we belong to him, that he can turn to us and rely on us. But the primary focus is not on the good we can do at the moment or promise for the future, but on the mere wish itself. However much we can do for each other and be to each other, there remains a far greater need, which only our wish can take account of. The life-threatening possibilities are so incalculable, sudden, and powerful, so obscure and alien, that ultimately we can protect neither ourselves nor each other against them. The closer our relationship is with others, the more palpable and painful is our impotence to give them, to guarantee them, what they need. All that is left for us to give is our wish.

This is most obvious *in extremis*, when death imposes separation. We are again close together, but mutually helpless. What else is left to do for each other at this crucial moment? And what form can a farewell greeting take, if it finds words at all? To commend the one who is on the point of departure to God, and to bless those who will remain? How hard it is to do this when things become serious! What right have we to commend someone to God? What power is there in a wish for blessing, that we can entrust others—and ourselves—to it? But this is the very question we are confronted with by the simplest, commonest forms of greeting that we use. What is the point of saying something like "Keep well" or "See you later"? That this should be does not lie within our power. For this very reason we feel constrained to wish, even if we do not know what a wish can do, or what to think about the power of wishes.

This is probably the most remarkable aspect of wishing, if we stop to think about it. Even when the mention of God in a greeting has become an empty form, or the greeting has lost all traces of religious language, there remains a deeply rooted agreement, when greetings are exchanged, to go beyond what we can do and enter the realm of what we can only wish for. If we address each other not for a particular purpose but in order to show mutual respect and friendship and establish the necessary sphere of confidence, we cannot escape the realization that we live together through an all-pervading giving power. We cannot live together in a manner that is humanly bearable without laying claim to this power on each other's behalf and repeatedly expressing this claim. We must wish each other well, whether in the sense of happiness, as the Greeks greeted each other, or strength, as conveyed by the Roman greeting, or the *shalom* imparted by the Jewish greeting, a peace that provides a safe and prosperous life.

The formula of greeting Paul uses in his letters is a Christian invention. Its basic form χάρις ὑμῖν καὶ εἰρήνη (*charis hymin kai eirēnē*, grace to you and peace) is used by Paul in 1 Thess. 1:1. The extended version with the addition ἀπὸ θεοῦ πατρὸς ἡμῶν καὶ κυρίου Ἰησοῦ Χριστοῦ (*apo theou patros hēmōn kai kyriou Iēsou Christou*, from God our Father and from the Lord Jesus Christ) appears in all the other letters like a liturgical text whose wording cannot be changed. It is impossible to decide with absolute confidence whether the simple basic form (χάρις ὑμῖν καὶ εἰρήνη) or even the definitive version (χάρις ὑμῖν καὶ εἰρήνη ἀπὸ θεοῦ πατρὸς ἡμῶν καὶ κυρίου Ἰησοῦ Χριστοῦ) was borrowed by Paul or whether he himself composed not only the longer but also the shorter form. His letters suggest the possibility of development; one might, therefore, tend to favor the theory that at least the longer definitive form of this greeting formula derives from Paul himself. This is supported by the formulation of the "from" phrase, which is typical of Paul's style. On the other hand, the importance of the term χάρις (*charis*, grace) for Pauline theology could also suggest that the very basis of the greeting formula, the juxtaposition of χάρις and εἰρήνη (*eirēnē*, peace), is Pauline in origin. For its interpretation, in any case, we must adhere to the meaning that the expression has for Paul.

The basis is undoubtedly the Jewish greeting *shalom*, which is translated into Greek as εἰρήνη. Jewish tradition also includes a bipartite formula: ἔλεος καὶ εἰρήνη (*eleos kai eirēnē*, mercy and peace). In reverse order, this formula appears at the conclusion of Galatians (6:16): "All who walk by this rule—peace and mercy be upon them and upon the Israel of God." It is not by accident that the word "mercy" appears in this sentence, with its echoes of the Old Testament, along with the phrase "Peace be upon Israel," a quotation from Ps. 125:5 and 128:6.[8] Its Hebrew equivalent *chesed* occurs primarily in the Psalms. Now when χάρις (*charis*, grace) instead of ἔλεος precedes εἰρήνη in the standard Pauline salutation, the choice of words bears a distinctively Christian stamp. This combination of χάρις and εἰρήνη has not been found outside of Christian texts, either as a salutation or in any other context. But the choice of the word χάρις also shows Christian influence with regard to its meaning. Its Hebrew equivalent *chen* plays a minor role theologically in the Old Testament. Significantly, it is not used at all in the prayers of the Psalter. Therefore the use of χάρις in the LXX cannot be considered a direct source for Paul's use of this word. It is true that the roots of the Hebrew words *chesed* and *chen* are closely related semantically; but in translating them, the LXX clearly prefers ἔλεος for *chesed* and χάρις for *chen*, putting the strictly theological emphasis on the former. It is probably the doctrine of justification that accounts for the insignificance of ἔλεος in Paul's language, while the word χάρις assumes an unexpected importance, without any precedent in the language of the Jewish Old Testament, not to mention Hellenistic usage.

At this point we can consider what has taken place here only from the perspective of accounting for the origin of the Christian salutation χάρις καὶ εἰρήνη (*charis kai eirēnē*, grace and peace). There are two possibilities to consider: either the catchword χάρις was added to the traditional Jewish greeting *shalom*, rendered as εἰρήνη, or χάρις was substituted deliberately for ἔλεος (*eleos*, mercy). Both possibilities open up several perspectives.

In the New Testament, εἰρήνη (*eirēnē*, peace, well-being) is used by itself as a greeting, albeit in oral discourse rather than in letters. When the disciples sent forth by Jesus enter a house, they are first to say, "Peace be to this house" (Luke 10:5). This has the mysterious force of a blessing. Peace with all its power is laid upon those who dwell there, but it returns to the speaker if the one blessed is not worthy of the blessing (Luke 10:6; Matt. 10:12–13). Now if this *shalom* salutation has merely been expanded by the addition of the word χάρις (*charis*, grace), we must face the question of the source and purpose of the addition.

With respect to the question of origin, a connection has been suggested with the common Greek salutation χαῖρε (*chaire*), the imperative of χαίρειν (*chairein*, rejoice, be happy). This is usually translated into English as a standard greeting such as "Hail" or "Hello." But we should always keep in mind the literal meaning, which a Greek would obviously be aware of. It is in fact a wonderful greeting to call on each other to rejoice and to wish each other happiness. This Greek salutation appears in the New Testament in both oral and epistolary usage. The angel greets Mary by saying χαῖρε, κεχαριτωμένη (*chaire, kecharitōmenē*, Rejoice, O favored one: Luke 1:28). The soldiers mock the man of sorrows by crying out χαῖρε, βασιλεῦ τῶν Ἰουδαίων (*chaire, basileu tōn Ioudaiōn*, Rejoice, King of the Jews: Matt. 27:29). The corresponding infinitive χαίρειν (*chairein*) serves as an epistolary salutation and appears, for example, in the *prescripts* of the so-called Apostolic Decree (Acts 15:23) and the Epistle of James (1:1).

The theory has been proposed that this Greek salutation was Christianized by the substitution of a word based on the same root—not, however, the substantive χαρά (*chara*, joy), but χάρις (*charis*, grace). In secular Greek usage this latter word includes overtones of rejoicing and can mean charm or favor. In Christian usage it takes on the religious meaning of divine favor and grace. If this explanation is right, the word χάρις was intended to give the Greek salutation a religious form, combining it with the Jewish *shalom* to create a new formula. There may even have been polemical overtones against the Greek form of greeting. At the same time, there may have been an intention to forge a link with the Jewish tradition of the Old Testament by alluding to the verb *chanan*. In contrast to the substantive *chen*, whose usage is very close to the meaning of χάρις in secular Greek, the verb *chanan* is very important in the Old Testament as a term for God's graciousness. Thus there may also have been a desire to revise the sense of εἰρήνη *(shalom)*, evincing criticism of the Jewish greeting as well. This derivation assumes, of course, that the Christian understanding of χάρις was already highly developed.

We arrive at the same result if we start with the other hypothesis, namely, that there was a conscious move to revise the bipartite Jewish salutation formula by substituting the word χάρις (*charis*, grace) for ἔλεος (*eleos*, mercy). A mere intent to echo the Greek form of greeting is hardly sufficient explanation for the change. Such a change of wording would carry conviction only if, in contrast to the concept of mercy, the word χάρις were better able to express a specifically Christian reality in the salutation formula and thus also give a more precisely Christian sense to the understanding of εἰρήνη (*eirēnē*, peace, well-being). Here again we are left with the same impression: the word χάρις could become a key word of the salutation formula only by virtue of having been given new meaning in Christian usage, thus taking on theological import. For such a notable linguistic development we have no evidence except the theology of Paul.

The centrality of this formula for Paul is made clear by the appended phrase indicating the source of χάρις (*charis*, grace) and εἰρήνη (*eirēnē*, peace): ἀπὸ θεοῦ πατρὸς ἡμῶν καὶ κυρίου Ἰησοῦ Χριστοῦ (*apo theou patros hēmōn kai kyriou Iēsou Christou*, from God our Father and from the Lord Jesus Christ). If we compare this with Paul's regular usage, we note the following:[9] the association of εἰρήνη with God is especially common with Paul, while χάρις is associated primarily with Jesus Christ. "The God of peace" is an expression encountered repeatedly in blessings (e.g., 1 Thess. 5:23; 2 Cor. 13:11; Rom. 15:33; 16:20; Phil. 4:9). The phrase "the grace of our Lord Jesus Christ" is likewise used frequently in such blessings (e.g., 1 Thess. 5:28; 1 Cor. 16:23; 2 Cor. 13:13; [Rom. 16:24]; Phil. 4:23). The complete apostolic salutation is thus structured chiastically. It begins with χάρις and closes with its associated διὰ κυρίου Ἰησοῦ Χριστοῦ (*dia kyriou Iēsou Christou*, through the Lord Jesus Christ), which thus enclose the other member, εἰρήνη, and its source διὰ θεοῦ πατρὸς ἡμῶν (*dia theou patros hēmōn*, through God our Father). This interweaving is meant to indicate that we are not dealing with two distinct things, but with a single thing, albeit internally differentiated. Ultimately χάρις and εἰρήνη constitute a hendiadys, a single concept expressed in two designations; the same is true of the bipartite statement of the source, "from God our Father and from the Lord Jesus Christ." In this most pregnant formula, soteriology and Christology are represented, each with its own structure and also in combination, so that the whole with its christological and soteriological relationships represents a kind of hendiadys. The essential nucleus of Christianity can hardly be formulated more fundamentally and compactly than in this salutation.

In this manner a Christian spirit has pervaded the universal human phenomenon of greeting. What is usually reduced to an empty formula this spirit seeks to fill with new life. What is usually vague and unclear it seeks to make clear and true. Of course there is also a suspect way of Christianizing life, which has the outward appearance of being superhuman and therefore raises the suspicion of being inhuman. But there is a touchstone to determine what is Christian: does it make relationships between persons more human? Here all stands within the sign of the incarnation of God, so that God the Father and Jesus Christ together constitute inseparably the single authority to which faith—and therefore also the salutation permeated by faith—can appeal. Of course what issued forth as a fresh stream from Paul's overflowing heart can itself harden into a mere formula and become a Christian convention. But this need not happen. For the unity of Father and Son also includes the Spirit, who breaks through the letter *[aus dem Buchstaben]* repeatedly, making it impossible to serve the letter alone.

In order to comprehend something of the spirit of this greeting we must trace its inner movement, which is responsible for the uniqueness of what fills the Christian salutation. It states explicitly the source of that which one Christian should wish another. This guarantees that we are not dealing merely with an empty or—as we say ironically—pious wish. In fact, this wish is authentically pious precisely because it bases itself on a fulfillment that has already taken place. It is consequently worth considering whether the missing verb in the formula should be supplied not as an optative (the usual form) but as a future indicative grounded on a perfect indicative. Even if we follow the usual optative interpretation, it must be understood in the following sense: this is not some vague wish promising pie in the sky. The salutation is grounded instead on what came down from the heavens without human intervention—from God our Father. Therefore the blessing does not look forward to whatever unknown possibilities may yet come from God. This would be a surrender to what is uncertain and transitory. What has already befallen one belongs to the past; it is, in a sense, already used up. Therefore, one must always look for something different, something new, just as it is necessary every day to wish someone good day afresh, because the fact that yesterday or the day before yesterday may have been a good or happy day does not promise or guarantee that today will be so. The apostolic blessing holds fast instead to what has already taken place, once and for all, at God's behest in the appearance of Jesus Christ.

This is the basis for everything promised in the salutation, everything that is offered because it is already present. Χάρις (*charis*, grace) and εἰρήνη (*eirēnē*, peace)—these are not vague and distant objects of desire, these are not transitory, but rather incarnate reality already vouchsafed to humankind. Of course even this wish needs to be constantly repeated. Not, however, because the gift that is wished for is uncertain and deceptive and might never appear, but because the recipients in their inconstancy are in danger of letting it slip by.

The wish thus takes on the character of a reminder, as though we were to greet each other by saying: Remember what has taken place, what has entered into our lives forever! The Christian greeting thus stands wholly within the sign of Jesus Christ. But it does not for this reason leave God out, as though now all that mattered were a single human being—as in the terrible days of the so-called Third Reich, when people greeted each other in the name of a human being, himself inhuman. For Paul, Jesus Christ and God are not fused in such a way as to turn the human Jesus into an idol that takes the place of God. It is possible to express what has taken place in Jesus only when he is distinguished from God the Father and when this distinction determines our understanding of their indivisible unity. Only thus can one hope for what this Christian greeting promises. Through Jesus Christ we receive something that human beings cannot give each other. But we are thereby able now to pass on, one to another, the very thing that we as human beings are not able of ourselves to give.

How does this apply to what Paul wishes in his salutation? We shall pave the way for elucidating this question by an even more searching examination of the relationship between God the Father and Jesus Christ. The entire *prescript* is, in a sense, organized around this relationship. Three times Paul speaks of both God the Father and Jesus Christ, in each case as a source. In

v. 1, the combination defines the source of Paul's apostleship: διὰ Ἰησοῦ Χριστοῦ καὶ θεοῦ πατρός (*dia Iēsou Christou kai theou patros*, through Jesus Christ and through God Father). In v. 3, it refers to the source of the gift with which all Christians are blessed: ἀπὸ θεοῦ πατρὸς ἡμῶν καὶ κυρίου Ἰησοῦ Χριστοῦ (*apo theou patros hēmōn kai kyriou Iēsou Christou*, from God our Father and from the Lord Jesus Christ). In vv. 4–5, finally, it designates the source of the Christ event itself: τοῦ δόντος ἑαυτὸν ὑπὲρ τῶν ἁμαρτιῶν ἡμῶν . . . κατὰ τὸ θέλημα τοῦ θεοῦ καὶ πατρὸς ἡμῶν (*tou dontos heauton hyper tōn hamartiōn hēmōn . . . kata to thelēma tou theou kai patros hēmōn*, who sacrificed himself for our sins . . . according to the will of the one who is God and our Father).

From the risen Lord, through whom God called Paul to be an apostle, reference is made to God, who raised Christ from the dead (v. 1). At the end, likewise, mention of the crucified Lord establishes an association with the will of God: Jesus' death is not contrary to this will, but rather (however incomprehensibly) so in agreement with it that God cannot be praised sufficiently (vv. 4–5). In the middle (v. 3), however, we find what might be called the natural sequence of God the Father and Jesus Christ, describing the total movement of God to us through Jesus Christ. This sequence is always presupposed even when it is reversed.

Paul's basic sequence of God the Father and Jesus Christ has been referred to as subordinationist. This designation is erroneous; it looks at Paul's words in the light of a trinitarian theology that did not develop until later. Paul has nothing to say on the question directly, if only because he is not discussing the relationship within the Trinity between God the Father and God the Son. The reference to "our Father"—not the Father who begets the Son eternally—emphasizes this point, as does the concentration on the incarnate, not the preexistent Son. Paul is addressing the situation determined by the historical appearance of Jesus Christ and our own involvement in it. How this relates to later trinitarian reflection may be passed over for now. We will consider only the Pauline text.

The juxtaposition of God the Father and Jesus Christ reveals a fundamental theological insight. There are repeated references to God as the source: he raises the dead (v. 1), he gives all good things (v. 3), his loving will is carried out on the cross (v. 4). The point is not to use what is presumably familiar, the nature of God, to derive and explain something else. Instead, underivative events and experiences are related to God and associated with him in such a way that there is revealed who God truly is in the light of such events and experiences. He who was slain proves to be alive. In a world without grace and peace humanity has found grace and peace. The self-sacrifice of the sinless one has atoning and redeeming power. These are the crucial signals for the Christian knowledge of God.

The sequence in which these signals are placed in the *prescript* defines a trajectory. One might say that it begins with the radiant glory of the resurrection, leads to the life experienced by Christian faith, in which the radiance is unfortunately not undimmed, and ends in the darkness of death on the cross. But the import of this sequence is not as it appears to our reason or emotion. Everything comes together in what is mentioned last; it is the common denominator for what has gone before. The risen Lord is the crucified Lord. And the fact that the source of χάρις (*charis*, grace) and εἰρήνη (*eirēnē*, peace) is to be sought in the crucified Lord is underlined by Paul in the kerygmatic addition that he only here appends to the salutation. From every side, whether from the encounter of the apostle with the risen Lord or from the spiritual experience of every Christian, reference is made to the fundamental event, the crucifixion of Jesus Christ. Here in the deepest depths knowledge of God finds its true foundation. It must hold fast to Jesus Christ and to the place of his utmost humiliation. Knowledge of God cannot be achieved by speculation, so that one might proceed by deductive reasoning. Knowledge of God in the Christian sense is dependent on life as it is lived and particularly where it has been realized unsurpassably through suffering and death.

Luther made this point with unusual clarity in commenting on v. 3: "Paulus semper connectit Iesum Christum cum patre, quia vult docere Theologiam christianam quae incipit non a summo, ut omnes aliae religiones, sed ab imo."[10] ("Paul always associates Jesus Christ with the Father, because his purpose is to teach Christian theology, which does not have its source in the utmost heights, as all other religions do, but in the utmost depths.") But this leads to the knowledge that God is in Christ and is at work in Christ: "Dare autem gratiam et remissionem peccatorum et vivificationem, iustificationem, liberationem a morte, peccatis non sunt opera creaturae sed unius, solius maiestatis."[11] ("But the giving of grace and forgiveness of sins and bringing to life, justification, liberation from death and from sins—these are not works of the creature, but of the one [divine] majesty alone.") "Non est alia res quam a patre habemus, quam a filio; alioqui aliter dixisset Paulus, sed coniungit duo simul, gratiam et pacem."[12] ("There is nothing that we have from the Father that we do not have from the Son, else Paul would have expressed himself differently; instead he joins the two things as one: grace and peace.")

The statement that God our Father and Jesus Christ the Lord are the source of what constitutes the substance of the blessing fundamentally alters our understanding of the wish expressed. First, as has already been empha-sized, we are dealing with something already vouchsafed. It is present; it needs only be perceived and acknowledged. All we could wish for ourselves or for each other finds here its ultimate measure, but also its guarantee of appropriate fulfillment. The second point follows: since it is already vouch-safed, the substance of the wish takes on new meaning. The meaning of grace and peace is no longer dependent on earlier ideas of what a wish should encompass. Instead, what has been brought to fulfillment by God the Father and Jesus Christ must be taken as the criterion for what is ultimately to be wished for, since it has already been given absolutely and without res-ervation. The two factors—the presence of fulfillment and the change of the criterion—interpenetrate, making us rethink what we should be wishing for. They must therefore be guarded against hasty misunderstanding.

The fact of presence does not eliminate the repeated need to overtake ful-fillment, because it is always ahead of us. It is, therefore, likewise possible for fulfillment in a sense to overtake and surpass itself, because it is never automatic and never grows stale. Constant repetition of the same wish is therefore not superfluous, but comports in fact with the superfluity that is here revealed and offered, because the blessing wished for always brings something new.

Similarly, the change of criterion does not mean that transitory, penulti-mate things do not have their proper place alongside the ultimate things of eschatology. It would be a misunderstanding of the spiritual thrust given the salutation by its appeal to the Christ to suppress and condemn, to silence the temporal, corporeal needs that control our woefully deficient lives, instead of including and thus purifying them. The appeal to God the Father is an ap-peal to the creator. And the appeal to Jesus Christ is an appeal to him whose human vulnerability and need are so emphasized by Paul: "born of a woman, born under the law" (Gal. 4:4). Neither element, the appeal to God the Father or the appeal to Jesus Christ, can tolerate a spiritualization that ceases to take human need seriously.

In the light of this preliminary caution, one must guard against sketching the requisite antithesis narrowly and crudely, simply defining the meaning of grace and peace in the apostolic blessing in opposition to Hellenistic Greek usage or the Jewish usage of the Old Testament. Of course, the differ-ences on both sides must be delineated, but not in an absolutely exclusive sense. The Pauline phrase "grace and peace" has much in common with pre-Christian and non-Christian ideas, with universal human usage.

To the Greek mind, εἰρήνη (*eirēnē*, peace) is primarily political in mean-ing: the word refers to a state of peace in contrast to the chaos of war. It is, therefore, often paired with the concept of quiet(ness) (ἡσυχία, hēsychia), not in the sense of idleness, inactivity, or sleep, but as a necessary condition if life is to go on happily and prosperously. Here it begins to converge with *shalom*, although the latter is not primarily political in meaning and generally speaking has a much wider semantic range. Its basic meaning is "wholeness." It also is used with respect to social relationships, whether well-being in society or easy and untroubled relations between individuals. Material implications are never overlooked. But since they are naturally considered to have God as their source, this ever-present reference to God introduces a disturbing restlessness into any overly self-evident and self-confident idea of *shalom*. The violent controversies over the optimistic school of prophecy bear witness to this disquiet, as does the challenge felt in the prosperity of the wicked. Both lead to a tendency to interpret *shalom* in an increasingly eschatological sense. It now takes on the comprehensive and radical meaning of "salvation," although without ignoring the corporeal and social sides of human life.

The Christian understanding of εἰρήνη has something in common with all these pre-Christian and non-Christian nuances in the concept. How could one as a Christian be other than sympathetic toward all sincere desire for peace and salvation, as well as toward both efforts on behalf of peace and knowledge of the limits imposed on human power? But now there are new aspects as well.

There is an immeasurably clearer awareness than before of what is the true root of lack of εἰρήνη and what is necessary to restore it. The opposite of εἰρήνη is now conceived in much more radical and universal terms, a point that will be discussed in the context of v. 4. What is now clear is that peace is determined by one's relationship with God. More is involved than dependence of peace on God in the sense that all the goods of this life must be asked for and received from him. Rather these goods themselves now take their value from one's relationship with God. Is the individual God's enemy or is he at peace with God? The understanding of peace has been radicalized and universalized, becoming salvation that affects both the individual and all humanity; this change derives from the assurance that the saving event is already present in Jesus Christ: "We have peace with God through Jesus Christ" (Rom. 5:1).

Without detracting from the future eschatological dimension revealed here, the aspect of such εἰρήνη that is already present itself has eschatological force. And without trivializing the problems of temporal peace and well-being, we now find our attention directed to what the human heart needs (e.g., Phil. 4:7), if peace and well-being are to be promoted even imperfectly and become a way of life. For a peace that is merely war carried on by other means and a prosperity that engenders all kinds of abuses—even something as trivial as the surliness and dissatisfaction of the spoiled!—are not worthy of the name. Therefore the Christian understanding of εἰρήνη calls for an antithetical statement: contrary to all the sham peace of this world, contrary to illusions of prosperity and promises of pseudo-salvation, true εἰρήνη must be understood on the basis of the peace of God that has become reality through Jesus Christ.

This perspective also deepens our understanding of χάρις (*charis*, grace). As we have already seen, it has a much narrower basis in secular usage. Undoubtedly, χάρις refers to that which is the source of εἰρήνη. This accounts for its position in the *salutation* formula. But it would not do justice to Paul's understanding if we were to follow our own common usage without any awareness of what has already been said about this word, interpreting χάρις as a gracious disposition on the part of God, an attribute of God from which the gift of peace and salvation derives. Even the Old Testament, when speaking of God, does not understand its predications as abstract attributes; it always derives them from corresponding acts on the part of God. Thus, God's grace is not to be thought of as *potentia* but as *actus*, an actual demonstration of grace.

Now if we note that Paul does not follow Old Testament usage, using χάρις instead of the term "mercy" (ἔλεος, *eleos*), we find the following nuance: mercy is shown to someone who is weak, whose strength is insufficient to the task. Grace, on the contrary, is shown to someone who is guilty, who has incurred guilt despite or even through his achievements. It is therefore precisely the strong and the righteous that are dependent on χάρις, although in their perverted self-assessment they are unwilling to acknowledge this dependence.

Now we have already determined that Paul usually associates χάρις with Jesus Christ and εἰρήνη with God.[13] At first glance, the chiastic construction here conceals this association, as does the use of the same preposition ἀπό (*apo*, from) to introduce both God and Jesus Christ. But Paul does often use the genitive phrase "the grace of our Lord Jesus Christ." What does it mean? To interpret it as referring to a gracious attitude would be totally out of place, suggesting that Christians should exchange the wish that Jesus Christ be gracious and not appear as an angry judge. Neither, however, is it easy to understand this genitive as meaning an act or demonstration of grace: what has taken place in Jesus Christ depends for its salvific meaning on the fact that in this event God himself has demonstrated that he is gracious. Here, as often in Paul, the genitive has a characteristically indefinite meaning, often best represented by an explicative phrase; here we might translate "Christ grace." In other words, the locus and nature of χάρις must be defined from the perspective of Jesus Christ. And this is what Paul goes on to do. But before we address our attention to this explication of χάρις, let us first consider an observation that might explain this sudden intensive use of χάρις in Paul on the basis of linguistic usage.

The Old Testament uses the Hebrew equivalent *chen* primarily to characterize interpersonal relationships: one person finds affection, favor, and friendly acceptance in the eyes of another. Two features characterize this situation. First, there is the statement of an effectual presence, expressing how important it is to one party that the other look on him in friendship. Second, there is the noteworthy frequency with which the verb "find" is used, as in Laban's words to Jacob: "Let me find grace in your eyes" (Gen. 30:27). In this encounter I experience something over which I have no control. The very glance of the other person alters my situation. This idiom is also used to express a relationship to God: "Noah found grace in the eyes of the Lord" (Gen. 6:8).

Here we find echoes of the forensic situation—with its original locus in the cult—that is fundamental to Paul's understanding of justification. The Old Testament idiom, which the Septuagint translates χάριν εὑρίσκειν ἐναντίον or ἐνώπιον or ἐν ὀφθαλμοῖς (*charin heuriskein enantion / enōpion / en ophthalmois*, find grace before / in the eyes of . . .), might possibly explain the linguistic origin of the Pauline concept of χάρις, at least in its central christological and soteriological usage. If so, the phrase ἡ χάρις τοῦ κυρίου ἡμῶν Ἰησοῦ Χριστοῦ (*hē charis tou kyriou hēmōn Iēsou Christou*, the grace of our Lord Jesus Christ) could be understood as defining the situation in which human beings find themselves before God through Christ. They are accepted, looked upon with loving favor. They themselves therefore reflect χάρις, solely because they are looked upon with such favor although in themselves they have nothing winsome or joyous to offer, no charm, nothing that might please God. A poetic metaphor from a hymn by Paul Gerhardt can summarize the situation: "The sun that smiles upon me is my Lord Jesus Christ."[14] That is the meaning of χάρις: a reality that fills all of life with joy brought by the coming of Jesus Christ.

This helps explain how χάρις can become for Paul an all-inclusive, almost atmospheric description of a situation analogous but contrary to being under the νόμος (*nomos*, law). This suggests that here, too, an antithetical interpretation suggests itself. The explanation would be more immediately accessible if put in the following terms: those who have their being in Christ under the grace of God are no longer dependent on how the rest of humanity and the world look upon them. They do not live by the world's grace and do not fear its wrath, even though they are especially concerned to live in peace with all. The antithesis of νόμος (*nomos*, law) and χάρις (*charis*, grace) will be examined later.

The *prescript* to Galatians is unique in not concluding with the liturgical formula of the apostolic benediction. In v. 4 there is appended a statement explaining how all that is contained in the benediction is grounded in Jesus Christ. Syntactically, this addition is joined to the final member of the greeting formula in participial apposition to ἀπό . . . κυρίου Ἰησοῦ Χριστοῦ (*apo . . . kyriou Iēsou Christou*, from . . . the Lord Jesus Christ). But it would be contrary to what we have observed concerning the structure of the *salutation formula* to interpret the extension as modifying the last member alone and not the whole formula. This apposition to Jesus Christ refers again explicitly to God the Father (in emphatic position at the end), insisting once more that in the Christ event God's will was fulfilled. Here, then, we find again the common stylistic feature of chiasmus: the sequence God—Christ in the *salutation formula* is now reversed in the appended elucidation, becoming Christ—God.

But the reference goes back even further. Since the understanding of χάρις (*charis*, grace) and εἰρήνη (*eirēnē*, peace) depends on the definition of their source ἀπὸ θεοῦ πατρὸς ἡμῶν καὶ κυρίου Ἰησοῦ Χριστοῦ (*apo theou patros hēmōn kai kyriou Iēsou Christou*, from God our Father and from the Lord Jesus Christ), this understanding, too, is further defined by the additional statement. Contrary to the apparent grammar, we are dealing with a significant elucidation of the entire salutation.

Why does Paul depart so seriously from the usual style of his *prescripts*? The *salutation formula*, which in Paul's other letters is likewise the only portion of the *prescript* that is repeated, marks the formal conclusion of the *prescript*; any continuation cannot help appearing stylistically inept at first glance. The reason for this unusual and apparently awkward divergence clearly lies in the situation of the letter. Interpretation of v. 3 revealed that this *salutation formula* expresses the essence of Christianity, the gospel, in an unusually pregnant and compact form. If this is so, it is fully consonant with the occasion of the Epistle to the Galatians—the imminent danger that this gospel of Christ will be perverted and turned into its opposite—for Paul to bring the meaning of this *salutation formula* to the awareness of the Galatians with all possible emphasis. What is endangering if not totally destroying the gospel among them is their disregard of that which is the foundation of the apostolic greeting. This foundation is now made explicit in v. 4. What is at stake is nothing less than the meaning of the cross of Christ.

Although the addition is polemically motivated and may appear didactic, Paul in fact observes even the stylistic requirements of an apostolic *prescript* as a religious message of major importance. He actually goes beyond the usual way of concluding a *prescript*: only here does he add a doxology with a final amen. He could not have chosen a more impressive introduction to a letter addressing so critical a situation.

It does not detract from this function of vv. 4ff. to observe that Paul is obviously using traditional language that is not his own in all respects. A major indication is his speaking in the plural of the sins for which Christ died. In his own theological language Paul always speaks of sin in the singular. The plural phrase ὑπέρ τῶν ἁμαρτιῶν ἡμῶν (*hyper tōn hamartiōn hēmōn*, for our sins) appears characteristically in the tradition of 1 Cor. 15:3. And the similar phrase παρεδόθη διὰ τὰ παραπτώματα ἡμῶν (*paredothē dia ta paraptōmata hēmōn*, he was handed over for our transgressions) appears also as a traditional expression in Rom. 4:25. All of these passages involve allusions to the notion of sacrifice that is found also in Isaiah 53, where the phrase διὰ or περὶ τὰς ἁμαρτίας ἡμῶν (*dia / peri tas hamartias hēmōn*, for our sins) appears frequently.

Traditional language may also be involved in speaking of Jesus Christ's giving himself, an expression that is also used by Paul in Gal. 2:20 (cf. Eph. 5:2, 25; 1 Tim. 2:6; Titus 2:14). The passive form "he was handed over for our sins," based on Isa. 53:12 (LXX: παρεδόθη [*paredothē*]), is also used in Rom. 4:25, as well as the active statement "God handed him over for us all" (Rom. 8:32). Whether this self-sacrifice formula represents a primitive stage of Christology based on the Jewish notion of martyrdom could be determined only by extensive investigation.

Finally, pre-Pauline language may also be suspected in the soteriological statement of purpose in v. 4: ὅπως ἐξέληται ἡμᾶς ἐκ τοῦ αἰῶνος τοῦ ἐνεστῶτος πονηροῦ (*hopōs exelētai hēmas ek tou aiōnos tou enestōtos ponērou*, to deliver us from the present evil age). In contrast to this expression, Paul speaks elsewhere only of αἰὼν οὗτος (*aiōn houtos*, this aeon), not of "the present evil aeon." But in isolation such observations rest on a very insecure foundation. One point, however, may well be important: by means of these echoes of early tradition, Paul emphasizes the liturgical character of this passage. At the same time, he is reminding the Galatians of elementary credal formulas. Naturally, he is able to take every word of this and make it his own.

The salvific significance of Jesus' death is understood here in terms of deliverance or liberation, as in Col. 1:13: "He has delivered us from the dominion of darkness and transferred us to the kingdom of his beloved Son."

In Colossians the prison is represented by the power of darkness; here it is called the present evil age. Both agree in representing humanity as being subject to a power by which it is held captive, from which it cannot set itself free.

The "present age" is not a historical period that will be replaced by another, not an evil era followed by one that is better. This age or aeon is the world as it exists until the eschatological irruption of the world to come, which will be God's new creation. This present age is called evil not with respect to its creatureliness but because sin is at work in it. Sin is the cause of the captivity in the present aeon. Deliverance does not consist in a transformation of circumstances, nor even simply in the change of aeons that is yet to come, but in the liberating power that proceeds from the atoning death of Jesus Christ. This deliverance consists neither in transforming the world nor in forsaking it. To be delivered from the present evil age means that a place has been prepared through Jesus Christ, a place not subject to any power belonging to the world (which for Paul includes both ἐνεστῶτα (*enestōta*, things present) and μέλλοντα (*mellonta*, things to come) and from which no one can be separated, the place to which those who believe in Christ are brought: the love of God in Christ Jesus (Rom. 8:39), the kingdom of his beloved Son (Col. 1:13). It is there that χάρις (*charis*, grace) and εἰρήνη (*eirēnē*, peace) reign. There they are constantly experienced afresh. And because the will of God is fulfilled there in the event of salvation, there God also receives the honor due him for all eternity.

By describing salvation as deliverance, Paul anticipates a primary theme of the letter. And by using "we" to include himself with the Galatians, he insists that the argument to follow, bitter as it may be, is conducted where all those who believe in Christ belong: under the cross of Christ, the place of God's love.

The Apostolic Curse

1:6–9

6 I am astonished that you are so quickly deserting him who called you [to be] in the grace of Christ and turning to a different gospel.

7 Not that there is another. But there are some who trouble you and want to turn the gospel of Christ into its opposite.

8 But even if we or an angel from heaven should preach to you a gospel contrary to that which we preached to you, let him be accursed.

9 As we have said before, so now I say again, If any one is preaching to you a gospel contrary to that which you received, let him be accursed.

The rules of ancient epistolary style are conceptualized in rhetoric; according to them, the *prescript* is followed by the *exordium*. The standard model for ancient rhetoric was a speech in defense of a person before a court or other public forum. The purpose of the *exordium* is, accordingly, "to gain the sympathy of the judge (or, more broadly, of the public) for the subject matter as represented by a partisan."[15] The formal requirements of a speech also apply to the written presentation of a position intended to gain the good will and understanding of those addressed.

It may seem artificial and grotesque to look for rhetorical forms in a Pauline letter, especially one composed so much on impulse. In the interpretation of Paul, this possibility has been assessed in various ways. Scholastic exegesis (for example, Thomas Aquinas or Nicholas of Lyra), in its efforts to analyze the text down to its smallest units, made frequent use of rhetorical forms. A knowledge of these was part of a basic education in the arts.

Surprisingly, Luther (probably at the urging of Melanchthon) likewise used the rhetorical approach in his interpretation, drawing on it for understanding. His concern, however, was less to analyze the text into units than to follow the movements of its language and its flow of emotion, although both—individual units and overall movement—go together when the text is understood correctly. The correct analysis of a text is not intended to drain the life from it so that it can be studied anatomically. It is meant, rather, to understand the life that pulses within it and follow its rhythm.

Among the modern commentators on Galatians, Hans Dieter Betz has emphasized the rhetorical background and made it a primary theme of his exegesis. It is undeniably true that we may assume Paul enjoyed a substantial measure of Hellenistic education along with his Hebrew rabbinic training; but it would be erroneous to assume that he always composed his letters on the basis of the proper rhetorical model. Such rules for the most part describe what takes place automatically when the speaker or writer devotes himself entirely to his cause and becomes totally involved in his situation.

The *exordium* is followed by (to use rhetorical terminology) the *narratio*, a statement of what will be shown in the *argumentatio* that follows. In the present case it is not clear where the introductory section ends. Even apart from formal compositional considerations, opinions differ as to whether the introduction to the letter, which clearly begins in v. 6, includes v. 10, or even vv. 11 and 12. The so-called *narratio* begins in the literal sense in v. 13, with the narrative recollection of the apostle's past. But the point at issue is not biographical details from his own life, of interest for its own sake to those addressed. Instead, the *narratio* lays out the problem that will be discussed in the letter.

In antiquity it was common to begin the letter proper (following the *salutation formula*) by establishing a personal point of contact with those addressed. In the generally prevalent religious atmosphere, this might involve assurances that the writer remembered the addressee in thanksgiving and intercession before the deity. Such sentiments are, therefore, not unique to Christian letters. But the letters of Paul furnish particularly impressive examples of how rich human communication can be in its modulations when it is permeated by the spirit of Christian prayer.

Let us take 1 Cor. 1:4–8 as an example. These verses constitute a single sentence so that the entire passage is merely an explication of its first word (εὐχαριστῶ [*eucharistō*, I thank]): "I thank my God always for you because of the grace of God which was given you in Christ Jesus, that in every way you were enriched in him with all speech and all knowledge—even as the testimony to Christ was confirmed among you—so that you are not lacking in any spiritual gift, as you wait for the revealing of our Lord Jesus Christ, who will sustain you to the end, guiltless in the day of our Lord Jesus Christ."

Toward the beginning of all his letters, Paul states warmly how he sees the community addressed and his relationship to it raised up in their common relationship with God. He is moved by the spiritual life of those he addresses. He has such a living relationship with them that their life is part of his own. This makes the contrast in the introduction to Galatians all the more striking. Not a word of thanks to God for the Christian communities of Galatia, not even a prayer for them, but only an expression of deepest alienation followed by a terrible curse.

Of course this obvious difference must not lead us to overlook the finer nuances. It would be wrong to describe the uniqueness of this letter's introduction in totally privative terms, as though the usual spiritual bridge section were simply omitted here, whether because Paul is in a hurry to get to his subject or because he is deeply wounded and, therefore, begins with words of blunt rejection instead of friendship. Here, too, Paul begins with the spiritual state of the Galatian communities and his own relationship to them, describing the situation frankly as it is in the eyes of God. There is no glossing over the fact that there is apostasy. The consequences, if one really stops to think about it, are terrible.

As Paul here describes the situation of the church, the possibility of prayer is frighteningly distant. But the very fact that prayer is presupposed and is adapted here to the extraordinary situation lends Paul's words a weight they could not possibly have if he were to give free rein to disillusionment and anger, to condemnation and threats, as would be quite understandable in this situation in human terms.

But the anathema that is pronounced here is totally different from a curse uttered in anger. That it is introduced not by εὐχαριστῶ (*eucharistō*, I give thanks) but by θαυμάζω (*thaumazō*, I am astonished) seems no less abrasive when one recognizes that Paul is clearly not attempting to insult his readers with irony or demolish them indiscriminately. He makes a clear distinction between those who are affected, with whom he feels an intimate sense of solidarity, and those who are responsible for the imminent catastrophe, with whom he wishes to have nothing to do, consigning them to God's judgment.

This section is no more dominated than the rest of the letter by the monotony of a judgment of wrath staged by Paul himself. Instead we find here at the very beginning the polyphony growing out of the fact that the gospel, because it is a message of joyous good news, is a matter of the utmost gravity. And precisely because the gospel is the ground of freedom it does not permit arbitrary deviation. Paradoxically, the gospel must be intolerant on behalf of freedom. Therefore we can already see in vv. 6–9 the intensity of Paul's struggle on behalf of the Galatians, which will later find expression in the moving words that imply an equally intense solidarity with them (cf. especially 4:12 ff.).

What happened in Galatia? The information conveyed by these verses appears to be slight. But if we look closely, they reveal more than a little. The Christian communities of Galatia are in the midst of a terrible crisis. Paul uses the verb μετατίθεσθαι (*metatithesthai*, become disloyal) to describe what is happening. If we take the verb in its literal sense, the Galatians are involved in a change of place. The same word is used in Heb. 11:5, for instance, to describe the assumption of Enoch. The Latin equivalent, used by the Vulgate, is *transferre*, cognate with English "transfer," as in the transfer of funds to a different monetary area. Verse 6 obviously refers to turning away, to disloyalty or apostasy; but there are overtones of a change of position or party, so that an element of sarcasm is probably involved. The opprobrious epithet ὁ μεταθέμενος (*ho metathemenos*, the renegade) was once applied to an Epicurean who went over to the Stoa. Such use of the verb has connotations of lack of character. And although the financial meaning alluded to above is a product of modern usage, it symbolizes vividly the change of values that accompanies the change of place, the subjection to an alien system.

The change goes beyond incidentals. There has been a change of sign affecting everything, even—to drop the image of transfer of funds—when the same words are used as before. They take on a totally different meaning. Even when one continues to speak of Christ or the gospel, these terms now mean something else. There has been a confusion of language, whether in consequence or in furtherance of mental confusion. Despite the appearance of close association with what has gone before, everything has in fact been turned upside down. Such a process of derangement has been taking place in Galatia.

History knows many instances, both small and large scale, of intellectual changes that suddenly erupt within a community or society and spread like a plague—unpredictable, almost inexplicable, and hard to influence. In Galatia the process is still going on, as we can see from the use of the present tense in vv. 6–7 (and later in 4:9, 21) and from a host of other symptoms in this letter. The outcome is still unknown. This is reason for excitement and encouragement but also for deep depression, depending on how one diagnoses the situation. Paul's verdict is not optimistic. He finds the situation extremely perilous and knows that it represents an extraordinary challenge. His language shows that everything is at stake. It also demands that modern readers, so distant from Paul, open themselves to such a situation of utmost danger if they are to understand him at all.

The situation in Galatia has all the earmarks of a sudden surprise. "So quickly"—this temporal adjective describing what has happened is ambiguous and depends on the point in time involved. Is Paul thinking of the time when he was carrying out his missionary work in Galatia? Or the more recent date of his second visit, if there was one? Or the first appearance of his opponents among the Galatian Christians? Or does he have in mind the speed with which the crisis is unfolding?

What does he actually mean to convey? It was not long ago that you were converted—are you already falling away? Or: I was with you just a short while ago—why this sudden change? Or: Those who would lure you away have just appeared on the scene—have you already gone astray? Or: You could have inquired of me and waited for what I might have to say—but no, you rush pell-mell to destruction!

Of the interpretations suggested, the first is the most likely. It is of a piece with the account of the Galatians' apostasy that follows. The terminus a quo is not identical with the time of their call but is closely related to it. Nevertheless, the phrase οὕτως ταχέως (*houtōs tacheōs*, so quickly) does not admit a more precise chronology. Paul does not mean that if more time had passed and the Galatians' apostasy had taken place ten years later it would have been easier to understand. All that really matters is the overwhelming magnitude of what had befallen the Galatians, which they have turned their backs on (cf. 3:5).

The breathless evanescence of their Christianity is at fundamental variance with its origin and basis. Therefore there is an element of truth in all the interpretations of οὕτως ταχέως. The suddenness is not a circumstantial accident. It points to an essential characteristic of all apostasy, which is also in striking competition with the expectant "soon" that characterizes the hope of the earliest Christians (e.g., Rom. 16:20; Rev. 2:16). But what is so astonishing and incomprehensible about apostasy has nothing to do with chronology. In the final analysis, οὕτως ταχέως merely underlines one's astonishment that such apostasy could take place. The bewilderment grows as one becomes increasingly aware of the miracle involved in the call to be a Christian. How can it happen that anyone can heedlessly reject such a gift?

The common charge that people have changed their position for political or ideological reasons is not directly applicable to the present situation. Seen from outside, this does appear to be what has happened. The Galatians had been Paul's adherents; now they have gone over to his opponents. Previously they had put their trust in his gospel; now they put their trust in another. For Paul, however, this description is wrong. The real shift in apostasy is not from him to others, nor from one doctrine to another. The terminus a quo is rather the source of all being: ἀπὸ τοῦ καλέσαντος ὑμᾶς ἐν χάριτι (*apo tou kalesantos hymas en chariti*, from him who called you in grace); the terminus ad quem is simply zero: εἰς ἕτερον εὐαγγέλιον, ὃ οὐκ ἔστιν ἄλλο (*eis heteron euangelion, ho ouk estin allo*, to a different gospel — not that there is another). Their apostasy is from God to something that simply does not exist. This is the fundamental image of the fall as described already in Genesis 3. How Paul describes the beginning and end of such a fall, however, needs to be examined more closely.

The Galatians might also be said to be deserting "Christ" or "the gospel." The reason why Paul does not put the matter thus might be explained by pointing out that he would be contradicting the facts. His opponents also are supporters of Jesus Christ. They also claim to be preaching gospel. The situation would be clearer (because it would be unambiguous) if the Galatians had simply deserted Christ and the gospel to return to paganism. But Paul had fallen afoul of a conflict between Christ and Christ, between gospel and gospel. How precarious the situation is can be seen from the difficulty in formulating the terminus ad quem of their apostasy: εἰς ἕτερον εὐαγγέλιον, ὃ οὐκ ἔστιν ἄλλο (eis heteron euangelion, ho ouk estin allo, a different gospel—not that there is another!). Different but not another! A gospel but not a gospel!

But such explanations can hardly explain why Paul does not say: "I am astonished that you are so quickly deserting Jesus Christ *or* the gospel." There can be no gainsaying that we must deal here with a conflict between Christ and another Christ, between the gospel and another gospel. Nor does Paul wish to mitigate this conflict. He wishes rather to intensify it by redefining the terminus a quo of the apostasy.

To the ears of Paul's opponents and the Galatians influenced by them, it must sound particularly severe, indeed almost absurd, to say that it is God himself who is being deserted. This is in fact Paul's meaning, even though he does not explicitly add the word "God" to the participial phrase ὁ καλέσας ὑμᾶς (ho kalesas hymas, him who called you). Just as v. 1 referred to διὰ θεοῦ πατρὸς τοῦ ἐγείραντος αὐτὸν ἐκ νεκρῶν (dia theou patros tou egeirantos auton ek nekrōn, through God the Father, who raised him from the dead), Paul could certainly have said: ἀπὸ θεοῦ πατρὸς τοῦ καλέσαντος ὑμᾶς ἐν χάριτι (apo theou patros tou kalesantos hymas en chariti, from God the Father, who called you in grace).

Paul can omit the word "God" because in his usage the participial ὁ καλέσας (ho kalesas, he who called) or ὁ καλῶν (ho kalōn, he who calls) is a standard term for God (Rom. 4:17; 9:12; Gal. 1:15; 5:8; 1 Thess. 2:12; 5:24). For Paul, "calling" is a fundamental element of God's nature. It is so typical of what God does that the same word can be used for God's historical call to salvation, his primordial calling of all things into being, and his eschatological call into life from death (cf. Rom. 4:17). Therefore the historical call the Galatians experienced is not a mere invitation; it is an efficacious word that brings about what it states. What has taken place is therefore all the more serious: not only has an invitation been refused, but God's own work has been vitiated and his word contradicted.

The declaration that God himself, rather than "Christ" or the "gospel," has been deserted makes for a blunter attack on Judaizing tendencies. The ultimate authority, Paul says, is involved, and the charge is transgression of the first commandment. Above all, however, Paul wishes to preclude any appeal to alternative positions, as though we were dealing here with one opinion confronting another, with one religious authority competing with another. This would also not be what his opponents had in mind. Paul's concern is to make explicit the decisive criterion. He does this by appealing not to principles or ideas but to an event, to what the Galatians have experienced. This mode of argumentation appears repeatedly in Galatians (especially in 3:2–5).

Christ—that could be confused with an idol. Gospel—that could be mistaken for an ideology. The Galatians must be absolutely clear about what they are on the point of doing; they must think about what has befallen them, about what they have actually experienced. Therefore, Paul refers here to God rather than using the name of Jesus Christ or the concept of the gospel. This way of referring to God denotes an event that involves the Galatians themselves, because they have been part of it. It is God who has called you, therefore you are those who have been called by God. By deserting this God you are deserting yourselves, you are deserting what you have become through the call of God, you are deserting what you have been called to by this call. By the appeal to experience, the "no" to God is made a self-contradictory denial of the Galatians themselves.

The range of this argumentation becomes clear when we see that it blocks all recourse to any neutral stance. Could Paul's opponents not argue likewise that God's call had gone to the Galatians no less through them than through Paul, however the relationship between the two calls might be conceived, whether as contradiction or as enhancement? Once more the Galatians have experienced something new—otherwise they could scarcely have been won over. To counter such a threatening way of stating the situation Paul introduces the phrase ἐν χάριτι (*en chariti*, in grace) into his description.

This crucial word introduces an exegetical problem. The appended genitive Χριστοῦ (*Christou*, of Christ) must be considered secondary from the point of view of textual criticism. If it is dropped, we seem well on the way to a kind of formalization. The specific χάρις Χριστοῦ (*charis Christou*, grace of Christ) threatens to fade into χάρις in general. And it is no longer possible to follow the line of interpretation taken by Calvin: Christ is already to be understood as the subject of καλεῖν (*kalein*, call). Calvin translates: "Miror quod ita cita transferimini in Christo, qui vos vocavit in gratia, ad aliud evangelium . . ."[16] ("I am astonished that you are so quickly deserting Christ, who called you in grace, for a different gospel . . ."). He makes the genitive Χριστοῦ (*Christou*, of Christ) depend not on ἐν χάριτι (*en chariti*, in grace), but on the preposition ἀπό (*apo*, from), and therefore connects Χριστοῦ with τοῦ καλέσαντος (*tou kalesantos*, he who called you).

This is impossible for various grammatical and textual reasons, however correct Calvin may be in his intent to stress the contradiction the Galatians are involving themselves in with respect to the work of Christ. They are left with nothing more than an imitation Christ, a dummy. As concerns the actual text, we must be content to observe that χάρις is here used absolutely, and both interpretations are left open: χάρις Χριστοῦ (*charis Christou*, the grace of Christ), or χάρις θεοῦ (*charis theou*, the grace of God), as the variation in the textual tradition reflects.

This brings us to the real difficulty in this passage: how are we to interpret the combination of καλεῖν (*kalein*, call) with the preposition ἐν (*en*, in)? It might be taken as an instrumental or causal use of ἐν. This would mean that grace was the instrument or basis of God's call; one might say it was the motive for the call. Then the phrase καλεῖν ἐν χάριτι (*kalein en chariti*, call in grace) would correspond to the construction used in v. 15: καλεῖν διὰ τῆς χάριτος αὐτοῦ (*kalein dia tēs charitos autou*, call through his grace). Verse 6, like v. 15, would then refer to the grace of God.

Although Paul usually associates χάρις with Christ, so that it appears as "Christ-grace," he also uses the phrase ἡ χάρις τοῦ θεοῦ (*hē charis tou theou*, the grace of God), as in the central statement of his argument in Galatians: "I do not nullify the grace of God; for if justification were through the law, then Christ died to no purpose" (2:21). Or 1 Cor. 1:4: "I give thanks to God always for you because of the grace of God which was given you in Christ Jesus." More examples could be cited. But they would only underline what we have already observed in the apostolic salutation: when Paul speaks of χάρις, it is impossible to distinguish the reference to God from the reference to Christ, playing one off against the other. It is, therefore, quite unlikely that in this passage Paul added the phrase ἐν χάριτι (*en chariti*, in grace) merely as a pious flourish, without significance, appended to the statement that God called the Galatians only to emphasize that the call resulted from his gracious state of mind.

Particularly if one interprets ἐν χάριτι as referring to God's motives, understood emphatically, the notion of God's purpose and goal is necessarily implied. Then it would be easy to misread the passage as though it said εἰς χάριν (*eis charin*, for grace). This is the basis of the Vulgate's translation: *qui vos vocavit in gratiam Christi*, who called you to the grace of Christ. Many modern interpreters give a similar translation: "God called you to grace, i.e., to a state of grace." In this case being in a state of grace would be the purpose and result of the call.

Now, if in fact the emphasis is here on election that comes through grace, Paul has already stated the terminus a quo of apostasy, making a crucial distinction: the Galatians have experienced God's call as a liberating power of grace, not as the enslaving power of the law.

Later, Paul will summarize his argument: "You are severed from Christ, you who would be justified by the law; you have fallen away from grace" (5:4). This theme is already announced here in the *exordium*: they have fallen away from him whose call is the reason why they are under grace.

The strange prepositional phrase καλεῖν ἐν χάριτι (*kalein en chariti*) is, therefore, best translated "under the sign of grace" or, more freely, "in the power of grace." In other words, this call from God, which is a *verbum efficax*, is the vehicle and instrument of grace. This is what the Galatians had experienced. From the moment of God's call, their very being was under the sign of grace and in the power of grace. Now that they have come to the terminus ad quem of their apostasy, they can no longer make this boast. The call that they now mean to follow stands clearly in contradiction to grace.

When Paul calls this opposite into which they are about to lapse ἕτερον εὐαγγέλιον (*heteron euangelion*, a different gospel), it is only in order to state by means of the oxymoron that they are destroying nothing less than the gospel itself because they are turning it into its opposite.

In pre-Christian usage, the term "gospel" was used for a variety of good news. There is no trace of exclusivity. Even when we look at the corresponding Hebrew word *baśar* and its use in the Old Testament, we do not find anything truly unique. The change that turned "gospel" into "the gospel," with a single referent, came about when the term was associated with Jesus Christ. In the history of the word εὐαγγέλιον (*euangelion*, good news), which we will not trace in detail here, the shift of meaning to the good news of Jesus Christ had already taken place before Paul and independently of him. But theological reflection on the meaning of this change and thus on the nature of the gospel itself is first observed in Paul; in fact, he probably initiated it.

It is therefore reasonable to assume that Paul's opponents in Galatia also claimed the word "gospel," although they had not thought through their use of it theologically. It is therefore even conceivable that they spoke of their message in contrast to that of Paul as "another gospel," without noting the self-contradiction involved in such a phrase. It was Paul who was acutely aware of this contradiction. It is not merely that he finds the presentation of another Jesus, another spirit, another gospel intolerable (cf. 2 Cor. 11:4); this would also hold true for his opponents, who were equally intolerant of competition. Instead, Paul sees clearly why the gospel is essentially one, admitting no alternative.

At first glance it appears that Paul is merely making an authoritarian claim that his gospel is the only true gospel. There is a suspicious air about Paul's frequent use of the first person singular or plural possessive pronoun with εὐαγγέλιον, referring to himself or himself and his fellow workers: τὸ εὐαγγέλιόν μου (to euangelion mou, my gospel; Rom. 2:16; 16:25); τὸ εὐαγγέλιον ἡμῶν (to euangelion hēmōn, our gospel; 1 Thess. 1:5; 2 Cor. 4:3). There are also passages where Paul speaks emphatically of the gospel that he preaches, for example, Gal. 2:2 and 1 Cor. 15:1. Is he linking the gospel with his own person? He denies this accusation out of hand: "For what we preach is not ourselves, but Jesus Christ as Lord, with ourselves as your servants for Jesus' sake" (2 Cor. 4:5).

Or is Paul insisting dogmatically that his version of the gospel is the only true one, making no allowance for anyone else? For us, thinking in historical terms, it is perhaps only too natural that each person may and must have his own theology; primitive Christianity must have offered a kaleidoscopic variety of competing theologies. This view was certainly foreign to Paul. But it would be anachronistic to expect him to make a conscious distinction between gospel and theology.

This certainly does not mean, however, that Paul failed to realize that even obvious differences do not necessarily preclude cooperation in the preaching of the gospel. What he says about his relationship with Apollos is significant in this regard (1 Cor. 3:4–9). Even when motives are mixed, he can say generously: "What then? All that matters is that Christ is proclaimed, whether in pretense or in truth; and in that I rejoice" (Phil. 1:15–18).

In all these instances the gospel is proclaimed differently, but it is not a different gospel. Gal. 2:7, which refers to the decision of the so-called apostolic council, makes a distinction between two gospels, one for the uncircumcised and one for the circumcised (εὐαγγέλιον τῆς ἀκροβυστίας / εὐαγγέλιον τῆς περιτομῆς, euangelion tēs akrobystias / euangelion tēs peritomēs), that is, between a gospel for the Gentiles and a gospel for the Jews. Whether this form of expression has any bearing on the "different gospel" in Gal. 1:17 will be discussed in the context of 2:7.[17] What we have observed already, however, should caution us against assuming that Paul made wholesale positivistic claims of exclusivity. But he does espouse the cause of an unambiguous and therefore exclusive understanding of the gospel. And he does suggest a criterion that permits appropriate verification: the antithesis between χάρις (*charis*, grace) and νόμος (*nomos*, law).

But it cannot be denied that we seem to encounter here features typical of later polemic against heresy. Paul refuses to engage in any discussion. He issues edicts and discredits his opponents to the point of ἀνάθεμα (*anathema*, accursed), just as later conciliar texts pronounce their anathemas and the confessions of the Reformation use *damnare*, subsequently weakened to *improbare*. The actions and motives of his opponents he describes solely from his own perspective. They are agitators sowing the seeds of disorder, with no other purpose than to pervert the gospel of Christ, whatever their claims to the contrary. Their way of life is as pernicious as their teaching. There is nothing good to say about them, or at least none is recognized.

The fact that he does not mention them by name but speaks only of "some" people appears to be a departure from later polemic against heresy, which turned at least certain representative names into horrible examples, highly stylized, to be named with dread long after those who bore the names had died and the substance of their teaching was only of historical interest. But ecclesiastical practice has also made use of *deletio memoriae*. All memory of the enemies of orthodoxy is blotted out and they become non-persons.

We cannot tell whether Paul has something like this in mind. In spite of everything, however, he cannot be described as the typical representative of all the charges laid against the church by the modern world—manifestly turning the forms of antiheretical polemic around, so that the church is now stereotyped every bit as much as it once stereotyped the heretics. The extent to which Paul's conduct does not fit the cliché of heresy hunting may be inferred in part from what has already been said; what follows will make the difference even clearer.

We are not told what moved the opponents of Paul, as seen through their own eyes, to set to work in the Galatian congregations. Of course, such cases always involve impure motives or at least thoughtlessness. We have no right, however, to base our analysis on such insinuations; we have every reason not to translate the problem into personal or ethical terms, thereby blunting its force or distorting it by poisoning the atmosphere. Without at this point exhausting all the relevant information in the letter, we can say this much with some assurance: the people involved were Jewish Christian missionaries or emissaries, who claimed that circumcision and other rites spelled out in the Torah were required of Christians. A messianic faith in Jesus was here combined with Jewish observance of the law, producing a Christian spirituality that kept within the limits of a Jewish sect. We do not know whether they saw themselves called to do missionary work among Gentiles, thus also gaining proselytes for Judaism, or merely trying to gain influence in already existing congregations of gentile Christians. We can only surmise that they were seriously convinced that the Christians of the Pauline mission, living without the law, had been deceived about true salvation.

Our interest in describing Paul's opponents can easily lead us to forget the equally important question of how the Galatian congregations could have been thrown into such a state of confusion. It will not suffice merely to speak of outside religious agitators. We must also inquire into what left the Galatian Christians so susceptible to such agitation. This leads in turn to a further question: what motivated them originally to become Christians in response to Paul's preaching? Most of these historical questions are shrouded in obscurity. All we can do is cite three major pieces of evidence.

First, the Galatians lived as Gentiles, as non-Jews, surrounded by a variety of religious options; they were probably much concerned with religious questions and passions. The details could be filled in on the basis of our historical knowledge, but if we restrict ourselves to the most elementary level, we will probably not go wrong in assuming that a profound dissatisfaction with the world and a restless search for personal fulfillment were the soil in which the seed of the gospel sprouted. The phrase "the present evil age" in v. 4 undoubtedly refers to the experience that explains why the Galatians were moved to listen to a Jew who came to them as an itinerant preacher but not trying to turn them into Jews. It takes some imagination to picture this missionary situation; but with respect to the deepest motivation on the part of the Galatians, it is hardly necessary to search further than our own hidden experiences.

Second, despite the many letters of Paul that we possess, and despite the account in Acts, it is not easy to arrive at a clear and convincing picture of what Paul's mission actually involved. Whether to assume, in the case of Galatia, a kind of infiltration through diaspora Judaism must remain an open question. In any case, one must realize that Paul brought with him the most important product of diaspora Judaism: the Greek translation of the Holy Scriptures of Judaism, the Septuagint. In large measure he had probably already learned them by heart. But he also had them in whole or in part in the form of a written text, at least the Torah and the Prophets. "Scripture" or "the Scriptures" is his term for the canonical corpus, the extent of which was not yet definitively determined. In our context, it is important to single out what was later to be called the Old Testament; there was as yet no trace of any New Testament as an addendum to it. It will help elucidate the double conversion of the Galatians: their conversion to Christianity of the Pauline sort, and their desertion of it under the influence of Judaizing Christians.

Paul uses the verb εὐαγγελίζεσϑαι (*euangelizesthai* [middle voice], proclaim the gospel) preferentially along with κηρύσσειν (*kēryssein*, proclaim publicly) to describe his missionary preaching. The subject of his preaching is not Scripture, but Jesus Christ. Of Paul's letters that are undoubtedly genuine, three—1 Thessalonians, Philippians, and Philemon—contain few if any references to the Old Testament. But the four other major letters are full of biblical allusions and quotations, and argue to a large extent on the basis of biblical exegesis.

It would certainly be false to assume that, in his mission to the Gentiles, Paul at first avoided the Old Testament and only later, primarily under pressure from Judaizing circles, made greater use of it in order to beat his opponents with their own weapon. Such an assumption would be totally at odds with the general nature of this highly educated scribe. His call to be an apostle of Jesus Christ did not distance him from Scripture but made it possible for him to understand Scripture through the Spirit of Jesus Christ. In 2 Cor. 3:4ff., referring to the change that has been brought about through Christ, Paul writes of the difference between the two dispensations and testaments as the antithesis between the letter that kills and the Spirit that gives life. As the introductory words show, this distinction is highly informative with respect to Paul's own person.

Now this change in the manner of understanding Scripture undoubtedly changed the way it was used. Paul's message was not proclaimed in the form of preaching on Old Testament texts. But it is safe to assume that he did familiarize the congregations he founded with Scripture, to the extent that the Septuagint was not already familiar to them as part of their religious heritage. Its dissemination in the Hellenistic world must not be underestimated. Of course the conflict with Judaism (probably not by itself) led Paul to make more intensive use of Scripture in the gentile Christian communities. But how can we assume that Paul's biblical argumentation in Galatians 3 and 4 was accessible to his addressees if it was only his opponents and not Paul himself who first introduced them to Scripture?

But in fact Scripture turned out to be a two-edged sword. It was far from clear that the Judaizers did not have the better argument with respect to Scripture. Even without any malicious outside influence, there was here a latent occasion of uncertainty for the Galatians.

Third, it is unlikely that their new conversion is to be explained on the basis of a change of mind about Scripture, as though its authority, which had been suggested to them by Paul, had now won the upper hand over the κύριος Ἰησοῦς Χριστός (*kyrios Iēsous Christos*, Lord Jesus Christ). The Judaizing emissaries may indeed have found a weak point here, but their primary interest was not in an exegetical principle as such but in the soteriological meaning of the law and what it meant to belong to the chosen people. The inner reason why the Galatians deserted Paul, it seems to me, cannot be derived primarily from the question of how Scripture is to be understood. The real reason for their instability must be connected with the liberating effect of the Spirit they had experienced when they first became Christians. There are indications later in the letter that this is where we should look for the sore point. Not in the sense that enthusiasm waned and freedom gave way once more to the pressures of daily life, as though the motive were inward exhaustion. This would have made reversion to paganism more likely. On the other hand, the Judaizers can hardly have precipitated a crisis not already in the making. Thus it is reasonable to suppose that the Galatians had been dizzied by their enthusiastic freedom, so that the transports of their religious experience left them finally without religious anchor. The Judaizing message rushed in to fill this vacuum.

It could be depicted as a necessary corrective to the first phase of their life as Christians, not diminishing their spirituality but enhancing and confirming it. Luther describes the appeal trenchantly: "'Christus ein feiner meister, incipit, sed Mose mus das gewelb schliessen.' Daran zeige sich diaboli natura: quando non potest perdere homines nocendo et insectando, facit meliorando."[18] ("'Christ's a fine master. He makes the beginning, but Moses must complete the structure.' The devil's nature shows itself therein: if he cannot ruin people by wronging and persecuting them, he will do it by improving them.") The Judaizers offered concrete guarantees and criteria for salvation. And it made more sense to consider Jesus the Christ—although he had been crucified—than, as Paul so offensively taught, because he had been crucified.

The very religious appeal of the Judaizing propaganda must have alarmed Paul. Erosion of the community through laxness and accommodation to the pagan environment would be less serious. Confusion about the essence of the gospel is incomparably more dangerous. The Galatians still speak of the "gospel," but it is law in gospel's clothing and therefore not that which alone deserves the name of gospel, having its ground and substance in the grace of Christ. And they still speak of Christ, though not as the Christ who set them free (Gal. 5:1) but as an adjunct to the law. In this way this gospel is annulled. For the "different gospel" that is no gospel ends up by saying that Christ died in vain (Gal. 2:21). Now, indeed, he is truly put to death and his resurrection denied.

Generally speaking, it is easy to destroy quickly and permanently something that has required great labor and sacrifice to build. In the case of Paul's work this is especially true. Anyone with any experience of what it means to bear the responsibility for the life of a Christian congregation will understand why Paul reacts so violently as soon as the heart of the Christian faith is threatened. In such a case it is out of place to criticize the response for being overly impassioned. Albert Bengel states the situation well: "Controversiae non modo [non] possunt, sed ne debent quidem sine affectu tractari; sed affectus debet esse sanctus."[19] (Controversies not only cannot but must not be carried on unemotionally; but the emotion must be holy.)

Now, we are dealing here not just with Paul's own work, but with the work God has accomplished in the person of Paul and used him as an agent to continue. Paul's Judaizing opponents are casting doubt on the very thing that made Paul an apostle and has determined his life ever since. His decision for the sake of Christ to count as refuse all that he could boast of as a Pharisaic Jew (Phil. 3:4–8) must now, to the extent that the Jewish Christian understanding of the law is involved, appear a blasphemous error. The advance of the Judaizers into Galatia is aimed at Paul's very heart; it not only seeks to rob him of his congregations, but also denies him personally righteousness before God, charging him before God with having gone astray and now seeking to lead the whole world astray. Here there can be no peaceful coexistence.

It is not the attack of the Judaizers that has unleashed a life-or-death struggle. The gospel itself is a matter of life or death, as the *prescript* explicitly reminds us. But the gospel is concerned with self-assertion, with a survival that seeks to evade death or even eliminates one's opponent in self-defense. People everywhere are engaged in such life-or-death battles. They infect the religious world in crusades and holy wars, in inquisitors or certain ayatollahs, but also in the hidden forms of calumny and violations of conscience.

In the light of Jesus Christ, however, the gospel speaks of a totally different kind of life-or-death struggle. There life has emerged out of death, because life has been sacrificed to death. The attitude of faith toward life is changed accordingly. "For to me to live is Christ, and to die is gain," Paul affirms (Phil. 1:21). This revaluation and interpenetration of life and death took place in Jesus Christ and can therefore be claimed by those who are in Jesus Christ (cf. Gal. 2:19–20). It would be contrary to the gospel as preached by Paul if he were to follow, in his conflict with his opponents, the universal human-inhuman practice of battle to the death: only one of us can survive. But how is a struggle that now truly involves life or death to be reconciled with the battle between life and death fought by Jesus Christ on the cross?

It appears incomprehensible that anyone should make use of a curse in the context of the gospel. Was Paul carried away by anger at this point, acting contrarily to the Lord's word that he elsewhere took to heart: "Bless those who persecute you; bless and do not curse them" (Rom. 12:14; cf. Matt. 5:24; Luke 6:28)? A slip of the tongue here, which would actually be more like a slip of the heart, is out of the question, if only on stylistic grounds. Every word has clearly been chosen with careful consideration. Furthermore, the composition of the epistolary introduction appears to require that the apostolic curse should follow immediately after the apostolic blessing pronounced at the outset. Toward the end of the letter the blessing is repeated twice: in the *postscript* (6:18) and two verses before (6:16). If we disregard the *prescript* and *postscript* with the two blessings that encompass the entire letter, we could also say that the body of the letter itself is framed by a curse (1:8–9) and a blessing (6:16).

But that is not all. In the middle of the letter, at the very center of its subject matter, we find a concentration of statements about blessing and cursing: the blessing of Abraham and the curse of the law, from which Christ has set us free, in which he became a curse for us in order that we might share in the blessing of Abraham (3:9–14). In these words, initially enigmatic, Paul makes the relationship between blessing and cursing the key to God's saving work, which constitutes the substance of the gospel.

These observations caution us against ignoring the apparently offensive curses in vv. 8–9 as atavistic remnants of a magical world view. Blessing and cursing are complementary, like the positive and negative poles of an electric charge. They bring us back to the basic substratum of experience of the holy, as enshrined in all religions that still preserve traces of an archaic approach to reality.

Blessing and curse together represent a basic religious phenomenon, for which comparative religion provides copious illustrations. The holy is a wellspring of life, but it can also be pernicious or destructive to the life of the wicked. Neither aspect, however, is an immediate action or reaction of the holy. Both are communicated through the medium of the word. Blessing and curse are antithetical (and therefore sometimes conjoint) aspects of words fraught with power, through which some of the mystery of reality can be perceived and take effect. Although pronounced by human beings, such words transcend human understanding and power.

Within this fundamental structure, the complementary phenomena of blessing and curse exhibit a wide variety of forms, from magical ceremonies and formulas to such sublime manifestations as prayer and spiritual authority. As extreme possibilities of human language, corresponding to the inmost needs and fears of humanity, they are always subject to misuse and perversion. This is particularly true of cursing. When it becomes the vehicle of hatred and vengeance, and attempts to use the power of the holy for private ends, cursing becomes an act of blasphemy and is therefore forbidden.

But it would be premature to assume that the spirit of Jesus put an end to cursing, so that only blessing remains. That cursing is also associated with Jesus is shown by the tradition that he cursed the fig tree (Mark 11:14, 21) and spoke of those who are cursed at the eschatological judgment (Matt. 25:41). The commandment to bless and not to curse (Luke 6:28) has to do with loving one's enemy; it forbids cursing someone out of personal enmity rather than ruling out the possibility of cursing in general. Even swearing, which probably originates as a kind of conditional self-curse, is forbidden only when misused as a substitute for direct and honest statement (Matt. 5:33–37). In the Old Testament, blessing and curse are included in the law as sanctions, as Leviticus 26 and Deuteronomy 28 clearly illustrate. And the story of the fall in Genesis 3 already speaks of the curse on all human history.

It would be wrong to wish that God could only bless and deny him the right to curse. It would likewise be foolish to make easy use of ecclesiastical blessings while rejecting the very idea of cursing as being simply un-Christian. Paul uses this problematic phenomenon of cursing in three contexts.

The first instance is Paul's curse upon himself, albeit in a characteristically altered form. He could wish himself accursed and cut off from Christ instead of and for the sake of his brethren and kinsmen (Rom. 9:3). This paradox illustrates how Paul in his own life seeks to follow the principle he imposes on his fellow Christians in parenesis: "Bless those who persecute you; bless and do not curse them" (Rom. 12:14). The self-curse is here the ultimate illustration of how he wills a blessing for those who curse him. But even this is a marginal thought. In practice, as Paul well knows, the effect would be blasphemy, as though he were able to coerce God and control his incomprehensible predestination.

We find another self-execration when Paul says: "Woe to me if I do not preach the gospel!" (1 Cor. 9:16), for imprecating woe is also a kind of curse. Finally, the possibility of Paul's cursing himself appears in Gal. 1:8, this time in the notion that Paul himself would not be excluded from his anathema against anyone who would counterfeit the gospel.

Here we have already moved on to another usage. In Gal. 1:8–9 a sanction is added to the gospel, just as a sanction is added to the law in the form of a conditional curse. There are noteworthy differences, however. In contrast to the situation with the law, blessing and curse are not dependent on the doing of what is commanded. The gospel itself is the blessing. And the curse, at least here, is not on those who refuse to accept the gospel or later reject it, but only on those who proclaim it falsely. This special case is so serious because it destroys the blessing brought by the gospel, so that all others are robbed of its blessing.

Of course, this means that the curse extends beyond the circle of the false evangelist. The other side of the blessing poured out through Jesus Christ in the gospel consists in the fact that the curse strikes those who do not love the Lord. The exclamation at the end of 1 Corinthians (16:22), εἴ τις οὐ φιλεῖ τὸν κύριον, ἤτω ἀνάθεμα (ei tis ou philei ton kyrion, ētō anathema, if anyone has no love for the Lord, let him be accursed), is probably a fragment of the early Christian eucharistic liturgy borrowed by Paul. It is even conceivable that the absence of love can grow into hate, expressed in the cry Ἀνάθεμα Ἰησοῦς (anathema Iēsous, Jesus be cursed!: 1 Cor. 12:3). This is the ultimate criterion of what is certainly not the voice of the Spirit, and it may in fact be meant only as a contrast to the positive statement that the affirmation κύριος Ἰησοῦς (kyrios Iēsous, Jesus is Lord) is in any case the mark of the Holy Spirit.

A third Pauline use of cursing is expulsion from the community in cases of flagrant immorality. Even if only in absentia, Paul delivers the person in question to Satan—a charismatic act in a way representing a soteriological last resort (1 Cor. 5:3–5). It must be noted, however, that the passage says nothing of a curse expressis verbis. And, since the purpose is ultimately soteriological, the "ban" of the Old Testament cannot be intended, for it involves total and definitive surrender of a person to God's wrath.

Up to now we have discussed the phenomenon of cursing in general, not taking terminological nuances into account. New Testament usage involves two words, ἀνάθεμα (anathema) and κατάρα (katara), and their derivatives. Both occur in Galatians: ἀνάθεμα here in 1:8–9, and κατάρα in the crucial christological passage 3:10, 13.

In the case of ἀνάθεμα, we are dealing with the particular form of curse found in the Old Testament ban. The Hebrew word ḥerem, which refers to the ban itself or that which is banned, is always translated ἀνάθεμα by the Septuagint. The original meaning of ἀνάθεμα was neutral: something deposited in the sanctuary, a votive offering. Only through the influence of the Septuagint did it take on the specifically Old Testament meaning of something set apart from secular use and consigned directly to God for destruction. This gave rise in turn to the usage found in Paul, which he appears to have had a part in forming. Paul's usage of $\dot{\alpha}\nu\dot{\alpha}\vartheta\varepsilon\mu\alpha$ shares with the tradition he borrows the idea of something given over definitively to God for destruction. Paul, however, uses the word exclusively in relationship to the gospel: here in Gal. 1:8–9, in the eucharistic anathema of 1 Cor. 16:22, in the notion of his own vicarious rejection and abandonment, and at least indirectly in the absurd possibility of declaring Jesus himself to be $\dot{\alpha}\nu\dot{\alpha}\vartheta\varepsilon\mu\alpha$.

The sole purpose of the anathema is to maintain the purity of the gospel and the blessing it brings. In this function, however, it points up the mysterious boundary that cannot be crossed by the gospel's power to bless. The gospel can, in fact, be counterfeited. And it is by no means successful with everyone. What provokes an anathema in the context of this ultimate, inexplicable boundary is not infringement on territory that is God's alone, but the inward necessity of drawing serious attention to this boundary. In this interpretation, the anathema has declaratory force. It states what is true ipso facto when the gospel is veiled and someone says "No" to Jesus Christ. What is thus separated from God is consigned to God and his judgment.

In contrast to the situation in 1 Cor. 5:3–5, the Pauline anathema does not involve an explicitly charismatic element, unless it is charismatic for someone to insist on that ultimate boundary with such gravity and resolution. It should be noted, though, that in both primary passages (1 Cor. 16:22 and Gal. 1:8) the anathema is pronounced conditionally and without mention of names. The universal and almost tautological situation is underlined emphatically: those who counterfeit and disdain the eschatological blessing of the gospel will lose it. Those who separate themselves from God in this fashion are separated from him definitively. But they are *eo ipso* handed over to God.

It remains to be explained why Paul pronounces the anathema twice. The hypothesis that he immediately repeats his words only for emphasis is stylistically untenable. On various occasions Paul uses the verb $\pi\varrho o\lambda\acute{\varepsilon}\gamma\varepsilon\iota\nu$ (*prolegein*, say before) to refer to statements he made on earlier occasions and not to the text immediately preceding (e.g., 1 Thess. 3:4; 4:6; 2 Cor. 7:3; 13:2; Gal. 5:21). We must, therefore, assume that Paul had already pronounced this anathema on another occasion, whether during his initial missionary activity or some later visit, or even in some unknown letter, already foreseeing the crises and dangers to come.

This conclusion is supported by some differences in the formulation of the curse. The conditional clause of the first anathema (v. 8) is formulated as a real possibility that cannot be ruled out a priori, even though it would be an extreme far surpassing all other possibilities and therefore encompassing them: that Paul himself or even an angel from heaven should preach a different gospel, contrary to the gospel Paul had brought. For Paul, angels are always potential messengers (cf. Gal. 3:19), and even angels can defect from God; conversely, Satan can disguise himself as an angel of light (2 Cor. 11:14); similarly, there can be no absolute trust in an apostle, not even in Paul himself. The crucial thing is to follow not Paul but the gospel, albeit the gospel that Paul had preached irrevocably.

In the case of the second anathema (v. 9), an event has actually taken place. The conditional clause is formulated in general terms with τὶς (*tis*, anyone), just as the earlier clause (v. 7) used τινές (*tines*, some). But the situation is as clear as day. Paul also states the absolute criterion differently in v. 8 than in v. 9. In v. 8, it is what Paul preached as gospel to the Galatians. In v. 9, the same form of expression is inherently possible, but Paul refers instead to what the Galatians have received. The change is not merely for the sake of stylistic variety; it is meant to burden the Galatians with what they have already accepted, bringing them together. Now, in the midst of the crisis, they already possess the criterion for judgment. To contradict it will bring about a situation which Paul must bluntly oppose. In such a case there can be no more "ifs" and "buts," but only the definitive "No!" of anathema.

We would be deceiving ourselves not to admit how alien we still find this text. But it would be too simple to keep our distance by calling it an "archaic mode of thought," or whatever other label we use for things that alienate us. What we call archaic can embody dimensions of life and experiences that may be closed off to us or buried but are not necessarily irrelevant or simply nonexistent. Of course, we are hardly in a position—are hardly likely ever to be in a position—to repeat such an anathema, not to mention have to pronounce it on our own authority. But no matter what has come between us and Paul to prevent our using his language, there is also the possibility that what is difficult or even inaccessible to us in the Pauline text is the fact that it speaks with such unshakable certainty and gravity about what is indeed a matter of life or death. In comparison to Paul, we are far removed from such total demands and commitment. But this does not give us the right to pass judgment on something which, as we must confess, we barely understand. It invites us rather to open our ears to a deeper understanding of such uncommon language.

The Source of
the Apostolic Gospel
1:10–12

10 Am I now seeking to persuade people or even God? Or am I trying to please people? If I still wanted to please people, I would not be a servant of Christ.

11 For I would have you know, brethren: the gospel that was preached by me is not a human gospel.

12 For I did not receive it nor was I taught it from a person, but through the revelation of Jesus Christ [it was revealed to me].

Interpreters are agreed that Paul, between his *exordium* that ends with the curse and his exposition of the question at issue, which begins as a biographical narrative, inserts a transitional passage. There is disagreement over its extent, however, depending on how the words are interpreted and the function they are assigned. This difference of opinion illustrates the transitional function of the text.

Its beginning, marked by the temporal adverb ἄρτι (*arti*, now: v. 10), consists in a reflection on what has just been said. What it leads up to, described by the phrase ἀποκάλυψις Ἰησοῦ Χριστοῦ (*apokalypsis Iēsou Christou*, the revelation of Jesus Christ: v. 12), is the source of Paul's apostleship. The point of this passage, however, is not to drop a subject that has been settled and can therefore be declared of secondary importance, so that the letter can finally address the primary issue. Instead, the bridge already serves to introduce the fundamental thesis for what follows. It appears in the form of v. 11 in the middle of this short section.

The preceding verse is not a piece of perfunctory self-irony linking the section with what has gone before. If this were the case, no special weight would attach to the two rhetorical questions with which it begins. But when we examine them more closely, we see that here, from the very beginning, Paul's train of thought is determined by the gospel. What seems to be a mere transition, appearing to turn from the negative curse to the positive revelation of Christ, is intended rather to join them both in an incontestable unity.

The gospel proclaimed by Paul already defined the purpose of the strange-sounding *exordium*. This gospel, which has its origin in the revelation of Jesus Christ granted to Paul and accepted by him, was espoused with total assurance in Paul's resounding "No!" to any other gospel. Luther[20] uses the phrase "securissime pronuntiare" (state with absolute assurance). This is not a way of using language that is inherently natural. Appearances to the contrary notwithstanding, in that "No!" one can already hear the language of the gospel. The contrast with the normal standards of human judgment and acceptance therefore permeates the whole transitional section.

This dubious human standard is apostrophized four times: in v. 10 in the phrases ἀνθρώπους πείθειν (anthrōpous peithein, persuade human individuals) and ἀνθρώποις ἀρέσκειν (anthrōpois areskein, please people), in v. 11 in the statement οὐκ ἔστιν κατὰ ἄνθρωπον (ouk estin kata anthrōpon, is not [a] human [gospel]), and in v. 12 in the affirmation οὐδὲ γὰρ ἐγὼ παρὰ ἀνθρώπου παρέλαβον αὐτό (oude gar egō para anthrōpou parelabon auto, I did not receive it from a person). Just as the revelation of Jesus Christ represents the antithesis of what human beings expect and what is expected of human beings, so, too, Paul's language stands under the sign of sovereign independence from human judgment.

The interpretation of v. 10 by itself encounters some problems. What is the relationship between the two components of the first question, πείθειν ἀνθρώπους (peithein anthrōpous, persuade people) and πείθειν τὸν θεόν (peithein ton theon, persuade God)? What does the latter expression actually mean? And what is the relationship of the second question to this first question? What is the relationship between the attempt to please people and the attempt to win them by words? Must these questions be understood as allusions to accusations of Paul's opponents? Or is Paul merely using these rhetorical questions to express his own purpose?

Just as in the preceding verse, the adjective ἄρτι (arti, now) in emphatic initial position refers to the present moment. Paul has now begun to address the Galatians, to persuade them. How has he done this? Obviously, not like a cunning rhetor, who knows how to dispose an auditorium favorably by means of a few gratuitous civilities. He has, instead, blurted out his position without regard for anyone's sensibilities. He has not hesitated to be totally candid so that one might well ask how the letter could possibly continue. All conversation with his opponents must be considered totally broken off, to whatever extent it might even have begun. Paul is, apparently, not among those who have unlimited confidence in discussion. Precisely because he values the word so highly, he knows the limits of the use of words as instruments of the human will. But he is driven to address the imperiled Galatians as his brothers in order to win them over.

How should someone, driven by such an inconceivably powerful sense of mission, do otherwise than strive to win as many as possible—Jews or non-Jews or even Christians whose faith has grown slack (1 Cor. 9:19–22)? But Paul does not use the word πείϑειν (*peithein*, persuade) for this activity. Although he often makes use of the intransitive and perfect passive forms of this verb (πέποιϑα, πέπεισμαι; *pepoitha*, *pepeismai*) in the sense of "be confident" and "be convinced," he distrusts the active form. Creation of confidence and assurance is not the function of human rhetorical skill, not even when powerfully persuasive words of wisdom are involved, such as are foreign to Paul's kerygma (1 Cor. 2:4), and certainly not when rhetoric makes use of dishonest tricks (cf. Gal. 5:8; Col. 2:4).

On one occasion Paul does appear to make positive use of the verb πείϑειν. With reference to his work as an apostle he speaks of his attempt to persuade human individuals (2 Cor. 5:11). In this passage, however, the word πείϑειν is probably being used in quotation marks, as an allusion introduced with some reservations either to the common jargon of philosophical propaganda or to specific allegations. For Paul uses this expression bracketed by knowing the fear of the Lord and being known to God, before whom nothing impure can endure; for this reason Paul addresses his proclamation to the conscience, not to reason and certainly not to credulity. Elsewhere Paul's pejorative understanding of πείϑειν is fully in harmony with the widespread contemporary distrust of a rhetoric that can put language to the service of any cause with unscrupulous virtuosity. Verse 10 could thus be paraphrased: Am I now acting like a rhetor who is trying to pull the wool over people's eyes? Luther[21] used the term "hofieren." We would speak instead of an advertising specialist or a public relations agent.

The shift to πείϑειν τὸν ϑεόν (*peithein ton theon*, persuade God) is then not nearly as difficult as it seems at first. It does not introduce the positive antithesis—"Of course I am not trying to influence people; I am concerned with God." Such an interpretation would see in this clause the antithesis to the next: to please not human individuals but God. But such a meaning would be premature. The phrase πείϑειν τὸν ϑεόν in the sense of "seek to persuade God, seek to influence him" is not unprecedented in Hellenistic Greek. It applies, for example, to the sacrifices through which one seeks to influence the deity.

Of course, Paul embarks on a detour by including this motif. The text would read more smoothly without such secondary ideas. But it calls attention to itself by referring back to the *exordium*. The phrase ἀνϑρώπους πείϑειν (*anthrōpous peithein*, persuade people) has its basis, grotesque as it may be, in the way Paul begins in vv. 7–8, with a directness that makes a mockery of rhetoric. The phrase πείϑειν τὸν ϑεόν (*peithein ton theon*, persuade God) could refer similarly to the curse in vv. 8–9. Is anyone insinuating that I am using rhetorical or even magical arts?

But Paul returns at once to the main course of the argument. When the desire to persuade is transformed into an effort to please people, we have the possibility of a theological antithesis. Not directly, of course. In the context of relationships with others, Paul can also refer to the desire to please in a positive sense, namely, when he contrasts the drive to live for one's own pleasure with the duty to live for the pleasure of others. But when he uses the expression in this sense, he finds himself forced to add: for his good, to edify him (εἰς τὸ ἀγαθὸν πρὸς οἰκοδομὴν; eis to agathon pros oiko-domēn). And he secures the proper interpretation by referring to Christ, who likewise did not live to please himself (Rom. 15:1–3). If the desire to please focused merely on a sexual partner, for example, it would still be egocentric. Pleasing oneself and its concomitant egocentric desire to please others must be revolutionized by a totally different approach to the desire to please others. It is, therefore, very important to Paul that one should please God (cf. Rom. 8:8; 1 Cor. 7:32; 1 Thess. 2:15; 4:1). In the matter of the gospel it is especially important not to speak in order to please others but to please God, who tests our hearts (1 Thess. 2:4).

When Paul, nevertheless, with reference to his own ministry, can affirm his intention of pleasing all in every respect (καθὼς κἀγὼ πάντα πᾶσιν ἀρέσκω, kathōs kagō panta pasin areskō, 1 Cor. 10:33), it is certainly not to his own advantage but for the deliverance of the many others. The word ἀνθρωπάρεσκος (anthrōpareskos), coined by the Septuagint (although it appears there only once [Ps. 52(53):6]) refers to someone who seeks to please others and thus becomes their servant; it occurs only in the Deutero-Pauline Epistles (Col. 3:22; Eph. 6:6), but is fully in line with Pauline thought (cf. 1 Cor. 7:23). Here, then, we do indeed find a real either/or: a desire to please others or a desire to please God, a desire to be a servant of others or a desire to be a servant of God.

The catchword ἀρέσκειν (areskein, please) in a sense opens a window with a view from the present situation in which Paul is speaking out over the broad expanse in which the gospel is proclaimed. Up to this point, Paul has been concerned to defend against misuse of language, whether rhetorical or magical. This now takes on concrete form in the turning point marked by his call to be an apostle. The temporal adjective ἔτι (eti, still) has, as its point of reference, Paul's conversion, when he became a δοῦλος Χριστοῦ (doulos Christou, servant of Christ). If he were still acting as he was before this point, he would not be Christ's servant. The dividing line drawn here separates him from efforts to please other people instead of God. Thus ἀνϑρώποις ἀρέσκειν (*anthrōpois areskein*, pleasing people) would be illustrated by Paul's conduct before his conversion: his efforts to win the applause of his compatriots through the radicalism of his obedience to the law and his hatred of Christians, and even to be able to boast of it before God. This is now shattered as a possibility for him. He cannot simply continue his efforts under different auspices.

His opponents may have some such idea of him. To this extent, there may in fact be specific accusations in the background: Paul has now changed course and is trying to please the Gentiles by proclaiming a gospel without the law, which amounts to cheap grace. Paul, however, undoubtedly identifies the present attitude of the Judaizers with his own dead past: they want to spare themselves and others the scandal of the cross (Gal. 5:11; 6:12). In requiring circumcision, they are seeking only their own glory (6:13). But Paul will now glory only in the cross of Christ (6:14; cf. 1 Cor. 1:18ff.), receiving his reward from every quarter in the form of hatred and persecution; he thus documents what has freed him from catering to others.

Thus, we are also given a profound insight into the fundamental human situation. What do people really use their language for? If we are not content to stop with what is right before our eyes, if we bore through the surface and penetrate to the hidden fiery core, asking what people ultimately want to hear and achieve with their words, we see the fundamental purpose: they want to be worth something, to establish their own worth.

Several verbs that are characteristic of Paul's usage come together here in a single complex: πείϑειν (*peithein*, persuade [used pejoratively]) and ἀρέσκειν (*areskein*, please), καυχᾶσϑαι (*kauchasthai*, boast, glory) with its derivatives, as well as ἑαυτὸν συνιστάνειν (*heauton synhistanein*, recommend oneself). The term ὑπόκρισις (*hypokrisis*, hypocrisy), familiar from the Synoptic tradition, is also closely associated with this complex. They all point to a basic human need, expressed today in various "self-" compounds such as self-preservation, self-discovery, self-realization, self-definition, self-security, self-confidence, and so forth. Not that all this is simply to be discarded. It is also a truism that self-praise and self-glorification are unseemly, and that self-criticism and self-accusation can be overdone. But why is this whole complex so explosive and ambivalent? Surely not just because one person stands in the way of others' efforts to be something and make something of their lives. It is also because we are all inclined to fool ourselves through self-deception and self-betrayal. For among all these compounds, self-knowledge is the rarest. All too often we perceive what is harmful as being beneficial. We take pleasure in things that in truth are not good at all. And in social situations we are all too ready to promote this confusion, to befuddle others to be befuddled in turn ourselves, to flatter others in order to be flattered. Everyday experience provides many examples.

But when we come to speak of God, it is not this mutual deception that comes into view but rather the fundamental hidden process that underlies the surface fluctuations of life. Some insights from this source have entered into our modern secular self-understanding, but a significant number of them have been suppressed or have utterly vanished. Here the antithetical symptoms of our era, clear-sightedness and blindness, do battle with each other. And this is the very point that determines to what extent the gospel—today as in the eyes of Paul—is not a human gospel (οὐκ ἔστιν κατὰ ἄνθρωπον, *ouk estin kata anthrōpon*: v. 11).

Paul is not thinking in terms of any abstract contrast between God and human beings. Neither is he trying to solve the problem and repair the damage by demanding self-renunciation and ascetic self-control. When God called him to be on the side of Christ, his call to be an apostle became his mission to humankind. Therefore, he ceased to be a servant of other people, because as a servant of Christ he was enabled truly to serve others. Because God's philanthropy was here revealed (cf. Titus 3:4), there was no longer any room for misanthropy. What is handed on as gospel must be something that is truly good and beneficial for humankind. It is not intended to cripple us but to heal us of our disabilities and make us whole once more. We are not to be robbed of joy but to be granted true joy. Having worth and boasting are not prohibited; on the contrary, they are now for the first time real possibilities.

But we are human, we refuse to be enlightened on this point, although it serves our enlightenment. When confronted with it we retreat even more into ourselves, although it is meant to free us from ourselves and give us true life. No wonder we are unwilling to hear that we are sinners before God and that all we undertake to justify ourselves makes the situation even worse. Therefore, the gospel does not in fact persuade and certainly does not flatter. But it awakens faith as an inward conviction, as the assurance that we are pleasing to God. This faith gives rise to a better freedom from the world and for the world, and through this freedom to the possibility of living an upright and edifying life for the pleasure of our neighbors.

In v. 11 Paul states the guiding principle for all that is to follow. He starts with γνωρίζω γὰρ ὑμῖν (*gnōrizō gar hymin*, I make known to you, I would have you know). Contrary to appearances, there is nothing new involved. The Galatians, now addressed for the first time as "brethren," are solemnly and emphatically reminded how the gospel was preached to them from the beginning and what Paul has already stated in v. 10 as the purpose of his introduction. The gospel he preaches is not a human gospel; it did not even come to him through human mediation, as is otherwise the case and as was true also in the case of the Galatians. How important this double statement is to him can be seen from his proleptic allusion to it at the beginning of the *prescript* (v. 1). What needs to be said to complete the idea is to be approached from the end of the section. In v. 1, Paul had formulated the source of his authority as an apostle in two phrases: "through Jesus Christ and through God Father, who raised him from the dead." Now he summarizes his call in a single statement, but adds the explanatory phrase "through a revelation of Jesus Christ." What does this mean? We shall begin with linguistic observations, then concentrate on the process referred to, and finally inquire into the nature and meaning of the immediacy that Paul claims.

The last phrase, "through a revelation of Jesus Christ," stands independently. The verb that goes with it cannot simply be supplied from one of the verbs used in the negative part of the sentence. The word παραλαμβάνειν (*paralambanein*, receive) is in fact used with reference to the gospel (1 Cor. 15:1, 3; Gal. 1:9, 12), but it involves the process of human παράδοσις (*paradosis*, tradition), which is directly antithetical to the phrase "through a revelation of Jesus Christ." And certainly the word διδάσκειν (*didaskein*, teach) would be out of place. This holds true quite generally for the gospel. There is much to teach and much to learn in connection with it, but the content of the gospel itself is the object not of teaching but of εὐαγγελίζεσθαι (*euangelizesthai*, bring good news) and κηρύσσειν (*kēryssein*, proclaim, preach). It addresses itself not to human reason but to conscience as the mainspring of human life. In this case, then, it is probably best to derive the appropriate verb from the noun itself and say pleonastically: "It was revealed to me through a revelation of Jesus Christ."

The genitive phrase "revelation of Jesus Christ" is explicated by transformation into a verbal construction in v. 16 as an objective genitive, with God as the subject who does the revealing. But this does not rule out the possibility that the nominalized form has overtones of a subjective genitive, especially in the context of this sentence, where the semantic object is actually the gospel. But it would do violence to the text to take the relationship intended by Paul between Jesus Christ, the gospel, and the revelation he had received, and analyze it in the schematic terms of a grammar based on metaphysical notions of substance.

The word ἀποκάλυψις (*apokalypsis*, revelation) likewise does not provide a firm basis for interpretation. Paul sometimes uses it eschatologically for the revelation at the end of time (Rom. 2:5; 8:19; but with reference to Jesus Christ only in 1 Cor. 1:7: "as you wait for the future ἀποκάλυψις of our Lord Jesus Christ," that is, his parousia). Elsewhere he uses it of prophetic and visionary experiences (1 Cor. 14:6, 26; Gal. 2:2; 2 Cor. 12:1, 7; in 2 Cor. 12:1 it also refers to Christ, but in the plural: "visions and revelations of the Lord"). The verb ἀποκαλύπτειν (apokalyptein, reveal), too, is used with reference to the eschatological future (Rom. 8:18; 1 Cor. 3:13) as well as the eschatological present or past (Rom. 1:17–18; Gal. 3:23; 1 Cor. 2:10; 14:30; Phil. 3:15). If we consider also the other New Testament root meaning "reveal," φανεροῦν (phaneroun) and its derivatives, we will observe further distinctions but also further points of contact. Although there are recognizable differences between the two word-groups, Paul can, for example, use both verbs to express the revelation of the righteousness of God (Rom. 1:17; 3:21). Even if one were to claim to find nuances of meaning in this context, this would hardly alter the fact that Paul speaks of revelation in a great variety of ways; he does not use carefully defined terminology.

Now there can be no doubt that the revelation of which Paul speaks here represents something unique for him. It is not at all comparable to the visions and revelations of the Lord mentioned in 2 Cor. 12:1. The explanation in Gal. 1:16 makes it perfectly clear that he is referring to the experience of his call to be the apostle to the Gentiles, the same experience recounted in three different versions by Acts (9:1–19; 22:3–16; 26:4–18). But this peculiar textual witness in Acts itself precludes any attempt to interpret Paul's words on the basis of these accounts with their legendary elaborations, in order to identify particular details.

Apart from Gal. 1:12, 16, Paul speaks of his conversion only three times in his letters. Of these, Phil. 3:4–11 is totally ruled out as a description of the event itself; here Paul describes the fact of his conversion to Christ from being a zealously devout Jew and persecutor of the Christians only as a radical change of opinion, without any reference to the actual event. In 1 Cor. 9:1, alluding to the basis of his apostleship, he says only that he has seen Jesus the Lord; in 1 Cor. 15:8–10 he adds the tradition of Christ that he himself had received. He is the last, he says, in the series of appearances of the risen Lord, is the least of the apostles in view of his past as a persecutor of the community of God, and yet surpasses them all with respect to his labors, which, however, are due solely to the grace of God. We learn nothing more from Paul about his so-called Damascus experience, except that Gal. 1:17 appears to confirm the location given in Acts. To call it a "conversion," as is usually done, is misleading in that the event is identical with his call to be an apostle and is described only from that perspective.

In the light of these observations, what are we to make of his absolute denial of any human mediation? We might interpret it as an amplification of v.

1. There he apparently dealt only with the origin of his apostleship; now he traces the substance of the gospel itself directly to the revelation of Jesus Christ revealed to him. Despite all cautions against psychologizing attempts to fill the gaps in our historical knowledge, no attempt at historical reconstruction can avoid making certain connections between the extant bits of evidence. Drawing on the principle of analogy (which must be used with caution), we may therefore take into account the nature of Paul's own life.

As an active opponent of the new Christian sect, possibly connected with the Jewish upper class in Jerusalem and in any case superbly trained in theology, Paul obviously knew something about Jesus and the Christian faith even before his call. It is inconceivable that he was attacking something with which he was unacquainted. One must realize, furthermore, that only a period of two or three years—very short in retrospect—separated him from the crucifixion of Jesus. Since that time, of course, the situation had changed radically. In Damascus, as in many other places, there were already groups of people who had been baptized in the name of Jesus Christ and understood themselves to be members of the ἐκκλησία τοῦ θεοῦ (*ekklēsia tou theou*, community of God). What had originally been a Palestinian movement had already invaded diaspora Judaism and had probably also partially moved into the gentile world. The situation was still in a state of ferment. How could anyone know within such a short period of time where things might lead?

There were already incipient traditions, liturgical forms and formulas, and even institutional structures. But it is scarcely possible to exaggerate the fluidity of the earliest manifestations of Christianity, the various attempts, separate or interwoven, to articulate the meaning of faith in Christ. Even in contemporary Judaism there were various groupings of inherently incompatible movements emphasizing observance of the law, apocalyptic hopes, or ecstatic visionary experiences; such unstable combinations also appeared in primitive Christianity. They drew upon motifs that were somehow associated with Jesus while there were as yet no accepted criteria to determine what was authentically Christian. It is also necessary to remember that proximity to the event did not necessarily make it easier to comprehend. But it is impossible that Paul had not the slightest knowledge, direct or indirect, of Jesus and the beginnings of the Christian faith when his life underwent its undoubtedly sudden transformation.

Similar conjectures are natural for the subsequent period, although in the biographical sketch that Paul presents in the remainder of chapter 1 he seems to play down the importance of his contacts with those who were Christians or even apostles before him. Paul does not expressly confirm the statement in Acts that he was baptized in Damascus after receiving the revelation of Jesus Christ, but there can be hardly any doubt that this is what happened. There was undoubtedly much occasion for talk and discussion. The sensational incident led not only to talk but also to prayer and common study of Scripture. Similarly, the visit to Peter a few years later must have led to substantial discussion, even if it was brief. People can say much to each other in two weeks.

Such notions are confirmed by Paul's letters, sometimes directly, sometimes indirectly. In two passages of central importance Paul emphasizes the continuity of the tradition in which he stands: with reference to the institution of the Lord's Supper (1 Cor. 11:23–26) and again with reference to the kerygma of the death and resurrection of Christ, together with the appended list of the risen Lord's appearances (1 Cor. 15:3–6). Paul also commends the Corinthians in general terms for maintaining the traditions as he delivered them (1 Cor. 11:2). In these passages Paul uses the technical terms παραδιδόναι (*paradidonai*, hand on as a tradition) and παραλαμβάνειν (*paralambanein*, receive as a tradition), used in Judaism and also in Hellenistic education (1 Cor. 11:23; 15:1, 3). What he himself received he has handed on to those who have received it in turn from him.

In 1 Cor. 15:1 Paul explicitly introduces the substance of the tradition with expressions that also appear in Gal. 1:8–12: γνωρίζω δὲ ὑμῖν, ἀδελφοί, τὸ εὐαγγέλιον ὃ εὐηγγελισάμην ὑμῖν, ὃ καὶ παρελάβετε . . . (*gnōrizō de hymin, adelphoi, to euangelion ho euēngelisamēn hymin, ho kai parelabete*, But I remind you, brethren, of the gospel that I preached to you, and which you received . . .). There follows almost immediately in 1 Cor. 15:3, introducing the quotation of the tradition, the technical term for the chain of tradition in which Paul himself stands: παρέδωκα . . . ὃ καὶ παρέλαβον (*paredōka . . . ho kai parelabon*, I handed on . . . what I also received). It almost sounds like a contradiction of Gal. 1:11–12, as though he had received the gospel he preached through the process of a human chain of tradition.

But the phrase ὃ καὶ παρέλαβον does not refer directly to the gospel preached by Paul but only to the traditional formula that he proceeds to quote, which of course did play an important role in his missionary enterprise. But it cannot simply be identified with what Paul means when he speaks of the gospel he preached.

We hit another problem in 1 Cor. 11:23. Here, it seems, the human chain of tradition is expressly denied: ἐγὼ γὰρ παρέλαβον ἀπὸ τοῦ κυρίου (*egō gar parelabon apo tou kyriou*, for I received from the Lord). Is Paul making the same point in 1 Corinthians 15, when he passes directly from the tradition to what he himself received when the risen Lord appeared to him? Is he meaning to suggest that he knows the risen Lord not merely through this tradition, but through personal experience? But how is one to picture Paul's receiving the tradition of the Lord's Supper directly from the κύριος (kyrios, Lord)? It would be absurd to think that Paul means to claim that he received the actual wording of this text in an audition directly from the risen Lord without human mediation. The words "from the Lord" mean here that this tradition was established and authorized by Jesus himself, and that, despite having come through human mediation, it still has for him the immediacy of its origin. One is almost tempted to say, "Of course!" An original utterance even when enshrined in tradition remains original.

What we have observed in the case of the two central texts could be supported by a wealth of further evidence. The letters of Paul, above all 1 Corinthians, exhibit an assimilation, albeit very limited, of the Jesus tradition, as well as a substantial borrowing of pre-Pauline Christian language. We must also remember that the information available to him and absorbed by him was naturally more extensive than the largely random selection of his extant letters suggests. But the details are not at issue; here opinions can diverge markedly. The issue is how the situation just outlined affects Paul's statement in v. 12 about the origin of the gospel he preached. There are two major aspects of the problem to focus on: Paul's undeniable participation in the chain of early Christian tradition and his persuasive identification of the revelation of Christ to him with his mission outside Judaism to the gentile world. The following solution suggests itself without doing violence to the text.

The enlightenment that Paul received, accompanied by a visionary experience of the exalted Christ, had its inner meaning in an understanding of the gospel as a universal message of salvation, based exclusively on grace and therefore free of the law. Paul could rightly claim that he did not receive this understanding from any human person, certainly not in the form of a doctrine. What suddenly overwhelmed him, completely transforming his life and claiming his total allegiance, was the manifestation of Jesus Christ in a clear and decisive soteriological context that those who believed in Christ had previously grasped only tentatively and vaguely. To claim immediacy for this insight did not in the least contradict Paul's undeniable reliance on tradition. Failure to insist on this immediacy would not have been merely a modest refusal to claim originality. It would have meant giving up an irreducible event, which not only imposed its absolute demand on the apostle himself but through him inescapably required clarity and decision of Christendom as a whole.

Enlightenment of this sort did not involve particular notions, ideas, and doctrines, even though they followed from it. The enlightenment as such had Jesus Christ himself as its content, because it illuminated for the first time his significance, the truth of the gospel. The primacy of this event therefore finds expression in the seemingly paradoxical combination of mediation and immediacy. For Paul, although it is not a product of tradition, neither is it a break with tradition; it is the full breakthrough of that faith to which others had witnessed before Paul, albeit not with full knowledge of its implications.

Paul does not bring another Jesus, another Spirit, another gospel (cf. 2 Cor. 11:4). The source of his gospel is in fact identical with the historical source of the universal gospel. Abstract analysis might separate the three elements of the ἀποκάλυψις Ἰησοῦ Χριστοῦ (apokalypsis Iēsou Christou, revelation of Jesus Christ) Paul received, but for Paul himself they constituted an inseparable unity: his conversion to faith in Jesus Christ, his call to be an apostle of Jesus Christ, and his enlightenment with respect to the essential nature of the gospel of Jesus Christ. But the significance of the identity of these three elements is revealed only when the equation is, as it were, read backwards.

The Independence of
Paul's Apostleship
1:13–24

13 You have heard of my former life in Judaism, how I persecuted the community of God immoderately and tried to destroy it;

14 and I advanced in Judaism beyond many of my own age among my people, so extremely zealous was I for the traditions of my fathers.

15 But when it pleased him who had set me apart from my mother's womb and called me through his grace

16 to reveal his Son in me, in order that I might preach him as gospel among the Gentiles, then—without any hesitation—I did not confer with flesh and blood,

17 nor did I go up to Jerusalem to those [who had already been called to be] apostles before me; but I went away into Arabia and then I returned to Damascus.

18 Not until three years later did I go up to Jerusalem to visit Cephas, and remained with him two weeks.

19 But I saw none of the other apostles—except [I did see] James the Lord's brother.

20 What I am writing to you, note well: before God, I do not lie!

21 Then I went into the regions of Syria and Cilicia.

22 But to the Christian communities of Judea I was still not known by sight.

23 They knew only by hearsay: Our former persecutor is now preaching the faith he once tried to destroy.

24 And they glorified God because of me.

In vv. 11ff., Paul introduced the subject of the debate in the form of a thesis. Now he begins to elaborate the *status controversiae* in more detail. This necessarily takes the form of a biographical narrative. Its purpose, of course, is not biographical but theological. But there are some historical constellations in which person and cause are indissolubly fused—not because the personal elements push themselves unduly and inappropriately to the fore so as to attract all the attention, but because a cause has so taken possession of a person that it has left deep marks on his life. In them one can perceive the decisions in and through which not this particular person but, rather, the cause itself that dominates him has come to a focus. In this sense, the life of Paul is exemplary to an unusual degree. The distinction between law and gospel has shaped this biography.

The purpose of the *narratio* can be determined only from its total compass. It runs to the end of the second chapter and passes so confidently to the crucial point at issue that it is impossible to tell precisely where, toward the end of the chapter (around 2:15ff.), the narrative stops and the Galatians are addressed directly. We pass unconsciously from Paul's remonstrance with Peter to the concluding summary in which he turns to the Galatians themselves.

The preceding narrative comprises three sections. The second and third are clearly defined episodes: the account of the apostolic council in Jerusalem (2:1–10) and the description of Paul's conflict with Peter at Antioch (2:11–14[?]). Or, to point up the contrast between the two events: the agreement of the apostles about the gospel is followed by the conflict of the apostles over the gospel. Unlike these two sections, the first (1:13–24) exhibits such internal variety that one might hesitate to call it also a single unit.

A long trajectory from the time of Paul's call through subsequent events down to the apostolic council at Jerusalem is here described in two stages: from Paul's call to his first visit to Jerusalem three years later (1:13–20), then the fourteen years leading to his second trip to Jerusalem (1:21–24). The second and third sections of the narrative concern distinct events: what took place at Jerusalem and at Antioch; the first section (1:13–24), however, covers an extended period: at least fifteen or sixteen years, if we do not include the time before Paul's conversion and also take into account the Greek practice of counting the beginning year (like counting starting time as the first hour of work). The section does, however, constitute a rounded whole: the persecution motif with which it begins (v. 13) is heard once more at its conclusion (vv. 23–24). And the course of events during this long period of Paul's life is not centered on his conversion—it is mentioned only in a subordinate clause—as we would expect in a straightforward biography, but on his first visit to Jerusalem following his conversion.

This chimes with a second observation: each of the three narrative sections is devoted to an encounter with the other apostles, or, more precisely, primarily with one of them, Cephas (Peter). In the first, events before and after the encounter (which is itself not given prominence) emphasize the independence of Paul's apostleship. In the second, the Pauline gospel is explicitly recognized in a critical situation. And the third is tantamount to a reprimand from the mouth of Paul. Although in each case the person of Cephas is unmistakably emphasized, and Paul's relationship to him constitutes the focus of interest, James the brother of the Lord is also mentioned: the first time (1:19) only in passing, as a marginal figure; the second time (2:9) as the first in the official order of precedence; and the third time (2:12) in the background, as the antagonist.

The overall structure of the narrative thus illustrates a progressive development from formal contact through respectful cooperation to open hostility, which is clearly related to events in Galatia. In this sense Paul is merely recounting what led up to the explosion among the Galatian Christians. But his purpose goes beyond describing the background of what is now a bitter conflict over the gospel in Galatia, a conflict that cannot be resolved by any compromise. He is also, even primarily, concerned to prove that the Pauline gospel has preserved its independence of the authorities in Jerusalem through all the years and all the changing situations, and that the authorities themselves conceded him this independence, which is therefore not a mark of separation but, in spite of everything, a mark of unity. Even the clash with Cephas at Antioch, the painful but not hopeless settlement of a conflict with the weakening brother, bears witness to this unity. We are reminded here of Gal. 6:1: "Brethren, if anyone is overtaken in any trespass, you who are spiritual should restore him in a spirit of gentleness."

A commentary on Paul's narrative would actually require a historical account of primitive Christianity. Even if such an account were possible, however, there is no room for it here or for comparison with the account given in Acts. We shall only bring out the theologically relevant accents in Paul's statements.

Paul begins by emphatically recalling his Jewish past (vv. 13–14). This is in line with his theological intention. Of course, his own background is a matter of common knowledge; he would never be able to conceal it. The Galatians naturally have been told about it: Ἠκούσατε (*ēkousate*, you have heard: v. 13). But Paul does not want to conceal anything. In other passages, too, he makes explicit reference to his past (1 Cor. 15:9; Phil. 3:6). It is doubly relevant. This past of his can only underline the fact that he has experienced God's grace and that the gospel itself is pure grace. He can also stress that the position of his opponents had once been his own way of life, pursued with infinitely greater rigor. He knows their concern by personal experience and is more familiar with it than they are themselves. His persecution of the Christians was, in a sense, only the tip of the iceberg, the extreme consequence of his religious devotion as he then understood and practiced it.

It is unlikely, of course, that Paul was active in Jerusalem, as described by Luke. Paul, the diaspora Jew, should probably be pictured as a Jewish

missionary to the Gentiles, a representative of the strictest form of observance, requiring full obedience to the law on the part of proselytes, including
circumcision. He later (5:11) recalls: "But if I still preach circumcision, why
am I still persecuted?" In his work he was like a bloodhound on the trail of
the Jewish Christian communities in the diaspora that were not sufficiently
strict in observing the law, that is, the so-called Hellenists (Acts 6:1), who
had been banished from Jerusalem and were now living in such places as
Damascus. Force would be used only within the framework of synagogue
discipline, for example, the punitive lashing that was later inflicted on Paul
(2 Cor. 11:24). Paul's description of himself thus involves a double paradox
from the very outset: the Jewish diaspora missionary is a persecutor of the
chosen community of God! The persecutor of the community of God is its
apostle, chosen by God!

We know nothing of the success of his diaspora mission. Despite all his
obstinate efforts, the result may have been quite modest, like the description
of a similar enterprise in Matt. 23:15: "You traverse sea and land, to convert
just a single person to Judaism." Neither do we know anything about the extent to which the Christian communities were disrupted as a result of his persecution. But from the attention that its termination attracted we can
conclude that its effect was considerable. In any case, through all of this
Paul reached a peak of impassioned zeal for the law. These two verses
(13–14) contain an exceptionally large number of elatives, expressions that
are comparative or superlative in meaning: καθ' ὑπερβολήν (kath' hyper-
bolēn, immoderately), προκόπτειν (prokoptein, advance), περισσοτέρως
(perissoterōs, to a much higher degree). The word "zealot" does not refer
here to a member of a political party. As a devout Pharisee, Paul's concern
was not for political action; he concentrated entirely on religious observance
of the Torah together with the Halakhah. He always strove for perfection,
which argues against any gradual approach to the Christians, leading rather
to increasing distance from them.

Paul can only have understood the change that took place as being analogous to a prophetic call (cf. echoes of Jer. 1:5 and Isa. 49:1 in v. 15). It
would never occur to him to reflect psychologically on the event. This does
not prevent us from engaging in such reflections; but in the nature of the
case there is nothing they can explain, being limited to describing the outward and inward circumstances of such a break with one's own past. The
radical nature of this break is not lessened by the observation that even after-
wards the theme in a sense remains the same: worldwide dissemination of
what had been vouchsafed to Israel. The earthshaking change for Paul consists in this: what had been expected of the law now holds true of Jesus

Christ. Grace has become the determining factor. In the case of Paul himself, it outweighs all his efforts to resist. Divine election had been at work even before he saw the light of day. Grace is always prevenient, and there is nothing that it cannot overcome. With respect to Christ, Paul's blindness was turned into sight through God's revelation of his Son to him. This ends any speculation as to whether the revelation could have been the result of Paul's own seeking and finding. What he says of the Galatians is true of Paul himself: to know is in this case to be known (Gal. 4:9).

This does not conflict with a literal interpretation of Paul's statement that the revelation was ἐν ἐμοί (*en emoi*, in me). Under such circumstances, what is the difference between "inward" and "outward"? "Whether in the body or out of the body I do not know, God knows"—thus Paul describes his own personal state when faced with such an experience (2 Cor. 12:2–3). The vision comes as something outward and external but penetrates the innermost human depths. And only in this way could Paul have been reached by what God did in this case. Distrust of mystical-sounding expressions like "Christ lives in me" (Gal. 2:20) is not necessarily helpful in interpreting Paul's language. In this case, of course, whether the preposition ἐν (*en*, in) is emphatic or merely replaces the dative is a philological question not essential to the meaning of what is said. The revelation came to Paul from without; because it affected him inwardly, it also demanded outward expression. The ἀποκάλυψις Ἰησοῦ Χριστοῦ (*apokalypsis Iēsou Christou*, revelation of Jesus Christ) and the commission to proclaim this Jesus Christ as gospel among the Gentiles are not two different things. This is even clearer if one takes αὐτόν (*auton*, him) emphatically, as the content of the message, replacing the law, which Paul had formerly considered necessary and desirable to bring to the Gentiles: "That I might preach him as gospel [instead of the law as supposed gospel] among the Gentiles."

The subordinate clause in which Paul describes his sudden transformation, weighty as it is, functions here only to set the stage for what follows. Paul's opponents can hardly have questioned Paul's experience of revelation, but rather his response to it. Here Paul clearly makes use of formulaic language such as is found in other conversion accounts. The word εὐθέως (*eutheōs*, at once) expresses the prompt reaction of the one who receives a call (e.g., Matt. 4:20, 22), his unhesitating obedience, as a sign that God's word immediately effects what it says.

Although Paul's conduct is described initially in negative terms, the text must not be interpreted as though it read οὐκ εὐθέως (*ouk eutheōs*, not at once), meaning that Paul did not confer with others at once, but only later. His prompt response consisted, in fact, in his unhesitating renunciation, once and for all, of any such action. Paul here uses the Hebrew idiom of "flesh and blood" to refer to human beings with whom he might have conferred, suggesting an antithesis: God's revelation runs contrary to what one may expect of flesh and blood, of frail human beings. The same terminology is used of Peter's confession at Caesarea Philippi: "Flesh and blood has not revealed this to you, but my Father who is in heaven" (Matt. 16:17). It would be attractive to find a relationship between this tradition of the call of Peter and what Paul says of his own call, but we must probably be content with observing that they share characteristic features.

Now Paul's actual conduct in this situation is amazing. Nothing would have been more natural than to suspect his own experience and to confer with others about its meaning. And if someone is as confident as Paul of his own position, what would have been more appropriate than to establish immediate contact with the apostles in Jerusalem? Their seniority might well mean more than honorary precedence; even if not, it deserved at least respect. And it is highly unlikely that Paul hesitated to appear immediately in Jerusalem out of not illegitimate fear for his life.

Paul does not make it easy for the reader to perceive the real motivation behind his conduct. A mere demonstration of independence might be nothing more than a suspect sign of arrogance and unwillingness to cooperate. He obviously saw from the beginning that his enlightenment and call involved a decision about the understanding of the gospel such as had not previously appeared with such clarity and force among the followers of Christ.

He leaves us totally in the dark about what he actually did. Nowhere, not even here, does he speak of being baptized. There can be hardly any doubt that he was, in fact, baptized at once and therefore also had contacts with the Christians in Damascus. But for Paul anything connected with that event, even though it must not be minimized, could not serve to validate or supplement what had been revealed to him in the revelation of Jesus Christ.

The verb ἀπῆλθον (apēlthon, I went away) undoubtedly refers to a deliberate departure from Damascus. Paul probably went to northern Arabia, the region of modern Jordan. Whether he did so for quiet retreat, which would be understandable, or in order to work as a missionary must remain an open question. We are not even told anything about how long he stayed before returning to Damascus. During this entire time (easily two to three years) before his first visit to Jerusalem, Paul probably attracted considerable public attention, as may be seen in his perilous escape from Damascus, which probably belongs to this period.

Paul's first visit to Jerusalem (vv. 18–19) constitutes the focal point of this section of his account, as its overall purpose shows. In opposition to his

Galatian enemies, he wishes to demonstrate the independence of his apostleship. His primary, if not exclusive, interest is therefore his relationship to the authorities of the primitive community in Jerusalem. Up to this point he has spoken only in negative terms: he had avoided all contact with them. Now, however, two or three years after his conversion, he visits them there. This journey attracts attention. It was obviously known to his opponents and probably played a role in their arguments, albeit in a different version. Therefore, Paul underlines the truth of his divergent account with an oath.

This striking protestation reveals the critical point of the passage. Paul's journey to Jerusalem probably played an important role in the polemic of his opponents. It may have been linked with the claim that he had received instructions from the first apostles that he did not adhere to subsequently. This contact could, therefore, be doubly held against him: he himself recognized the superiority of the others and accepted their legitimation, but then (once more?) came into conflict with them. In any case his gospel was incompatible with the original gospel.

Paul's view of the matter is likewise only partially accessible. He describes his meeting with Cephas as being purely private, ascribes it to his own initiative, and limits its purpose to personal acquaintance. That he also, on this occasion, saw James the brother of the Lord is mentioned only in passing because it was of secondary importance. There was no official meeting with the circle of the apostles. There was, therefore, no official authorization, neither was he given any specific instructions. Up to this point, Paul's interpretation is perfectly clear. But we would like to know what brought this visit about and what took place. Paul's escape from Damascus may have been the immediate occasion for his journey to Jerusalem, but his motives remain unknown. All we can conclude from what he says is that he was particularly interested in meeting Cephas, but this leaves open a wide range of interpretations.

The most reasonable hypothesis is this: in Paul's opinion, Cephas was the most competent person to talk with concerning the gospel. His preference for Cephas over James agrees with their relative importance in the opinion of the primitive Christian community. But this cannot be separated from the fact that it was not James (who had joined the community only after Jesus' death) but Cephas who was the most important mediator of the tradition. We must assume that even before Paul's conversion he knew of the role Cephas played before and immediately after the death of Jesus. And it is likely that soon after his conversion Paul became acquainted with the Christ tradition of 1 Cor. 15:3–7, which names Cephas as the first witness to the resurrection. It is also reasonable to assume that even before Paul's first visit to

Jerusalem, that is, some five years after the crucifixion of Jesus, Peter's influence extended beyond Palestine. This is not confirmed by Paul himself until a time some twenty years later, with Cephas' appearance at Antioch (Gal. 2:11ff.), and in references to his missionary work (1 Cor. 9:5) and to the various parties at Corinth (1 Cor. 1:12; 3:22).

In any case, it is easy to understand that Paul put most store by personal contact with Peter. Because of the distortions of his opponents, he describes this meeting as irrelevant. But it certainly does not follow that it was meaningless or profitless for Paul himself. Throughout the entire account he limits himself to what is essential to his argument. In this respect, his conversation with Peter made no difference. Paul does not owe his apostolic commission or his understanding of the gospel to Peter, however harmonious and productive their meeting may have been.

How little Paul is concerned to provide a complete autobiographical account is shown by his passing over the next thirteen to fourteen years, the period of his first great missionary successes, with nothing more than the geographical statement that he then went to Syria and Cilicia. The most striking fact is that he does not mention the community at Antioch, although his belonging to it forms the transition to the next focus of his account, his second stay in Jerusalem. Paul refuses to divert attention from the point at issue by citing more details of his activity, not even contrasting the undoubtedly meager circumstances of the Jerusalem community with the cosmopolitan life of Antioch, the third largest city (after Rome and Alexandria) of the Hellenistic world.

What follows (vv. 22–24) does not continue the chronological account; it is only a postscript marking the end of the first section. The comment about the Judean communities, which naturally include the Jerusalem community above all, refers back to the account of Paul's visit to Cephas. In addition, however, it functions as a retrospective summary of the first section of the narrative. Once again Paul is defending himself against the picture of him painted by his opponents in Galatia. They themselves undoubtedly came from Judea and suggested that Paul was generally rejected there. In their centralizing ideology with its focus on God's work in history, they claimed a kind of primacy for the place where Christianity originated. Therefore, the supposedly negative opinion of Paul that was current there was meant to discredit him in the eyes of the Galatians. Paul points out to the contrary that he is not even personally known there. The rumors that have come to their ears are the well-known facts of his former persecution of the Christians and the miracle of his conversion.

Paul uses the past tense for his account and even quotes the Christians of

Judea in the first person. It is probably safe to conclude that we have here an echo of what he heard about himself during his first stay in Jerusalem. Then, at least, there could be no talk of hostility toward him. The news that he was proclaiming the faith was instead occasion to glorify God for the transformation. If, in the meantime, a different attitude toward him has appeared, it must be a secondary development, suggesting changes that bespeak a retreat from the original purity and simplicity.

The Agreement of the Apostles
About the Gospel
2:1–10

1 Then after fourteen years I went up again to Jerusalem with Barnabas, taking Titus along with me.

2 I went up in compliance with a revelation. And I laid before them the gospel which I preach among the Gentiles, and privately with those of repute, lest somehow I should be running or had run in vain.

3 But even Titus, who was with me, was not compelled to be circumcised, though he was a Greek.

4 But because of false brethren secretly brought in [matters came to a head], who slipped in to spy out our freedom that we have in Christ Jesus, that they might make us slaves.

5 To them we did not yield submission even for a moment, that the truth of the gospel might be preserved for you.

6 But from those reputed to be something (who they were makes no difference to me; God shows no partiality), those, I say, of repute imposed nothing upon me.

7 On the contrary, when they saw that I had been entrusted with the gospel to the uncircumcised, just as Peter [the "rock"] had been entrusted with the gospel to the circumcised

8 (for he who worked through Peter [the "rock"] for the apostleship among the circumcised worked through me also for the Gentiles)

9 and when they perceived the grace that was given to me, James and Cephas and John, who are reputed to be pillars, gave to me and Barnabas the right hand as a sign of fellowship, in the sense that we should go to the Gentiles and they to the circumcised.

10 Only they would have us remember the poor, which very thing I was eager to do.

Paul's first visit to Jerusalem was the focus of the first section of his autobiographical account; his second visit constitutes the focus of the account as a whole. The former involved a purely private encounter without public consequences; the latter included a highly official and momentous meeting. This incident has always attracted great attention, both because of its historical importance and also because of the theological problems discussed. The differences between the account in Galatians and the tradition in Acts combined with linguistic difficulties in the Pauline text itself provide a field day for historical-critical exegesis.

With respect to the former, we will not enter into a detailed comparison with Acts. It is generally agreed today that Acts 15:1–35 recounts this same event, but with substantial differences. With respect to the linguistic problems of Gal. 2:1–10, however, we shall begin with some general observations.

The style exhibits a high degree of internal tension. Twice in a row (vv. 4–5 and v. 6) we find a syntactic break, an anacoluthon. And everything said about the agreement (vv. 6–10) is compressed into a single sentence with several parentheses. It is too vague, although probably correct in itself, to explain these observations on the basis of Paul's agitation while dictating this especially important passage. What is the reason for such agitation? It can hardly be the direct result of the violent arguments reported, since they ultimately led to an outcome that was satisfactory to Paul. Furthermore, the event was already more than five years in the past. One could, of course, accuse Paul of being not really so certain of his position, so that he became especially nervous at this point in his account.

It is more likely, however, that the memory of that crucial event is affected by the news that had just come from Galatia. It contradicted the terms of the agreement and may also have suggested a contradictory account of the Jerusalem meeting. If so, the renewed challenge to what had been achieved then would be the source of an inner turmoil that is reflected in Paul's syntax.

But even this explanation is ambiguous. Is Paul seized with all too understandable anger at the intransigence and underhandedness of his opponents and at the damage they are doing? This would not necessarily be a sign of inward weakness, as is usually the case when anger erupts. Luther says that the Holy Spirit, who is speaking through Paul, must be allowed these syntactic irregularities: " . . . qui ardet loquendo, non potest simul tenere regulas grammaticas."[22] (Anyone who is inflamed while speaking cannot at the same time observe the grammatical rules.) Thus the supreme importance of the cause Paul is representing may interfere with orderly discourse.

In addition, a close study of the train of thought shows that words and ideas are not spewed forth chaotically, as from a volcano. Paul's language is always precise and coherent. Despite undeniable signs of impetuosity, it exhibits a sovereign self-control. The visible effort involved in stating what he has to say appears to be due primarily to his concern to show with the utmost pregnancy (in the literal sense of the word) how crucial this event was, how everything was at stake: his life's work, the truth of the gospel, the unity of the church. A person like Paul, so deeply involved in all these issues, must have sensed this in all its gravity, quite unlike an innocent and neutral observer.

If the *Kirchenkampf* [German church struggle under Hitler] of a few decades ago taught those of us who were involved anything, it is this: one can find oneself in critical situations in which, strictly speaking, no decision is required; all that matters is to stand by a decision made long before in which one has had no part; more is at stake than one's own life, even though one's personal contribution remains caught up in ambiguity, being little more than the human response of fear and anger.

The structure of the section clearly reveals the major points of Paul's argument. He first gives the background that led up to the meeting (vv. 1–2). Then he speaks of his absolutely fundamental resolution, which he would not even open to discussion, his uncompromising "No!" to the idea that Titus should be circumcised (vv. 3–5). Finally, in that omnibus sentence (vv. 6–10), he states the outcome of what was obviously a bitter conflict. This outcome was earlier stated in negative terms; now more precise details are given about its basis and formal definition: the mission of the apostles was divided up according to the simple formula "we to the Gentiles, they to the circumcised." The commitment to raise funds for the Jerusalem community, appended as a kind of postscript, is thus not a legal obligation (which would be incompatible with v. 6) but a free expression of the fellowship that had been sealed by handclasp.

These three subordinate units also introduce the three groups involved in the event. The delegation coming to Jerusalem includes Barnabas and Titus alongside Paul. Between them and those they came to meet with steps the group of false brethren, not mentioned by name, who try in vain to thwart the meeting. In the final section, the men who had been referred to briefly as δοκοῦντες (*dokountes*, those of repute), the prominent leadership of the Jerusalem community, are named: James, Cephas, and John. They lend their names to the agreement.

The common term "apostolic council" can easily give a false impression and is better avoided. The legal and ecclesiastical associations of the word "council," suggested by its later usage, are misleading. No formal institution is involved here, nor was there any official court of appeal. Even the term "apostle" must be used with some caution in this context. Since its usage varied, we cannot be certain that Barnabas was considered one of the apostles (despite Acts 14:4, 14), nor even that James belonged to the circle of the apostles in the narrow sense. In this account, apostleship is predicated explicitly only of Peter (v. 8). Otherwise, the title "apostle" appears to be avoided. If this observation may be considered significant, one might even conjecture that recognition of Paul's right to the title "apostle" was among the points of disagreement that remained unresolved after the meeting. If so, Paul's insistence on the title in Gal. 1:1 would have additional importance.

From all Paul says about the background of this meeting, a primary point emerges: Paul was not summoned to appear before a judicial court. He came forward as a free agent and even determined the outcome in essential points. The fourteen years mentioned in v. 1, with the appropriate subtraction, are probably to be counted from Paul's first visit to Jerusalem. This means a period of some sixteen years after Paul's call. It is probably A.D. 48. The fact that there was such a long time before an official meeting with the Jerusalem community and its leaders argues against the theory that Paul was finally looking for some kind of legitimation. What Acts 15:1–2 says concerning the occasion is probably correct: Judaizers had appeared at Antioch (just as they have now appeared in Galatia), insisting that for Christians circumcision was necessary for salvation. The resulting unrest sent Paul and Barnabas to Jerusalem. Their role, however, was more that of plaintiffs than defendants.

Whether Paul deliberately conceals the fact that they were sent by the Antiochene community or whether he was himself the motivating force behind the decision cannot be determined. Neither is it possible to determine what kind of ἀποκάλυψις (apokalypsis, revelation) was involved. Was it instruction through prophets of the Antiochene community (cf. Acts 13:1–2) or Paul's own inspiration (cf. Acts 16:6–7, 9)? The relation of the ἀποκάλυψις to the actual decision to go to Jerusalem must also remain an unresolved problem. Was it the motivating factor? Or did it possibly overcome Paul's initial reservations? In any case, he was now certain that this risky undertaking, so contrary to his previous conduct, was God's will.

In Paul's eyes, the initiative was neither Jerusalem's nor Antioch's nor his own. He does not think in terms of ecclesiastical politics and does not fight for positions of power. His only concern is the gospel—a claim, of course, that can easily disguise a desire for political power in the church and thus become an even more vicious instrument of ecclesiastical politics. The purity of such a claim is determined by how the claimant stands his ground in the face of temptation. Paul himself must be judged by this standard.

Paul set out on his journey accompanied by a Jewish Christian and a gentile Christian. A purpose is visible here, probably more than just the desire to demonstrate unity and fairness: the intention to provoke a decision in the controversy. Barnabas accompanied Paul ex officio. He had at one time brought Paul to Antioch (Acts 11:25–26), where he himself had previously come from Jerusalem (Acts 11:22–23). The two of them had developed their missionary program together, with Antioch as their home base (Acts 13:2ff.). In their relationship the center of gravity had slowly shifted in the direction of the latecomer, but fundamentally they were equals. This equality found expression both in their common errand in Jerusalem and in the role played by Barnabas together with Paul at the formal conclusion of the conference (v. 9).

Titus (who is never mentioned in Acts) was, by contrast, a Greek converted by Paul, who had joined Paul in his work. To take him along to Jerusalem was Paul's own personal decision. This difference can be seen from the way the two traveling companions are introduced in v. 1. By taking Titus as the only non-Jew to the conference, Paul not only created a test case but made up his own mind with respect to the basic question. Either Jerusalem would accept the uncircumcised Greek as a brother, or there would be a break with Jerusalem. It is inconceivable that Paul was expecting a decision from Jerusalem as to whether Titus should be circumcised. For Paul that was not a negotiable matter. But he wanted to do more than discuss the question in theoretical terms. The responsible parties in Jerusalem would be faced with a concrete case that would inevitably make them show their true colors.

This gives the appearance of being a clever stratagem. Fundamentally, however, it was the simplest and most straightforward procedure. In a sense, Titus represented in his own person the gospel Paul preached among the Gentiles. In a debate over whether circumcision was necessary for salvation, what would be more obvious for Paul than to present an uncircumcised Christian as a witness to the gospel without the law? Of course it was not sufficient just to bring him forward. Paul undoubtedly had to employ the full weight of his theological acumen and intellectual power to expound to this circle the gospel that he preached among the Gentiles. Titus' presence provided more than a concrete case, making a decision inescapable. It also made clear from the outset Paul's purpose in submitting to the Jewish Christian coryphaei the gospel that he preached among the Gentiles.

Paul states his purpose in v. 2: μή πως εἰς κενὸν τρέχω ἢ ἔδραμον (*mē pōs eis kenon trechō ē edramon*, lest somehow I should be running or had run in vain). Strangely, his statement is often interpreted in a sense directly opposite to the purpose he has already announced by taking Titus with him. Paul here expresses the fear that all his apostolic labors may have been in vain. But under what circumstances? If (it is suggested) the Jerusalem authorities decide against him. This interpretation can be varied with further nuances: either Paul was in fact uncertain of himself and is now seeking clarification and affirmation from the highest authorities, or he sees a conflict with Jerusalem as a catastrophe for his missionary work because the unity of the church would be breached and he would lose contact with its point of origin. Both possibilities converge, but they are also incompatible with Paul's position elsewhere. The end result, in any case, would be that he was making himself dependent on human authorities and harboring doubts about his commission and his understanding of the gospel.

Another interpretation sees in the subordinate clause an indirect question expecting a negative answer—not from Paul, but from the δοκοῦντες (dokountes, those of repute). They must now make up their minds whether he is running or has run in vain. He does not want to be rid of his own anxieties but to dissipate the apprehensions of others. The conjunction μή πως (mē pōs, lest somehow) would then be used as in 1 Thess. 3:5, where Paul says that he has sent Timothy to the Thessalonians to learn about their faith, for fear that somehow (μή πως) the tempter has tempted them and made his labor be in vain.

Now whenever Paul says he fears that something may be in vain or confidently denies the possibility, he is referring to the state of the Christian communities and of his own missionary work (cf. Phil. 2:16; 1 Thess. 2:1; 1 Cor. 15:10, 14; 2 Cor. 6:1). Therefore, it is most likely that in Gal. 2:2, also, he is thinking of his communities. He would have run in vain if confusion should arise about the gospel free of the law; what had almost happened at Antioch is now repeating itself in Galatia. His opponents have been saying to his converts: "Unless you are circumcised . . . , you cannot be saved" (Acts 15:1), so that their Christianity has been in vain. Paul turns this argument on its head: "If you receive circumcision, Christ will be of no avail to you" (Gal. 5:2), and all will have been in vain. What would represent a catastrophe for the Christianity of the Christian communities would also be a catastrophe for Paul's apostleship. He therefore goes to Jerusalem to force a decision and to settle the question at the very source of the threat to his missionary work.

Here, for the sake of the endangered communities, he resolutely expounds the gospel that he preaches among the Gentiles. The confusion must be checked at its source. Nothing can prevent such actions from continuing, but it must at least be made clear that those involved in them cannot claim the support of those of repute in Jerusalem. At least in this retrospective account of his successful appearance in Jerusalem, Paul does not even play with the notion of what might happen if the leading men in Jerusalem should fail him. From his words and from his subsequent conduct, we can only conclude that he assigned great importance to the unity of the ἐκκλησία τοῦ ϑεοῦ (*ekklēsia tou theou*, community of God). Therefore, a break with Jerusalem must, if at all possible, be avoided. But the price could never be surrender of that which constitutes the truth behind this unity. Obedience to the requirement of circumcision would run counter to the truth of the gospel and would therefore destroy, not preserve, the unity of the church.

Superficially, the purity and the unity of the church appear often to be conflicting goals. But when this is the case, we can be certain that neither is understood properly. For if the purity of the church depends on the truth of the gospel, then its unity is likewise determined by the same truth. This fundamental principle sounds very simple, indeed all too simple; it is therefore likely to evoke mistrust. But there is, in fact, no self-contradiction in the fact that the simplicity of the principle is entirely appropriate and yet conceals within itself difficult problems—problems of which this earliest known conflict over the purity and unity of the church is a highly instructive example.

It centers on two points, which are related but must nevertheless be kept distinct in their mutual relationship. The first is the requirement of circumcision. This is, in fact, what leads to the break—not between Paul and the δοκοῦντες (*dokountes*, those of repute), but between their various factions and between them and the separated false brethren. The other is the relationship between Paul and the δοκοῦντες. For in spite of everything there remains a great gulf between them, which does not, one hopefully assumes, destroy the unity of the church, however.

With respect to the first point, the major problem is why the question of circumcision should have led to a breach. With respect to the second, it remains an open question whether the agreement reached really results in a viable unity grounded in truth. In each subsection (vv. 3–5 and 6–10), we shall first examine the various textual problems in detail and then discuss the central problem.

Paul's successful refusal to require circumcision of his companion Titus, the only uncircumcised person in this homeland of circumcision, seems generally clear. Detailed examination of the text, however, raises several questions about this conclusion. Even the way v. 3 is linked with vv. 1–2 involves certain nuances. The use of ἀλλά (*alla*, but) makes the transition clearly adversative with respect to the negative suggestion immediately preceding—that Paul might have run in vain. This was not the result—quite the contrary! But the positive contrast is expressed in the form of a negation (v. 5). To what does οὐδέ (*oude*, and not, not even) refer? In the overall context, undoubtedly to the circumcision of Titus. The whole meaning would be reversed if all that were negated were the element of compulsion, so that Titus was indeed circumcised, but of his own free will rather than to satisfy a requirement.

Some textual witnesses, however, do follow this interpretation, dropping the words οἷς οὐδέ (*hois oude*, to whom . . . not even) at the beginning of v. 5. The relative clause resumes the negation of v. 3, but now negates submission to compulsion. When the two words are omitted, the meaning becomes: Paul was not compelled to have Titus circumcised, but in this single, exceptional case (πρὸς ὥραν, *pros hōran*), he complied for a moment with the wishes of others. According to Acts 16:1–3, he supposedly agreed to the circumcision of Timothy "for the sake of the Jews." But we have no need to waste time with this variant text and its absurd interpretation of events. Neither need we consider the proposal (primarily due to Marcion) that only the relative pronoun οἷς (*hois*, to whom) be dropped. This eliminates the anacoluthon and also suggests that the pressure was applied by those of repute themselves. Paul withstood them, in this reading, because of the even more radical false brethren, so as to exclude any conceivable abuse of a temporary submission.

But there is a further difficulty connected with the negation at the beginning of v. 3. The negator οὐδέ (*oude*, not even) can be used adversatively, copulatively, or even comparatively. In the present instance, the preceding ἀλλά (*alla*, but) already expresses the antithesis; the meaning is therefore probably comparative. The position of οὐδέ seems to make it apply directly to Titus: not even Titus was compelled to be circumcised. But who else could possibly be involved? The comparison clearly makes sense only with respect to other requirements, which are in fact alluded to in v. 6. In comparison with them, in this special case the requirement of circumcision would have been, so to speak, the absolute minimum. Then οὐδέ would apply to the entire clause: not even the circumcision of Titus was required. Of course this comparative ranking of circumcision would be valid only from the perspective of Paul's opponents; in his view, it was itself the absolutely crucial point. The other side saw it as a necessary minimum, whether in the universal sense of circumcision as a Judaistic sine qua non, or in the more restricted sense that at least the circumcision of Titus would be an act of polite respect for the sensitivities of the hosts. For Paul, however, this was an utterly unacceptable demand. It would have been tantamount to denial of the gospel. From Paul's perspective, then, οὐδέ could not possibly be comparative. It is, therefore, worth considering whether this negator is not used here merely to reemphasize the adversative conjunction. There are certainly grounds for such a reading: Paul's successful rejection of the requirement of circumcision is, in fact, the absolute opposite of the threatened failure of his entire missionary activity.

These problems connected with the meaning of the negation in v. 3 also confront us with the ambiguity of the verb ἀναγκάζειν (*anankazein*, compel, require). Does it mean here a mere attempt to compel, or a successful attempt? Which is negated? Is Paul saying that they did not even try to compel him, or that they were unable to compel him? And what subject should be supplied? If the meaning is that there was not even any attempt to compel Titus to be circumcised, it would clearly refer to the Jerusalem leadership. The radicals obviously made the attempt.

If, however, the meaning is that the pressure did not succeed, the subject of ἀναγκάζειν is not quite so clear. The radical Judaizers would certainly be included in the statement. Paul himself says in v. 5 that he did not submit to them even for a moment and did not yield. But the point of Paul's argument demands more: he must have been concerned above all to say something about the attitude of the δοκοῦντες (*dokountes*, those of repute) in this matter. However great the pressure applied by the false brethren, the really important thing to bring out is that not even the δοκοῦντες were able to compel him.

But is this really what Paul is trying to say? A total success that he could draw on effectively in his conflict with his opponents in Galatia would not take the form of a statement that the Jerusalem leadership tried to compel him but failed. The strongest card he could play would be to say: "The δοκοῦντες did not even try to compel me; the entire problem was created by the false brethren." This is probably also Paul's point when he begins the anacoluthon in v. 4 by mentioning the false brethren: διὰ τοὺς παρεισάκτους ψευδαδέλφους (*dia tous pareisaktous pseudadelphous*, because of false brethren secretly brought in). He wants to single them out as the troublemakers. Of course, one could also add: "On their account I did not give in to the general pressure, so as not to encourage further action on their part." But such conduct would, in fact, be irrational, as though Paul could have given in to pressure from the δοκοῦντες without enabling the radical Judaizers to capitalize on his submission. It is, therefore, probably more correct to add: "The entire problem was created and brought to a head only by them."

The more we look at this apparently simple text from various angles, the more we see that its central point is clear, but the details are remarkably hard to bring into focus. The various nuances of meaning change according to the parties involved. There are, therefore, limits to any attempt at absolute clarity. This is not because the text is formulated awkwardly, but because the style is extremely terse and pregnant. The careful and thoughtful reader is drawn into the complex relationships between the various persons in Jerusalem. Therefore, an exegesis that attempts to trace these nuances precisely but without coming to any firm conclusion is not just a pointless bead game involving various grammatical possibilities. Instead, it involves the reader himself in the event, so that he experiences something of the ambiguity of what was an open situation before Paul resolved it unambiguously.

Paul's verdict on his actual opponents sounds harsh and uncompromising. We are reminded of the observations already made with respect to 1:7. Once again, Paul describes his opponents from his own perspective. He calls them false brethren, implying that their Christianity is a lie. It is hardly safe to assume that the Jerusalem leadership used this terminology. Neither does Paul describe the purpose and conduct of his opponents objectively; he judges and condemns it. This does not satisfy our historical curiosity. We should like to know more details: What was Paul using terminology from the realm of political activism to attack? How were they "secretly brought in," and what was involved in their "spying"? Should we think primarily in terms of the Judaizing activity at Antioch or also of certain events during the negotiations at Jerusalem? Did the false brethren force their way into a private meeting of the inner circle, alluded to by Paul in v. 2, or even overhear confidential conversations? They themselves would undoubtedly have described what happened in different terms; they would certainly not have referred to their purpose as "the desire to enslave others."

But this very expression shows that Paul is not descending to invective. His purpose is to state the point at issue in the most precise terms possible. The thorn in the side of Paul's opponents is the freedom that, according to Paul, we have in Christ Jesus, which constitutes the truth of the gospel. Anyone who subverts this freedom is undoing what has been done through Christ, returning the victims to slavery and leaving them at the mercy of untruth. If this were to happen, Paul would indeed have run in vain as an apostle.

He emphasizes this by making what is happening in Galatia suddenly shine through his account of what happened at Jerusalem. In v. 4 he already uses an emphatic first person plural, extending his own involvement to include those he is addressing; he speaks of "our" freedom which we have in Christ Jesus, and the intention of his opponents to enslave "us." In v. 5, in the midst of his narrative, he turns totally to address the Galatians. He did not yield submission even for a moment, that the truth of the gospel might be preserved "for you," the Galatians. What he did more than five years previously at Jerusalem, when he had as yet no inkling of the critical developments in the Galatian Christian communities, was done "for you." The "No!" that he said there was also a "Yes!" to the Galatians, and a no less absolute "No!" to what they are on the point of doing: surrendering the truth of the gospel.

How is it possible to attach such importance to the question of circumcision? One could at least allow that the intentions of the Judaizers were pure. Their concern is membership in the lineage of Abraham. Does it not distort their understanding of circumcision to accuse them of a legalism that turns the rite of circumcision into a meritorious work of which one can boast? Can circumcision not be understood as a sign of promise, which does not convey salvation *ex opere operato*? What, in fact, is the fundamental difference between circumcision and baptism? Is baptism not also a ritual that is equally, if not even more greatly, open to being misinterpreted as guaranteeing salvation?

But even if one does not share the view that circumcision is a necessary sign of salvation even for the Gentile who becomes a Christian, is it necessary to react as harshly as Paul? Would it not, in fact, be a mark of Christian freedom to display generosity in this question? The argument might run as follows.

Circumcision is nothing more than a ritual—what harm can it do? It is a matter of indifference. It may be performed or omitted, depending on the situation. If those who see circumcision as being necessary for salvation feel attacked by a different opinion, would it not be best to give in for their sakes, not merely letting them alone when they make use of this means of salvation but accommodating them by agreeing to be circumcised so as not to cause a scandal by refusing? Did not Paul himself establish the principle that one must become a Jew to the Jews in order to win Jews (1 Cor. 9:20)? Suppose with their trust in circumcision they do consider themselves strong in faith, while others truly see in it a sign of weakness—does not this very fact demand a love so free that it sometimes refuses to avail itself of freedom in matters of religious ceremonies, as Paul himself says: "For though I am free from all, I have made myself a slave to all, that I might win the more" (1 Cor. 9:19)? Is not the result, in effect, the same whether I make myself the slave of others or others make me a slave and I permit this to happen?

To have regard for the weak means that I make a paradoxical use of my freedom by renouncing it freely. In many cases the need for such regard can be acute. That this should be true with respect to circumcision, however, is hard for us to conceive. It is no longer among those things that can assert an inward claim on us and become a problem in one way or another. This is not just the result of modern enlightenment. Amazingly soon after Paul's violent conflict over the question of circumcision, the theme had become a dead issue in the early church. It was considered obvious that a gentile Christian does not have to be circumcised. This opinion was justified by the argument that the law of the Old Testament had been partially abrogated; these sections retained only typological or allegorical meaning. It appears as though Paul had swept the field. In truth, however, no one had understood how crucial the question of circumcision was for him in his struggle for the gospel free of the law.

The questions that arise in connection with the theme of circumcision cannot be discussed solely on the basis of the text that recounts the episode of Titus in Jerusalem. For Paul, this problem is the focus of his conflict both with his opponents and with his own past. Therefore, it cannot be fully understood apart from the argument of the entire letter. We shall merely give a few indications of why circumcision became such an explosive matter that it could not be disposed of as a matter of indifference.

Paul explicitly rejects the necessity of circumcision only for non-Jews who become Christians. This statement appears trivial. For whom but a non-Jew could the question arise? Therefore the problem came up only in the mission to the Gentiles. But it takes on clear shape only when we realize that Paul apparently had no objections to the practice of circumcision among Jewish Christians. A Jew who becomes a Christian need not be ashamed of having been circumcised. He should not, for instance, attempt cosmetic measures to conceal the operation that was performed on him, as was occasionally done by men who wanted to conform to their Hellenistic environment (e.g., 1 Macc. 1:15), for reasons having nothing to do with Christianity.

When Paul rejects denying one's own circumcision, it is by the same argument as his "No!" to the reverse practice of circumcising a Gentile when he becomes a Christian: "Were you called as a Jew? You need not conceal your circumcision. Were you called as a non-Jew? You do not need to be circumcised" (1 Cor. 7:18). Both come under the principle that all should remain in the state in which they were called to be Christians (1 Cor. 7:20).

The same holds true, for example, in the case of a slave. He should cheerfully continue in this social status even if he could be freed. This attitude expresses the fact that becoming a Christian must not be falsified by being linked with change of social status. Similarly, it must not be confused with conversion within the framework of existing religious alternatives, which depend on one's ethnic background. It follows, therefore, that—although Paul nowhere says anything on the subject—he would consider it appropriate for Christians of Jewish descent to continue to circumcise their male off-spring. It would clearly be contrary to his views to proclaim a general prohibition of circumcision among Christians and simply claim that this element of the Torah had been abrogated.

Of course, Paul would also not agree with the statement that circumcision is necessary for salvation for Christians of Jewish descent. It is an element of the tradition from which a Jewish Christian has no compelling reason to break free. In so doing he might in fact run the opposite danger of turning absolute rejection of circumcision into a religious "good work" in reverse.

Our evaluation of Paul's position will be determined by its motivation. Paul can sometimes speak as though everything of religious importance to the ancient world were indifferent. "Neither circumcision counts for anything nor uncircumcision" (1 Cor. 7:19). But as the continuation shows, this relativity is not based on enlightened indifference to religion but on a higher religious perspective that makes this apparently fundamental religious distinction merely relative: "Neither circumcision counts for anything nor uncircumcision—all that matters is keeping the commandments of God" (1 Cor. 7:19). Even more precisely: "In Christ Jesus neither circumcision nor uncircumcision is of any avail, but faith working through love" (Gal. 5:6). And: "Neither circumcision counts for anything, nor uncircumcision, but only the new creation" (Gal. 6:15).

This formula of indifference in the question of circumcision chimes with the even more frequent Pauline formula of identification with respect to Jews and Greeks or Jews and Gentiles. The gospel is for both Jews and Greeks (Rom. 1:16). Both are equally sinners (Rom. 3:9). Both are baptized to form a single body (1 Cor. 12:13; Gal. 3:27–28). There is thus no difference between Jews and Greeks. Christ is the same Lord for all (Rom. 10:12; cf. also Rom. 2:9–10; 3:29; 9:24; 1 Cor. 1:22–24). Neither formula is based on an abstract principle of equality; both derive from the fundamental soteriological turning point of the Christ event. The historical pivot rests in Judaism, but its earthshaking significance has transformed the situation of Judaism no less than that of all the nations.

To this extent, then, there is no formal equivalence between the indifference formula and the identity formula. The special position of Judaism is already visible in a variety of outward signs. The Jews are always mentioned before the Greeks or Gentiles when both appear together. This is sometimes underlined by the addition of πρῶτον (*prōton*, first: particularly Rom. 1:16; 2:2, 10). The distinction is also already present in the perspective of Judaism itself, as can be seen above all by the use of the collective term "nations" or "peoples" in contrast to the chosen people of God. Similarly for

Paul the frequent antithesis between περιτομή (*peritomē*, circumcision) and ἀκροβυστία (*akrobystia*, foreskin) is totally dependent on the former term, which refers to the ritual act and the status it effects; the meaning of the latter term is merely privative, referring to the state of being uncircumcised.

We should also note the obvious fact that circumcision is not discussed here as a universal religious and ethnological phenomenon. Today as in the past it is still practiced by many peoples, and there is also a female equivalent. Paul, however, deals only with its Jewish manifestation, limited to the male sex and forming part of a very specific religious tradition. When the indifference formula emphasizes that neither circumcision nor uncircumcision is of any avail, it is not the distinctive religious rituals of the Jews and the other nations that are up for discussion. Paul is concerned exclusively with circumcision as the sign of God's covenant with his chosen people, going back to Abraham, and the question of who shares in this covenant.

The difficulties raised by circumcision cannot simply be transferred at will to some other religious ritual, such as a particular sacrificial cult. The uncompromising "No!" of early Christianity to the cult of the Emperor, for example, is by its very nature entirely different from the absolute "No!" of Paul to the circumcision of Gentiles who wish to become Christians. It is simply out of the question for any Christian to participate in the cult of the Emperor. But participation in the ritual of circumcision still remains open to Jewish Christians. Only for Christians from among the Gentiles is it incompatible with being a Christian. For them it is true that "If you receive circumcision, Christ will be of no avail to you" (Gal. 5:2). Those to whom Christ is of no avail are lost, and hopelessly lost.

This somewhat circuitous approach has been necessary to clarify the problem, in order that the crucial point may be stated with rigor. In opposition to the Judaizers' claim, "Unless you are circumcised . . . , you cannot be saved" (Acts 15:1), so that Christ would be of no avail, in Paul's judgment circumcision stands in forbidden competition with Christ himself for gentile Christians. If circumcision is made a condition necessary for salvation, it contradicts the unconditional nature of Christ's grace. The Torah remains the universal source of salvation; Christ is incorporated into it, where he is admitted as a mere supplementary datum. Thus, the meaning of the Christ event is radically altered. Instead of opening the way of freedom, it shares in subjecting proselytes to the Torah. Instead of canceling human differences, the Christ event serves to reinforce them. Despite the expansion of the boundaries of Judaism, the separative function of circumcision remains in effect and leaves everything as it had been: the distinction between Jews and Gentiles, and the religious superiority of the male sex to the female. Instead of inspiring courage to accept grace, the Christ event when linked with such a special demand encourages trust in one's own obedience and thereby self-glorification.

Not only does this obscure for gentile Christians who follow this course the meaning of what took place in Jesus Christ; it also conceals from Jewish Christians the difference the Christ event makes for them, precisely with respect to their own relationship to circumcision. Refusal to be ashamed of it is not the same thing as boasting of it. Thus, the treatment of circumcision becomes a test of the Christian faith. In historical terms, it must be decided whether Christianity is something other than a new Jewish sect. In theological terms, the decision is whether one's relationship to Christ is dependent on being under the law, or the relationship to the law is dependent on being in Christ.

Thus, there are two strangely conflicting answers to the question of whether circumcision is not a matter of indifference. Initially, in fact, everything seems to suggest that it is: neither circumcision nor uncircumcision is of any avail. On this basis it is quite possible that, for love's sake and out of consideration for others, someone who is already a Christian may be circumcised. Acts 16:1–3 tells of such an instance: Paul circumcised Timothy, a Christian, whose father was a Greek, but whose mother was a Jew who had already become a Christian. The reason for performing the circumcision in this case was that Paul wanted to take Timothy on his missionary journey and thought that he should respect the feelings of the Jews in the area. We need not examine in greater detail the status of a half-Jew in this period; neither is it necessary to consider the historicity of this event. The behavior ascribed to Paul can easily be harmonized with his general attitude.

It would be wrong to find a contradiction between this case and that of Titus. First, the two men were from different ethnic backgrounds; second, the situation did not involve a crucial decision over a fundamental question. The hypothetical question as to what Paul would have done if Timothy instead of Titus had been in Jerusalem may therefore be answered as follows: faced with the argument that circumcision was necessary for salvation, Paul even now would not have yielded to pressure, although in this case an argument could have been made for circumcision.

There is no such thing as a matter that is absolutely indifferent; indifference is always relative to concomitant circumstances and conditions. If the truth of the gospel is at stake, that is, *in casu confessionis*, what appears to be indifferent ceases to be so. If circumcision is linked with the moral constraint that it is necessary to salvation, the answer must be an uncompromising "No!" Shifting the problem to the context of the Reformation period,

Luther has this to say about our text: "If the Pope were to give me the seemingly innocent order to take a spoonful of milk, with the injunction that it was necessary to salvation, I would not do it, because the truth of the gospel would be tarnished."[23]

Above all, it is impossible to claim indifference when one is faced, as Paul was, with a decision of incalculable importance for the understanding of the gospel. Paul's firmness still affects us today. Imagine the theological and historical consequences of a careless surrender in this case! There could have been no appeal to Christian freedom, for the requirement of circumcision would have called this freedom into question, not just in this particular case but in general. To forgo the use of freedom is an expression of freedom only when it can still be seen that the choice is based on freedom and when that by which freedom lives is preserved. If the basis of Christian freedom is surrendered together with the truth of the gospel, this cannot be justified as an act of freedom.

Neither could there have been an appeal to love as grounds for yielding. Love does require us to submit to many things that are repugnant to us. But it would not be love to deny the very ground of true love, the love of God confessed by faith in Jesus Christ. In matters of faith, then, love can do nothing contrary to truth. There are situations, therefore, in which a direct "No!" in disputes about the faith is by no means irreconcilable with love. Indeed, such a "No!" as an act of faith is also an act of love.

These reflections do not furnish a prescription. They can take concrete form only in the presence of alert responsibility. Nevertheless, we have now probably found the point of contact with our own concerns. We may lack the necessary experience, knowledge, and training, so that it is difficult for us to discover the *casus confessionis* in the context of our own lives. But when the Christian faith is lived, somehow the question will always arise whether some particular action does not suddenly confront us with a crucial decision involving the truth of the gospel. This is not like the similar question that arises out of a legalistic spirituality: must I now obey this requirement or observe this prohibition? Instead, I have to examine myself in order to see how, in the given situation, I may live out the freedom for which Christ has set me free. Paul's conflict over the question of circumcision can help us grasp this crucial question of what it means to live as a Christian.

It would be totally wrong to think of the situation as arising out of two conflicting legal precepts, as though the Judaizers were holding fast to the commandment requiring circumcision while Paul was insisting that it was prohibited. It would also be totally mistaken to find here a conflict between legal rigor and laxity or even libertinism. The one side is in fact defending a precept, a specifically religious precept. Obedience to it is linked with soteriological hope. And the precept is central. On it depends a whole body of commandments and prohibitions having to do with ritual purity.

Paul, on the other hand, is defending the change in our relationship with God brought about by the appearance of Jesus Christ. It must be seen and believed, its truth must be accepted. This change is so fundamental that it is no longer the Torah but Jesus Christ who is crucial to our relationship with God. One law does not take the place of another; the very nature of the proceedings has changed.

This finds expression not least in a reversal of soteriological perspective. Righteousness before God and peace with God in the definitive sense no longer lie in a distant future that must be waited and worked for. They are already present through Jesus Christ for the faith that believes in him. In the life that still stands before us, all that matters is to maintain this faith, open ourselves to its manifestations, and await the ultimate revelation. When life is lived under the sign of the Torah—represented by circumcision as a token of the covenant—it cannot be determined by the freedom that we already have, nor by the love that is grounded in the unsurpassable and irrevocable demonstration of God's love. Therefore, the change in our relationship with God profoundly affects the definition of this relationship.

At the same time, the situation now allows a universal solidarity among all people. This is quite different from the ability to gain proselytes, which was always a possibility despite the separation of the Jews from the Gentiles. The serious differences between nations, races, classes, and sexes do not simply cease to exist. But they become totally irrelevant to the ultimate meaning of being human. This is the fruit of the freedom that Paul says we have in Jesus Christ. To defend it against the requirement of circumcision means nothing less than to preserve the truth of the gospel, the very essence of which is liberation from the state of servitude.

What was then the burning question has become a dead issue for us. But it was, in a sense, the catalyst through which the truth of the gospel came to be recognized in all its transforming power. This truth is far from being a dead issue. Therefore, the problem posed by the initial situation retains an irreplaceable hermeneutical function in helping us continue to grasp the truth of the gospel in its full depth. This claim will be honored in the subsequent course of our exegesis, when we come to explicate the concepts already introduced proleptically in such formulas as the "Christ event" or the term "freedom" without further definition.

In his account of the meeting at Jerusalem, Paul makes a clear distinction between the question of Titus and the agreement reached. In the case of the former, he is dealing immediately with those false brethren who, though perhaps not personally identical with the Judaizers who have appeared in Galatia, are in full agreement with them. In the case of the latter, Paul is dealing with the Jerusalem leadership. Unlike the former group, they are named individually but are also given a collective title. The list raises a variety of problems.

The sequence in v. 9 (James, Cephas, John) should probably be taken as reflecting rank. From it we may conclude that during the twelve to thirteen years since Paul's first visit to Jerusalem, the situation within the local community had led to a primacy of the Lord's brother. Apparently, however, we are dealing not with a monarchic episcopate but with a kind of triumvirate. For the moment we shall ignore the question of why Cephas is called by his Greek name Peter in vv. 7–8.

The collective term οἱ δοκοῦντες (*hoi dokountes*, those of repute) that Paul uses for these people clearly is not the title they had in Jerusalem, to the extent that they enjoyed any common title there. At least in the case of James it is dubious whether they all belonged to the circle of the apostles, whom Paul referred to in 1:17 as οἱ πρὸ ἐμοῦ ἀπόστολοι (*hoi pro emou apostoloi*, those who were apostles before me). Furthermore, we do not know how far the circle of the apostles extended. It probably included more than two or three persons. Therefore, the collective term "apostles" would hardly be appropriate here. Paul's terminology probably represents his own personal attempt to find a collective designation for those in question. But it would also be possible to theorize that Paul introduced this title so as to avoid using an official term of authority claimed by these men.

The term οἱ δοκοῦντες itself was not invented by Paul. It was a neutral social designation, which, like "notables," was commonly used both positively and ironically. It was already introduced by Paul in v. 2 and is now picked up in vv. 6 and 9. Aware of its verbal meaning, Paul links the phrase οἱ δοκοῦντες with interpretive additions: the dignitaries (as one might translate the absolute form οἱ δοκοῦντες in vv. 2 and 6) are those who are of some repute. The expanded form οἱ δοκοῦντες εἶναί τι (*hoi dokountes einai ti*, who are reputed to be something: v. 6) merely represents a more emphatic mode of expression. Here, too, the verb must probably be taken intransitively, in the sense of the respect someone enjoys. It should not be interpreted transitively on the analogy of Gal. 6:3, referring to the opinion someone has of himself, which may even turn out to be a self-deception—someone who thinks he is something although he is nothing.

The extension in v. 9 likewise conveys the meaning "dignitaries": οἱ δοκοῦντες στῦλοι εἶναι (*hoi dokountes styloi einai*, those reputed to be pillars). Here the term δοϰοῦντες is linked with an equally common synonym. As pillars they function to support the community. This term may actually have been applied to them in Jerusalem. This form of expression was probably least likely to involve ironic overtones; we can, therefore, assume that this is the case here. If Paul had intended to sound disdainful, he would have debased the agreement, which was in fact meant to deny his opponents the right to claim the Jerusalem authorities were on their side against him.

These stylistic observations concerning the titles of Paul's opposites in the discussion give no reason, in my opinion, to interpret the different expressions as referring to different groups of people. It is of course possible that the three στῦλοι (*styloi*, pillars) constituted an inner circle within the δοϰοῦντες (*dokountes*, those of repute), but the use of the phrase οἱ δοϰοῦντες στῦλοι εἶναι (*hoi dokountes styloi einai*, those reputed to be pillars) in v. 9, picking up the expression οἱ δοϰοῦντες from vv. 2 and 6, argues against this theory.

But even if there is nothing derogatory about this term, it does indicate a kind of aloofness. This arises from the dilemma in which Paul finds himself. He can deny that his opponents have the Jerusalem authorities on their side and can even appeal to their agreement with him. But for this very reason he has to protect himself against the insinuation that he recognizes them as a court of appeal. Therefore, as soon as he comes to speak of their position he adds a parenthetical reservation: he refuses to be impressed by who they are and will not be dependent on them. The verb used here, διαφέρειν (*diapherein*, be distinct, be different), in fact allows us to say that for him they belong in the category of adiaphora, things that are indifferent.

It is not immediately clear what personal qualifications of his partners Paul has in mind. The context makes it quite unlikely that he has in mind negative characteristics such as lack of education or character defects on the part of the δοϰοῦντες (*dokountes*, those of repute). The reference could be simply to the aura surrounding them in the eyes of others, but possibly also (more concretely) to the advantage they supposedly possessed on account of their pre-Easter acquaintance with Jesus.

No conclusions can be drawn from the change of tenses in this parenthesis. The use of the past tense ἦσαν (*ēsan*, they were) arises out of the narrative itself. The particle ποτέ (*pote*, formerly) is probably used in a generalizing rather than temporal sense. The present tense οὐδέν μοι διαφέρει (*ouden moi diapherei*, it is a matter of indifference to me) is typical of proverbial expressions. Of course, the emphasis is on what Paul is now saying to his addressees: the special distinction attaching to his former partners in the discussion does not matter to him; he appeals to their stated opinion then, but does not base his claims for himself on their authority. He appeals to them with an eye to his opponents, not out of personal need.

This also accounts for the weighty theological argument Paul uses to tip the scales. Because the leaders in Jerusalem were thought to have special religious qualifications, Paul finds it necessary to confront this human judgment with God's judgment. His opponents would, of course, be totally astonished that Paul should make any reference here to the common theological axiom of the Old Testament and of Judaism that God is not biased or venal, that he is a righteous and not a corrupt judge (e.g., Deut. 10:17; 2 Chron. 19:7; cf. also Acts 10:34; Rom. 2:11; 1 Pet. 1:17; etc.). Here (they would object) there is no question of anything unjust, which naturally cannot influence God's judgment, but of a privilege granted by God himself, remaining in force precisely because it is God's will. But Paul thinks otherwise.

He certainly does not wish to deny that in a sense the δοκοῦντες (*dokountes*, those of repute) enjoy a certain privilege bestowed by God and deserve human respect. They should be honored in their role as pillars of the first Christian community. But it is something else to claim to derive from this privilege an authority in matters of the gospel, an authority to which Paul would have to submit if it should ordain something different from what he himself had received through the ἀποκάλυψις ᾽Ιησοῦ Χριστοῦ (*apokalypsis Iēsou Christou*: cf. Gal. 1:12). When the question comes down to this—and this very possibility was raised by the negotiations in Jerusalem—Paul must hold fast to God's way of judging. God will not be blinded by human prerogatives or what human beings allow themselves to be impressed by (perhaps even with reason) in worldly matters. When the cause is the gospel as the revelation of God's righteousness, Paul will, therefore, not worry about human respect and judgment.

As the result of the conference Paul can report total success—as he already could in the matter of Titus. At least in negative terms he states with lapidary brevity that nothing was required of him. Apart from circumcision, this includes all kinds of ritual regulations and possibly also hierarchic and disciplinary obligations. In the light of Acts 15 one might ask whether the emphatic introductory ἐμοί (*emoi*, me) suggests some such limitation as: in contrast to their usual attitude toward others, they required nothing of me. The two accounts, which are mutually contradictory on this point, cannot be harmonized. Acts 15 shows that many thought that at some time the gentile Christians had been placed under an obligation to observe a bare minimum of the regulations governing purity: to abstain from food offered to idols, from blood, from meat that had not been fully drained of blood, and from unchastity (vv. 20, 29). According to Paul, this is out of the question. In his own conduct he could, in fact, generally follow such requirements. But he could never have agreed to add this requirement of a minimal assimilation to the Jewish way of life as a universal condition to the gospel to be proclaimed among the Gentiles.

The δοϰοῦντες (*dokountes*, those of repute), however, not only refused to impose such obligations, but on the contrary confirmed (not inaugurated!) the solidarity of the Christian community through the right hand of fellowship and agreed to a regulation of this solidarity in the church's missionary work. This section of the account is also brief and to the point, at least if one skips over the three additional parentheses in vv. 7, 8, and 9a, so that the ἀλλὰ τοὐναντίον (*alla tounantion*, but on the contrary) at the beginning of v. 7 is followed immediately by v. 9b: "But on the contrary . . . James and Cephas and John, reputed to be pillars, gave to me and Barnabas the right hand of fellowship, with the understanding that we should go to the Gentiles and they to the circumcised."

This would be a smooth text with no lacunae. But this observation obviously does not give us the right to consider the intervening passages a later addition, not least because they play a very important role. They all serve to show how the agreement came about. Even if we did not have the undoubtedly accurate statement of Acts 15:7 to the effect that there had been much debate, it would be reasonable to assume that the conversations were difficult and that the result was reached only with difficulty. Paul certainly oversimplifies when he emphasizes the conflict over Titus while presenting elsewhere a picture of peaceful unanimity, almost like a posed photograph for the press. Even if the interpolation in the main clause does nothing more than suggest the basis for the agreement, it reveals something of the background tension that is not mentioned directly.

If we examine the interpolation in greater detail, it displays surprising peculiarities even on the formal level. It would be tempting to find in them traces of the event that underlies Paul's account. The most striking evidence is the repeated use of the name "Peter" in vv. 7 and 8. Elsewhere Paul uses only the name "Cephas," as he does at once again in vv. 9 and 11ff. This has led to an hypothesis espoused by various scholars, with individual nuances.[24] The primary idea consists in the suggestion that a protocol of the Jerusalem conference has been incorporated at this point. Now of the three parentheses (vv. 7, 8, 9a), the first two can in fact be removed from the text without leaving a gap. The linking formula ἰδόντες ὅτι (*idontes hoti*, when they saw that: v. 7) is as it were the hinge that fastens the first parenthesis to the rest of the sentence. If it is omitted, a simple main clause emerges: "I was entrusted with the gospel to the uncircumcised, just as Peter was entrusted with the gospel to the circumcised." This statement is followed in the second parenthesis (v. 8) by an analogous justification: "For he who worked through Peter for the apostleship among the uncircumcised worked through me also for the Gentiles." In any case this double clause, also chiastic in form, provides a polished summary. It corresponds in content to the agreement as recorded in v. 9, likewise in the briefest possible form: "We to the Gentiles, they to the circumcised [i.e., the Jews]."

But there remain two unresolved problems. The fact that these two sentences are in the first person obviously eliminates the possibility of literal quotation. If Paul did borrow the text, he at least recast it in this form, thus adapting it to his own text. But that would lessen the value of an official document to which Paul could appeal for support. In addition, the first verb πεπίστευμαι (*pepisteumai*, I have been entrusted with) is an expression Paul uses elsewhere, so that it would be reasonable to assume that Paul's alteration of the language here went beyond mere shift to the first person singular.

On the other hand, there are traces of language that cannot easily be considered Pauline. An example is the genitive phrase εὐαγγέλιον τῆς ἀκροβυστίας or τῆς περιτομῆς (*euangelion tēs akrobystias* or *tēs peritomēs*, the gospel to the uncircumcised / circumcised), which does not appear elsewhere. The context rules out any interpretation that would see in this expression an antithesis between the gospel of Christ and some other gospel; according to Paul there is no such other gospel (1:6–7). Nevertheless, it is not entirely easy to accommodate the double formula to Pauline thought.

The passage clearly presupposes that the gospel is one by its very nature. The genitive phrase only indicates the different groups to which it is addressed, just as Paul refers to himself primarily as the apostle of the Gentiles (Rom. 11:13). Also Pauline is the use of the catchwords ἀκροβυστία (*akrobystia*, foreskin) and περιτομή (*peritomē*, circumcision), understood collectively, to indicate the difference between Gentiles and Jews. But in the situation of the discussion, this way of referring to the different groups to which the gospel is addressed suggests overtones of a different content as well. The gospel for the uncircumcised is free of the law, while the gospel for the circumcised is linked with observance of the Torah. Even this could be interpreted in Pauline terms. Observation of the Torah on the part of Jewish Christians would have to be so interpreted as to preserve the truth of the gospel in the sense of inward freedom from the law. The expression nevertheless remains ambiguous, betraying a use of language based on compromise.

Doubts might also be raised by the observation that the term ἀποστολή (*apostolē*, apostleship), which Paul uses elsewhere to describe his office and (perhaps accidentally) in no other context (Rom. 1:5; 1 Cor. 9:2), is used here only in connection with Peter. Of course, we must be on our guard against overly subtle interpretation. Since we know that Paul's apostleship and, therefore, also his claim to be called an apostle were matters of dispute, it is naturally tempting to sense a trace of these tensions here. But our observation can be explained quite naturally by the pregnant formulation of the two verses. In v. 7, the catchword εὐαγγέλιον (*euangelion*, gospel) appears only in connection with Paul and must be supplied in connection with Peter; the analogous situation obtains in reverse with respect to the catchword ἀποστολή (*apostolē*, apostleship) in v. 8. One might conclude (always assuming that the passage is based on an official text) that this passage no more denies Paul's apostleship than it denies recognition that Peter proclaims the gospel. The obviously delicate balance may have required a formulation somewhat different from what Paul would have chosen for himself, especially in a statement with polemic intent—if in fact Paul's title as an apostle was under discussion at Jerusalem and his calling himself "apostle of the Gentiles" was not a later development.

But the main evidence for the influence of non-Pauline language is (as already mentioned) the name "Peter." It is noteworthy that Paul uses this form only here in vv. 7–8. But there is yet another observation: the Aramaic synonym, transcribed in the Greek form Cephas, is used nine times in the New Testament: eight times by Paul, and otherwise only in John 1:42, which like Matt. 16:18 recounts Jesus' renaming of his disciple Simon. In contrast to Matt. 16:18, John uses the Hellenized Aramaic form Cephas and then immediately cites the translation in the Greek form *Petros* (Peter). This is a truly puzzling situation. The unusual distribution of the names within the New Testament could be explained as follows: in the earliest original texts, the Pauline Epistles, we find the earliest (Aramaic) form of the name. All the later texts, that is, primarily the Gospels and Acts (with the exception of the reminiscence in John), use only the Greek form, even when they claim to be telling how Jesus renamed Simon, as is the case in Matthew 16. In the texts as they exist today, therefore, we find only the Greek name. Paul alone uses the original Aramaic form, which may have been the only form current then.

This explanation would work out beautifully except for the appearance of the form "Peter" here in vv. 7–8. Various attempts to alleviate the difficulty through conjectural emendation or by the theory that someone else is spoken of here all do violence to the text. If the theory of a separate document did not involve other problems, it would be an evident solution: at Jerusalem the form "Cephas" was used, and so it appeared in the Aramaic version of the document. In the Greek version, however, the name itself was translated so as to make its meaning clear to those who understood only Greek. This meaning was important, since the appellation "Rock" was a unique distinction.

We shall not spend more time on the difficult question of how this name originated, but we must keep in mind that even for Paul this honorific title was so firmly fixed that he used it by itself to refer to this disciple of Jesus, fully aware of its meaning. In the Gospels, the personal name "Simon," itself already the Hellenized form of the Aramaic name "Simeon," often appears with the honorific "Peter." Paul never uses the personal name. For him, this disciple is identified totally with the new name that has been granted him. Paul has no desire to dispute his right to the unusual name "Rock." Since this name is already found in the tradition recorded in 1 Cor. 15:5, which Paul undoubtedly received immediately after his conversion, some two or three years after Jesus' death, it is highly probable that the name was bestowed by Jesus himself.

Now in our passage (Gal. 2:7–8), contrary to his practice elsewhere, Paul introduces the name in its Greek translation. This must attract the reader's attention, because to this point "Peter" was not a Greek name. The purpose therefore must be to indicate the meaning of the name "Cephas" to readers who understood only Greek. If the Greek translation of a separate document is not responsible, the only explanation is that Paul himself wishes to underline the special role of Cephas by translating the name for the reader.

Of course, consideration of the parties involved in the negotiations also played a part, not necessarily in the sense of deference to all of them. They should not be pictured as a monolithic block; there must have been internal tensions within the group. As we have already noted in the context of Paul's first visit to Jerusalem, there is some evidence that Paul enjoyed a fairly close relationship with Cephas, with whom he may have found the greatest understanding. It may have been important to Paul on this occasion to emphasize his special relationship with Cephas, perhaps even capitalizing on it against the other participants. Our text might preserve a trace of such tensions in vv. 7–8, which focus on the relationship between Peter and Paul. By contrast, the concluding formula in v. 9c uses the plural for both parties: the "we" includes not only Paul but also Barnabas and others involved in the gentile mission; $\alpha\dot{v}\tau o\acute{i}$ (*autoi*, they) includes not only Peter but also the other Jerusalem pillars. The difference between this passage and vv. 7–8, where only Peter is named, is especially striking. Could James, for example, be considered a missionary along with Peter? Or was Peter himself being tied firmly to the circle of the Jerusalem leadership, so as to keep him on the side of Jewish Christianity and prevent his involvement in a gentile mission that was free of the law?

I am unable to offer a completely satisfying solution to the complex of problems. It is most likely, I think, that the concluding formula in v. 9c, "We to the Gentiles, they to the circumcised," represents the literal text of the agreement, with the first and third person plural pronouns being interchangeable, depending on who was quoting the formula. The passage in vv. 7–8 seems to me clearest as Paul's summary from his own perspective, appropriate to the given situation and formulated with the necessary caution. His concern was equality with Cephas, whose honorific name he cites in such a way as to bring out its meaning. The effect should be echoed by using "Rock" in the English translation.

Notwithstanding these influences that have acted to modify the language employed, the point of the text is the thesis that Paul himself defended in Jerusalem, to which he received the assent of the others: "I was entrusted with the gospel to the uncircumcised, just as the Rock was entrusted with the gospel to the circumcised; for he who worked through the Rock for the apostleship among the circumcised worked through me also for the Gentiles." This, as Paul emphasizes, the men in Jerusalem agreed with. This understanding of his they made their own. The balance of the equation clearly runs from Peter to Paul. What may be considered a given with respect to Peter holds true for Paul also. He, too, can point to a call; he, too, can point to success.

It may seem strange that the agreement over Paul's preaching of the gospel was not recorded in the form of theological propositions but in a mere recognition of the facts. One has the impression that when Paul expounded to the others the gospel that he preached among the Gentiles, he was giving an account not so much of his theology as of his missionary work. It was not theses about the gospel without the law that impressed and persuaded the Jerusalem leadership, but what happened when it was preached. This was the pivotal evidence in support of the call that Paul had received. This is shown by the way v. 8 is presented in support of v. 7.

We should not misjudge the relative correctness of such reasoning. If the gospel is preached, the matter does not rest with the ideas that are communicated; a train of events is set in motion. Later, when Paul comes to dispute with the Galatians (3:2), he bases his argument on their experience of the Spirit. Of course Paul did not bring forward a collection of statistics, but he did point to the dynamics of a spiritual process that began with his missionary activity. More is involved than a comparison of outward success when he sees a parallel between his ministry and that of Peter. The evidence points to God as the identical source of such effective preaching. The impression that the same Spirit is at work in both cases reinforces the certainty that the same gospel is involved in both, although it has taken different forms because of the very different circles addressed.

But there can be no evading the fact that the agreement achieved finally broke down because of insufficient theological depth. Paul obviously did not feel called upon to instruct the others and help them improve their theology, for which there would certainly have been occasion. He was content that there should be a fundamental understanding based on the Jerusalem leadership's acceptance of what had been granted him. He did not surrender anything for the sake of the agreement; he did not listen to reason as expressed in the arguments of his opponents and yield to a superior understanding. The decisive change was that the δοκοῦντες (dokountes, those of repute) came to see something. Therefore Paul can prefix his summary statement in vv. 7–8 with the expression ἰδόντες ὅτι (idontes hoti, when they saw), and pick up this idea again (v. 9; cf. also 2:16) with the participle γνόντες (gnontes, when they perceived). Here he can speak his own language again, not having to compete with anyone else: "They perceived the grace that was given to me." This is certainly no longer a direct quotation of the words he had used in Jerusalem to summarize his position. They have been condensed again into a very simple formula. The noun χάρις (charis, grace) stands not only for what Paul had experienced personally as his call, but also for the very essence of the gospel he proclaimed.

In v. 10 the obligation to provide financial support for the original community is appended. Its members call themselves "the poor," a term linking their social status with a form of religiosity deriving from Judaism. Paul states clearly that the others initiated this request, but he agreed gladly and wholeheartedly. The Galatians are aware of the matter because they have already participated in the collection. His organization of the fund raising there is also suggested to the Corinthians as a model: on the first day of the week everyone is to set aside a contribution (1 Cor. 16:1–3). The Galatians themselves are thus witnesses that he has been faithful to the agreement.

He presumably also informed them of the meaning of this undertaking, as he expressed himself movingly on this subject elsewhere, especially in 2 Corinthians 8 and 9. He was concerned to translate into action his understanding of the unity of the church, although it was not identical with that of the Jerusalem community: on his last trip to Jerusalem, to deliver the collection, this difference created an uproar and led to his arrest. Paul's service of love to the Jewish Christians thus paved the way for his martyrdom, underlining how seriously he was concerned for the unity of the body of Christ.

The fundamental problem posed by the agreement reached at Jerusalem involves the theological and particularly the ecclesiological meaning of the formula of division: "We to the Gentiles, they to the Jews" (v. 9). Was this merely a pragmatic decision, so as not to interfere with each other's missionary work? Even in this sense it would be of no little significance. Paul himself considered it important not to preach the gospel where Christ was already known, lest he build on someone else's foundation (Rom. 15:20). And he was forced to make the bitter discovery that others had invaded his own territory, as in the case of Galatia.

But even if nothing more than this was meant, even if there was no tacit division into two churches—how was the agreement to be put into practice? Did it mean restriction of the Jewish mission to Palestine, where the Jews (before their political catastrophe) lived as a relatively closed community? How was the gentile mission to be carried out separately in the light of the sizeable Jewish diaspora? In fact, mutual interference was inevitable. Paul usually began his preaching among those who had some contact with the synagogue. And there are signs suggesting that Peter did not limit his work to Palestine.

It would be premature, however, to charge the formula of division with being ill-advised. It was an expression of good will, of the desire for peaceful coexistence, which did not anticipate the problems that could arise in practice. Procedural decisions in ecclesiastical matters often involve such experiments and compromises, which then either work out in practice or require revision when they fail.

More problematic than the wholesale division of missionary territories was the fact that everyone clearly failed to deal with the burning issue: how should a Christian community comprising both Jews and Gentiles live together? Should instead separate communities be the goal? That would divide the body of Christ, to which Jews and Gentiles equally belong. Or should one group accommodate itself to the other, the Jewish Christians having table fellowship with the gentile Christians notwithstanding the laws governing purity, or the gentile Christians observing the obligations imposed on the Jewish Christians? Neither the division of the missionary territories nor the refusal to require circumcision of gentile Christians did the trick. The next meeting between Cephas and Paul, this time at Antioch, revealed that the problems remained unresolved despite the Jerusalem agreement.

The Conflict of the Apostles
over the Gospel
2:11–14

11 But when Cephas came to Antioch, I opposed him to his face, because
he stood condemned.
12 For before certain men came from James, he ate with the Gentiles [i.e.,
gentile Christians]; but when they came he drew back and separated
himself, fearing the circumcision party.
13 And with him the rest of the Jews [i.e., Jewish Christians] acted hypo-
critically, so that even Barnabas was carried away by their hypocrisy.
14 But when I saw that they were not straightforward about the truth of
the gospel, I said to Cephas before them all, "If you, though a Jew, live
like a Gentile and not like a Jew, how can you compel the Gentiles
[i.e., gentile Christians] to live like Jews?"

Paul's account now comes to its end. If he were concerned only to demonstrate his independence of the Jerusalem authorities, it would be clear at
once that the story has reached a high note: at the outset Paul had not both-
ered with the apostles who preceded him; only after some time did he make
personal contact with Peter. At the official conference in Jerusalem he had
carried the day and remained independent. Now he even reprimands the man
who stood closest to him and refuses to shrink from conflict. But if we look
at the account as a whole from the perspective of Christian unity, we are
forced to say that it ends on a low note of shrill dissonance. The agreement
sealed in Jerusalem by the right hand of fellowship broke down immediately
at Antioch.

The criterion by which to judge the direction of the narrative is neither
Paul's personal independence nor concern for the unity of the church, considered in isolation. The very palpable climax appears in the clearer definition of the gospel preached by Paul—not clearer to Paul himself, who at the
very beginning of his apostolic work had received the crucial insight through
the revelation of Jesus Christ (although this does not rule out development in
his thought), but clearer to the Jerusalem authorities.

Independence from human authorities was, in fact, of primary importance. But it was also important to fight for equal rights for the gentile mis-

sion based on the gospel free of the law, alongside the mission among the Jews that emanated from Jerusalem. Finally, however, it was necessary to determine to what extent freedom from the law was also the sine qua non of the gospel for the Jewish Christians. Only when this has been decided does the narrative turn into a more precise definition of the substance of the gospel. At this point the narrative sequence merges into the theological lesson that Paul has to give the Galatians.

Such a purposive composition might arouse suspicions that the account has been adapted for apologetic and polemical purposes. The point at issue has, in fact, determined the principle of selection and the emphases, since this retrospective account was occasioned by the critical situation of the Galatian communities, which it was intended to clarify. But there are no grounds for doubting its trustworthiness. The history of Christian beginnings during these first two decades was a painful process of self-definition, through which it was necessary to clarify the actual meaning of the gospel.

Paul states at once that the events he is now describing involved a conflict. Their natural conclusion, depicted in v. 14, he anticipates in v. 11 as a statement and verdict. Paul's encounter with Cephas at Antioch is important only because the senior apostle stood condemned, and Paul had to oppose him personally. The details remain largely obscure.

When did this take place? Paul does not furnish any chronological information, not even a relative chronology as before (1:18 and 2:1). Presumably, it was not long after the Jerusalem agreement, to which the events that followed provided a critical epilogue.

Why had Cephas come to Antioch? Surely not out of hostility toward Paul, as his participation in the life of the Christian community there shows.

Who were the other visitors from Jerusalem, and why had they come? They can hardly be identified with the false brethren of 2:4. They had probably been sent by James, less out of concern over Paul than over Cephas. Possibly, rumors about the latter's conduct had made their way to Jerusalem. The result was that Cephas experienced at Antioch, with some change in roles, what Paul had experienced previously at Jerusalem: they wanted to spy out the freedom that he claimed for himself and make him listen to reason, that is, require that he faithfully observe the law or (in Cephas' case) abide by the Jerusalem agreement (cf. 2:4).

How was the drama finally resolved? Paul says nothing on the matter. His addressees may have known, although even at that time it was already hard to see beyond the immediate consequences. There could be several explanations for Paul's failure to describe Cephas' reaction. It is easy to imagine an exchange of words that left them totally divided. The separation of Paul from Barnabas, which Acts describes in different terms (Acts 15:36–40), was probably also connected with this disenchanting experience. But it is also possible that Cephas—not for the first time—showed the courage to repent. And it is conceivable that Paul did not succumb to the temptation to debase spiritual admonition by triumphing afterward over its success (cf. Gal. 6:1).

Nothing more is said about Paul's subsequent relations with Antioch. The next source of historical information about the Antiochene community is the letters of its bishop Ignatius, some two generations later. Does this perhaps explain why Antioch was not mentioned in 1:21? Did Paul have to leave the Antiochene community as a result of the quarrel and suffer at least an outward defeat? The argument that he would hardly have been likely in this case to mention the event does not hold water. Even if, as seems likely, he stood totally alone, even if he were the only Christian of Jewish origin who maintained solidarity with the gentile Christians, he had no reason to be ashamed in the eyes of the Galatians. In all these questions and conjectures we are groping in the dark. What Paul does state clearly and precisely concerns the problem that gave rise to the crisis and the theological reason for his crucial protest.

The facts of the case are simple: Cephas had been sharing in table fellowship with the gentile Christians; this was obviously the usual practice at Antioch despite the significant number of Jewish Christians in the community. And it involved both the agape and the Lord's Supper itself, which were still closely connected in this early period. In response to the emissaries from James, Peter then altered his behavior. Because of his authority, he thus (probably unintentionally) brought about a breakdown of the earlier practice. The Jewish Christians joined in this separation without exception, even Barnabas. The result must have been a division of the Christian community into a Jewish section and a gentile section, at least with respect to table fellowship. Thus, the very foundation of the life of the Christian community was called into question.

Since there is no statement by Cephas concerning these events, his motives must remain conjectural; but these conjectures are of high probability. It is quite possible that he had followed the Antiochene practice out of conviction. Like the Jewish Christians at Antioch under the leadership of Paul and Barnabas, Cephas, too, probably had the inner freedom in this situation to feel released from the Jewish purity regulations without transgressing the Jerusalem agreement and thus without violating his conscience. For him, too, unity through Jesus Christ was stronger than the separating power of the Torah (cf. 2:15–16). For him the question of purity was decided ultimately by faith, not by ritual. It did not depend on whom one ate with and what one ate, but on one's own heart. Impurity did not come from without but from within.

The meaning of purity of heart, however, had been transformed by the possibility of belonging to Jesus. Cephas and the other Jewish Christian theologians had not thought out the theological implications of this change wrought by Jesus Christ, but this need not have lessened their conviction of its reality. Where would we be—not just in matters of faith but in all realms of life—if we were to accept only what we fully understand intellectually? But a conflict will reveal the spirit that dwells within.

When the emissaries from James appeared, the moment of truth had come. It was clear from the outset that they could not approve the conduct of Cephas. At Jerusalem such table fellowship with gentile Christians would have been impossible. Remonstrances were probably not even necessary. For Cephas the mere idea that his fellow Christians from Jerusalem were offended was sufficient. It therefore seemed best to him silently to alter course and adapt to the changed situation.

Of course, he was probably also worried about the effect on his position in Jerusalem if he held out. But it would probably be an injustice to consider his behavior tactically motivated. His previous participation in the Antiochene freedom from the law proved vulnerable in the presence of people from Jerusalem who were faithful to the law, even by the terms of the Jerusalem agreement. The immediate juxtaposition of the two extreme manifestations of Christian faith created uncertainty for Cephas and presented him with a dilemma from which there was no escape. His conscience, formed within Judaism, cast doubt on whether his careless conduct had been proper. In any case, he lacked the confidence to stand by what he had done.

There were only two honest possibilities. He could openly continue his previous conduct, making it clear to the emissaries that he was not motivated by neglect of the law but by the freedom that comes through faith. Or he could equally openly heed his brethren from Jerusalem and try to explain to the Antiochene Christians that he was motivated not by a sense of faithfulness to the law as being somehow necessary to salvation, but by a love for which faith had set him free.

Faced with conflicting arguments, Cephas apparently embraced Paul's own chosen principle of conduct, which he had espoused in questions dealing with the Christian way of life that involved Jews and Greeks, the strong and the weak: "For though I am free from all, I have made myself a slave to all, that I might win the more. To the Jews I became as a Jew, in order to win Jews; to those under the law I became as one under the law—though not being myself under the law—that I might win those under the law. To those outside the law I became as one outside the law—not being without law toward God but under the law of Christ—that I might win those outside the law. To the weak I became weak, that I might win the weak. I have become all things to all, that I might by all means save some. I do it all for the sake of the gospel, that I may share in its blessings" (1 Cor. 9:19–23).

If Cephas' conduct at Antioch is taken as a commentary on this passage, that is, if Cephas is allowed, as it were, to appeal to Paul, Paul seems to be forced into a self-contradictory posture. The principle of adapting carefully to all is realizable at most when life is lived at an appropriate distance, not in a dialectic of opposites present in the same place. In such a situation of conflict, this motto of Paul's becomes a *reductio ad absurdum*, as he himself is forced to realize. In this particular situation it is like trying to square the circle when Paul says, "Give no offense to Jews or to Greeks or to the community of God . . . " (1 Cor. 10:32). Under the circumstances it is impossible to please everyone.

It is tempting to state the aporia by saying that Cephas acted, by and large, according to Paul's principles, thus apparently forcing Paul to retreat. This comports with the common understanding of what Paul says but not with its true meaning. This interpretation mistakes the purpose of Paul's instruction. When he speaks of desiring to win some, it is not a winning that Paul enters to his own credit, at the cost of those who are won. To win them for the gospel means to bring the gospel to them, to deliver them, to see that they are changed from what they are. To strengthen the Jews in their devotion to the law through accommodation, to strengthen the Gentiles only in their libertinism (cf. Rom. 1:18 ff.) or their soaring speculations, to strengthen the weak only in a weakness that they wrongly consider strength—that would win nothing.

Clearly, what Paul means is this: when for the sake of the gospel one becomes like those who are to be won for the gospel, one must be like them in other ways than they are by nature. By virtue of the gospel they are themselves not meant to remain as they were. To become a Jew to the Jews in accordance with the gospel, a Greek to the Greeks, weak to the weak, is not simply to mimic them—that would be to deceive them concerning the gospel. It means to enter into full solidarity with them, not in an accommodation that leaves them untouched but in a manner that changes them. What the Jews and the Greeks and the so-called weak Christians think is their strength must be shown to be a burden, must be shared and shouldered. The purpose is not familiarity and a partisan solidarity that merely reinforces the others in their illusions, but a liberating solidarity. This solidarity does not impose an alien law on the others, but helps deliver them from the specific form of their enslavement.

When circumstances permit, an outward accommodation can help demonstrate understanding, gain confidence, and avoid the mistake that what is wanted is a change of party affiliation within the old system. But such an accommodation can be helpful only when it shows forth the intent of the gospel all the more purely. If it leads only to obfuscation and confusion, then one has merely temporarily become something or other for one's own sake, not to help others transform their basic situation. Understood correctly, Paul's principle does not call for a constant change of roles. The point is, rather, under the particular circumstances and with an eye to the differences one confronts, to maintain one and the same role—the role of one who is responsible for the gospel, not imitating one way of life after another, but being true to oneself—which means, in this context, being true to one's mandate.

This lays the groundwork for our understanding of how Paul sees the situation. Note in the first place that he does not attack the emissaries from James as the mischief makers. Neither does he accuse anyone of breaking the Jerusalem agreement. The highly general nature of that agreement makes it unlikely in any case that this is what happened. But what took place did transgress against the spirit of the κοινωνία (*koinōnia*, communion) that had been confirmed by the right hand of fellowship.

But why did Paul censure only Cephas? It is certainly significant that he was the leading figure in the reversal whom the rest only followed. More important than the visible results, however, was Cephas' intention if possible to avoid the limelight and deal with the precarious situation by removing the stumbling block, returning, as it were, to the regular status of a Jewish Christian of Jerusalem. As even the outward consequences show, this unobtrusive settlement could neither remain unobtrusive nor lead to a real settlement. This is what aroused Paul's open opposition. What Cephas was trying to cover up had to be named by its right name publicly before the entire community. Only so could the gospel be served in this situation. Here it would have been inappropriate to speak to Cephas alone in private or to judge him behind his back after his departure. He stood condemned ipso facto, as Paul states in v. 11. Anything that might be cited to exonerate him could only confirm that he had not been straightforward about the truth of the gospel. He had been guilty of hypocrisy by acting as though he could revoke the truth to which he had borne witness through table fellowship with the gentile Christians without inflicting damage on every side. The more he might cite pastoral considerations, such as concern for the religious sensitivities of the emissaries from James, the worse became his hypocrisy when viewed objectively.

What was at stake was not a private concern of Cephas, not even his own personal veracity, but his public witness to the gospel and to its truth. The phrase ἡ ἀλήθεια τοῦ εὐαγγελίου (*hē alētheia tou euangeliou*, the truth of the gospel), which appeared already in v. 5, appears again here in v. 14. It does more than raise the question of whether the gospel is true in itself, in contrast to other messages and doctrines; it emphasizes the obligation that the gospel be proclaimed and preserved in all its purity and inward consistency. Cephas' conduct had the opposite effect and now had to be exposed by the light of the gospel.

Paul, therefore, focuses attention solely on the theological basis of his protest, bringing to light a hidden consequence of Cephas' conduct, which Cephas himself had been unaware of. Cephas had bowed to pressure from the Jewish Christians. By so doing he had in turn placed the gentile Christians under constraint. The moral constraint that had been avoided in Jerusalem (v. 3), thanks both to the perspicacity of the "pillars" there and to Paul's obduracy, had now reappeared with a vengeance. It is not the fact that Cephas, for whatever reason, had let himself be constrained that obscured the truth of the gospel, but the fact that he had himself thereby imposed a constraint. Paul does not blame Cephas, a Jew, for acting in Christian freedom as though he were not a Jew, feeling himself not bound by the strict Jewish way of life. Paul does not even consider the theoretical possibility of taking such conduct as imposing moral constraint, this time on Jewish Christians. This moral constraint is imposed with full force by Cephas' retreat: the gentile Christians can only conclude that he had originally made a mistake; the Torah remained fully in force, and its observance was required even of non-Jews who wished to be Christians.

I have deliberately rendered the words ἔθνη (*ethnē*) and ἐθνικῶς (*ethnikōs*) as "non-Jewish" or "Gentile," avoiding the literal translation "heathen" or "pagan." For us these words are antonyms of "Christian" rather than "Jewish." It is characteristic that Christianity has here followed the path of Judaism, defining itself in negative contrast to paganism. Dietrich Bonhoeffer's poem "Christians and Pagans" expresses this usage pointedly. Where Paul speaks of "Jews and pagans" we now find "Christians and pagans":

> God goes to all people in their need,
> Gives his bread their soul and body to feed,
> For Christian and pagan likewise
> Upon the cross he dies,
> And forgives them both.[25]

Christians must indeed ask themselves whether in their self-understanding they do not still need to come to terms with what Paul was fighting for in his insistence on the equality of "Jews and pagans/Gentiles." It is quite possible that a quasi-Jewish legalism may have taken possession of Christianity, so that the term "pagan/Gentile" is necessarily misunderstood in a Jewish Christian sense.

We shall not pursue this train of thought further. It is meant only to draw attention to the strange disequilibrium in Paul's words. The terms cannot be interchanged freely: moral constraint or consideration, gentile Christians or Jewish Christians. If all that mattered were for Gentiles and Jews to be able to live together without violation of either group, the only possibility would be the course of Jewish segregation, with its effects moderated as much as possible. The distinction established by the Torah permits no other solution. This is the nub of the problem. But when a whole new perspective is opened, so that Jews and Gentiles find themselves in the same situation with respect to the gospel, and this very fact is central to the substance of the gospel, an inequality appears. On account of the Torah, a more fundamental change is required of the Jews. Of course they can continue to maintain the Jewish way of life; they are not constrained to give it up. But this presupposes that their relationship to it differs fundamentally from the absolute faithfulness to the Torah of their previous understanding.

If the church is one body, made up of Jewish and gentile Christians—and on this point the gospel itself stands or falls—and if the gentile Christians are not to be defrauded of the gospel by being subjected to the Torah, the only possibility open is for the Jews in mixed communities to renounce their own way of life at crucial points. To speak of renunciation is, in fact, not germane, because we are dealing here only with a manifestation of Christian freedom, whereas the subjection of gentile Christians to the Torah cannot by its very nature be an expression of Christian freedom. It is, therefore, now high time for Paul to push on to the true root of the freedom he is thinking of. He does this in the section that follows.

The Truth of the Gospel

2:15–21

15 We ourselves, who are Jews by birth and not gentile sinners,
16 yet who know that no one can be justified by works of the law but through faith in Jesus Christ, even we have come to faith in Christ Jesus, in order to be justified by faith in Christ, and not by works of the law, because by works of the law "shall no flesh be justified."
17 But if, in our endeavor to be justified in Christ, we ourselves were found to be sinners, is Christ then an agent of sin? Certainly not!
18 But if I build up again those things which I tore down, then I prove myself a transgressor.
19 For as for me, through the law I died to the law, that I might live to God. I have been crucified with Christ.
20 It is no longer I who live, but Christ who lives in me; and the life I now live in the flesh I live by faith in the Son of God, who loved me and gave himself for me.
21 I do not nullify the grace of God; for if righteousness were through the law, then Christ would have died to no purpose.

It is impossible to give a direct answer to the much debated question as to how much (if any) of this discussion merely records what Paul said to Cephas at Antioch. The argument is linked directly to the episode there. At the same time, however, it is a commentary on the entire account from 1:13 on, focusing on the primary issue. At its conclusion Paul provides a definition of the gospel he preaches (cf. 1:11), propounding the thesis that he will later (starting in 3:1) justify and elaborate theologically. As before, it is the Galatians who are really addressed in these verses. For their benefit Paul formulates the conclusion of what he has just been saying.

This is true despite the change in grammatical subject. The "we" in vv. 15–17 includes Paul not with the gentile Christian Galatians but with the Jewish Christians and especially (in light of v. 14) Cephas. The "I" in v. 18, by the nature of the argument, cannot refer to Paul. Precisely because the previous "we" falls apart at this point, Paul changes the grammatical subject. He is now referring to Cephas and Jewish Christians who act like him. If he nevertheless uses the first person singular it is in a generalized sense, perhaps to remove from his words the all too personal allusion to the confrontation at Antioch and give them rather the character of a fundamental principle. The emphatic "I" at the beginning of v. 19, which remains the subject through v. 21, marks the transition from the shared "we" to Paul's own position.

But despite the explicitly confessional note, these statements in the first person singular are not limited to Paul. They exemplify the situation of every Christian. The Galatians are thus invited for their own good to identify with this "I" in contrast to the other "I" of v. 18, which referred at least indirectly to the Judaizers with whom the Galatians are on the point of identifying themselves, with disastrous consequences. As Gentiles by birth, the Galatians cannot identify totally with the Jewish Christian "we" of vv. 15–17. Nevertheless, they can find in these words a persuasive argument against the Judaizers who would lead them astray. And for the most part they can in fact join in this "we." The fundamental principle stated in v. 16 applies to all, whether Jewish Christians or gentile Christians; it is the core of the gospel that is preached among the Gentiles also. How could the faith of the Jewish Christians be formulated without destroying the Jewish Christian "we" and replacing it with a "we" that includes the gentile Christians?

These observations on the grammatical and semantic subject already pave the way for an understanding of how this section is organized. The argumentation begins with the Jewish Christian agreement (vv. 15–16). It then indicates the critical point of disagreement (vv. 17–18) and goes on to describe the sublation of the Jewish Christian agreement in the universal Christian truth of the gospel (vv. 19–20). The concluding sentence (v. 21) may be read by itself or in connection with the last subsection.

Stylistically, these verses are marked by an extreme density of expression. As a result they pose significant problems of interpretation, in part with respect to the meaning of the terse theological formulas, in part with respect to the logical structure of the argument.

Paul sets out to begin his argument with the crucial point at issue, the role played by the Torah for faith in Christ. He therefore takes what can bring a Jew to faith in Jesus Christ as his point of departure. The mere fact of being Jewish does not appear to be sufficient motivation—quite the contrary! Belonging to the chosen people gives a sense of soteriological privilege that places the Jew on a fundamentally different plane from the non-Jew. From the Jewish perspective, Gentiles stand accursed from birth, because they dwell outside the bounds of that which promises righteousness in the eyes of God. Gentiles, as such, are sinners. Just as Jews are Jews φύσει (*physei*, by nature), so Gentiles are sinners φύσει, quite apart from what they do or fail to do.

Of course, Jews are well aware, indeed infinitely more aware than Gentiles, that they are likewise threatened and repeatedly overtaken by sin. Where else in the pre-Christian and non-Christian world would we find so intense a sense of sin and so great a desire to overcome sin as in the Old Testament? But sin is not the primary concern here. It is not based on a given existential status but has the nature of a specific individual transgression. The sense of sin is awakened by the very thing that sets the Jew apart from the gentile sinner and is also the basis of hope for righteousness and an occasion for thanksgiving and glorying. On the basis of his own life as a Jew, Paul frequently mentions the various claims of which Jews may boast and in which they may set their hope (Rom. 11:1; 2 Cor. 11:22; Phil. 3:5–7; cf. also Rom. 9:1–5). On the one hand, these are the various genealogical statements defining membership in the chosen people: born of the seed of Abraham, a Hebrew of the Hebrews, of the people of Israel, and—in Paul's case—of the tribe of Benjamin. On the other, they are badges of religious devotion: circumcised on the prescribed date, a week after birth; a strictly Pharisaic attitude toward the Torah; and the proud sense of being blameless with respect to righteousness as defined by the law.

We should not oversimplify our evaluation of such self-esteem, which is grounded in a religious devotion that permeates all of life. Pharisaic piety, it is often said, bears, as such, the stain of hypocrisy and sanctimony. But for this cliché we cannot cite the man who ultimately counted all this to be so much garbage and in his own accounting entered as a loss what should have been gain (Phil. 3:7–8). Imagine the enormous demands a person opens himself to by exposing his entire life to God's judgment and living life accordingly. Furthermore, God's election takes absolute precedence over anything a Jew may point to as his own doing: birth is no more one's own doing than is circumcision on the eighth day afterward. And the crucial point about the Torah is that it bears witness to the election of Israel and the incomprehensible gift of God's revealed will, his deeds and promises, his commandments and prohibitions. The interweaving of ethical and ritual strands to form a single indivisible religious approach to reality must be understood as a sign that the Torah is all-inclusive, encompassing all of life, indeed the whole world. Human beings are more than merely ethical creatures. They are caught in tension between the holy and the unholy and must take care to protect themselves against impurity and to keep themselves pure. Like God's election itself, the regulations intended to protect and maintain the separateness of Israel have no rational basis. The interweaving finds its most powerful expression in the Sabbath commandment, which maintains the sacred order of God's world through the cessation of all human activities. By keeping at least some suggestion of this principle before our eyes, we may see quite clearly—even if we cannot really understand what we see—that such a people knows that it is uniquely different from all other peoples and nations, and that it is concerned to give full value to this difference as an effectual sign.

This is the background of the faith of the Jewish Christians. What moved them to go beyond what is given and required in the Torah, to look for another basis on which to be declared righteous and find it in Jesus Christ? No Jewish Christian before and besides Paul understood this question in such radical terms that answering it brought the Torah and Jesus Christ into mutual antithesis: "But whatever gain I had, I counted as loss for the sake of Christ. Indeed I count everything as loss because of the surpassing worth of knowing Christ Jesus my Lord. For his sake I have suffered the loss of all things, and count them as refuse, in order that I may gain Christ and be found in him, not having a righteousness of my own, based on the law, but that which is through faith in Christ, the righteousness from God that depends on faith" (Phil. 3:7–9).

Thus there came a rupture between Jewish descent and embracing Jesus Christ. This rupture appears also in the syntax of vv. 15–16. The appositive to the introductory "we" in v. 15 has no verb, but must be taken as a participial construction and interpreted concessively: not because, but although we are Jews by nature and not gentile sinners we have come to faith in Jesus Christ. The participle εἰδότες (eidotes, knowing) that follows in v. 16, however, has causal meaning. It gives the grounds for having come to faith and therefore stands in adversative relationship to what has preceded: "But because we know. . . ."

Verse 16 appears remarkably convoluted, both because the same expressions are repeated frequently and because the syntax initially seems somewhat obscure. Closer examination, however, removes the difficulties. In the middle of the verse stands the main clause of vv. 15–16, the statement: καὶ ἡμεῖς εἰς Χριστὸν ᾽Ιησοῦν ἐπιστεύσαμεν (kai hēmeis eis Christon Iēsoun episteusamen, even we have come to faith in Christ Jesus)—we, as described in v. 15. The ἡμεῖς (hēmeis, we) of v. 15 is now repeated emphatically and is further intensified by the preceding καί (kai, and, even). The verb of this main clause, πιστεύειν (pisteuein, believe, have faith), when used in the aorist, has the meaning "to have come to faith" (cf. Rom. 10:14; 13:11; 1 Cor. 15:2, 11). It thus refers to the event of embracing Christ, not as something in the past but as something that constantly determines the present and the future.

Now this main clause is embedded in explanatory material that makes clear the meaning of coming to faith in Jesus Christ. The main clause is preceded by a motivation clause (εἰδότες . . . , *eidotes*, because we know . . .) and followed by a purpose clause (ἵνα . . . , *hina*, in order to . . .). The complete sentence thus describes the movement from the motivation through the event itself to the intended goal. The whole is brought to a conclusion by another causal clause, which this time provides not a motivation but a scriptural proof: ὅτι ἐξ ἔργων νόμου οὐ δικαιωθήσεται πᾶσα σάρξ (*hoti ex ergōn nomou ou dikaiōthēsetai pāsa sarx*, because by works of the law shall no flesh be justified).

The impression of unnecessary complexity is due to the repetition of the same expressions at all stages of the process. This is illustrated first of all by the negation οὐκ ἐξ ἔργων νόμου (*ouk ex ergōn nomou*, not by works of the law). This phrase appears both in the motivation clause (v. 16a) and the purpose clause (v. 16c) as well as in the scriptural proof (v. 16d). Its positive counterpart διὰ or ἐκ πίστεως Χριστοῦ (*dia / ek pisteōs Christou*, through faith in Christ) accordingly also appears three times: in the motivation clause (v. 16a), in the purpose clause (v. 16c), and (transformed into a verbal construction) in the intervening main clause (v. 16b).

Also repeated three times is the verb δικαιοῦσθαι (*dikaiousthai*, be justified), which expresses the antithesis between ἔργα νόμου (*erga nomou*, works of the law) and πίστις Ἰησοῦ Χριστοῦ (*pistis Iēsou Christou*, faith in Jesus Christ): it appears in the three subordinate clauses (v. 16a, c, d) and is thus the central element in all the appended explanations. Human righteousness is decided by whether or not one embraces faith in Jesus Christ.

Contrary to first appearances, therefore, the structure of v. 16 is quite clear. But this poses a question: what is the purpose of this artful structure, when both form and content merely repeat the same fundamental statement: righteousness comes not by works of the law but through faith in Christ? The linguistic exuberance, which seems almost baroque in comparison to the all too frugal language of the surrounding verses, is probably due to the fact that something incredible is being stated. The same formula is used repeatedly to hammer home the crucial point and make it perfectly clear. In v. 15 Paul had referred to the Jewish self-understanding, which is reasonable and does not require further explanation. Now he tells why, in an act that defies all reason, Jews have become Christians. Here it is impossible to repeat the same thing often enough, because what is said of faith sounds so incredible.

But Paul immediately makes a further claim: just as there is an undisputed agreement for the Jews, so too for the Jewish Christians. The Jews know that what unites them is what makes them different from the Gentiles. The agreement that unites the Jewish Christians, on the contrary, is the incredible statement that righteousness is not attained through works of the law but through faith in Christ. The point does not really even require discussion; it is fundamentally agreed on.

But there is an implication here that must not be overlooked. The formula that Paul repeats so often can hardly have been commonplace among Paul's Jewish Christian predecessors and contemporaries, and they undoubtedly did not share his understanding of it. But can there be any other understanding for a Jew who has embraced faith in Christ? Does not this conversion necessarily require the admission that the righteousness that is quite properly so important to the Jews is never attained through fulfillment of the law? This is precisely why people have turned to Jesus Christ, because in him righteousness is in fact revealed and imparted in a very different way.

Paul is thus placing a heavy burden on the Jewish Christians with this interpretation of their acceptance of Jesus Christ. Any other reasons pale into insignificance beside the motivation that would lead a Jew to take such a step. It is at this point in the letter, therefore, that Paul first speaks explicitly of the law. For every Jewish Christian must have a clear idea of what it means to harmonize faith in Jesus Christ with fidelity to the law. In any case, this cannot be done if the understanding of righteousness is maintained with unbroken continuity. All Jewish Christians have in fact turned from reliance on works of the law to faith in Jesus Christ; Paul therefore takes this conversion as the point of departure for his subsequent argument. Why is there any need for Christ if the law really gives you what you need to be righteous?

Of course it takes more than formulaic repetition to gain general acceptance for what Paul takes to be the decisive reason that Jews have come to faith in Christ. And in fact the structure of v. 16 does more than this. The repetition proceeds in such a way that the same point is made with a different emphasis each time, so that it is increasingly illuminated.

One might suppose that the scriptural quotation would suffice for a Jew. Its importance here should not be underestimated. The fact that it comes at the end does not devalue it, but makes it summarize all that has gone before. But there are several reasons why it is insufficient in itself. Ps. 143(142):2 contains the cry of the petitioner to God: "Enter not into judgment with thy servant; for no living person is righteous before thee." The Greek translation of the second line reads: ὅτι οὐ δικαιωθήσεται ἐνώπιόν σου πᾶς ζῶν (*hoti ou dikaiōthēsetai enōpion sou pas zōn*, for no one who lives will be justified before thee). Paul changes the wording somewhat. In contrast to Rom. 3:20, where he uses the same quotation, he here omits the phrase "before thee."

This may be considered insignificant; the idea is obviously presupposed, and in any case the verse is not quoted in its entirety.

It may not be by accident, however, that both here and in Rom. 3:20 Paul replaces πᾶς ζῶν (*pas zōn,* everyone who lives) with πᾶσα σάρξ (*pasa sarx,* all flesh). There is no basis for this change in the Hebrew text. Obviously Paul wishes to emphasize human impotence in matters of righteousness before God, as though the text read "every mortal" rather than "every living person." It is also possible that this change was influenced by another Old Testament quotation that is likewise important for Paul's understanding of justification. In Hab. 2:4, the concept of life is closely linked with the righteousness of faith: ὁ δίκαιος ἐκ πίστεως ζήσεται (*ho dikaios ek pisteōs zēsetai,* the righteous will live by faith; cf. Rom. 1:17; Gal. 3:11). It would create tension if the notion of "living" were neutralized with respect to the theme of righteousness. For this very reason, the idea that belonging to Christ gives life plays an extremely important role in the discussion that follows. In vv. 19–20 the verb "live" occurs no less than five times, in a dialectical context that raises the question of what life really is; it is therefore with good reason anchored to a thrice-repeated reference to the death of Christ (vv. 19, 20, and 21).

Now this scriptural proof appears to contain a serious failing: the crucial phrase for Paul, ἐξ ἔργων νόμου (*ex ergōn nomou,* by works of the law), does not appear at all in the text. As in Rom. 3:20, Paul adds it as an interpretive gloss. It is for him an appropriate explanation. The statement that no one is declared righteous before God is certainly not true in the totally unrestricted sense that there is no prospect for righteousness before God. It is just this that Paul denies through his appeal to Jesus Christ. It is true, however, that no one is declared righteous before God strictly on the basis of one's own contribution to one's righteousness, namely nothing at all. But this must also be stated in such a way as to apply not only to the Gentiles, who are sinners by nature, but also to the Jews, despite the advantages they enjoy thanks to the Torah. On account of the Jews, therefore, the meaning of the quotation must be clarified by the addition of ἐξ ἔργων νόμου: "Because by works of the law shall no flesh be justified."

Of course, this scriptural quotation covers only the negative aspect of what Paul has to say about justification. But this does not lessen its applicability here. In the formula expressing the Jewish Christian agreement, the primary emphasis is on the statement that no one is justified by works of the law. Strictly speaking, this applies only to the Jews; only they can point to works of the law, because only they possess the Torah.

Important as the scriptural quotation is, it is far from sufficient by itself to account for the radical change that leads a Jew to faith in Jesus Christ. As we have already seen, the positive aspect of what Paul has to say about justification cannot be found in the quotation from the Psalm. And without this positive aspect there would be no need for the more precise interpretation of the quotation: ἐξ ἔργων νόμου (ex ergōn nomou, by works of the law). But it is also important to keep in mind that whatever references to faith and promises of the coming Christ Scripture may contain, it would be a gross illusion to think that faith in Christ can and must be simply derived from Scripture. Paul speaks explicitly of the veil that still lies over the reading of the Old Testament, which is removed only through Christ (2 Cor. 3:14).

Something must therefore have taken place, faith must have come (Gal. 3:23, 25), Jesus Christ must have appeared (Gal. 4:4–5), the Spirit must have been sent (Gal. 4:6), that people's eyes might be opened to this faith and that it might also be found in Scripture. Therefore Jews have not come to faith in Jesus Christ simply through studying the Scriptures. Quite the contrary: through the coming of faith and the coming of Jesus Christ and the sending of the Spirit, something has come to these Jews that has given them a new understanding of the Scriptures.

Therefore, the actual motivation is stated before the scriptural proof. It is introduced (v. 16) by εἰδότες (eidotes, because we know). This refers to a knowledge that cannot possibly be achieved through study of the Scriptures alone. It is based rather on an oral message that came to these Jews and changed them. And this oral message, in turn, grew out of an event that had taken place not long before. Now the source of this knowledge also changes its nature. It is not learned by rote but entered into through personal experience, which is itself made possible only by the message of faith (ἀκοὴ πίστεως, akoē pisteōs, Gal. 3:2, 5).

This accounts for the double motivation in v. 16: first (at the beginning of the verse) the experience of faith based on the message of faith, then (at the end) the witness of Scripture, which can be understood only by virtue of that faith event. Because this knowledge is not learned but lived, it has enormous motivating power. Knowledge of faith is not enough. How could such a mere knowledge of faith be any match for the ἔργα νόμου (erga nomou, works of the law)? Instead, πίστις (pistis, faith) now takes place as a verb, πιστεύειν (pisteuein, "[have, act on, come to] faith"), not every now and then, but at a radical turning point of decisive importance for all of life: καὶ ἡμεῖς εἰς Χριστὸν Ἰησοῦν ἐπιστεύσαμεν (kai hēmeis eis Christon Iēsoun episteusamen, even we have come to faith in Christ Jesus).

It is totally appropriate to the experiential knowledge involved here that the motivation clause should speak not only of the πίστις Χριστοῦ ᾿Ιησοῦ (*pistis Christou Iēsou*, faith in Christ Jesus) and its justifying power, but also of the critical rejection of powerless ἔργα νόμου (*erga nomou*, works of the law). Without such a "No!" the "Yes!" of faith in Christ could not be straightforward and consistent for a Jew. In the ὅτι (*hoti*, that) clause dependent on εἰδότες (*eidotes*, because we know) the negation appears twice: οὐ . . . ἐὰν μή (*ou . . . ean mē*, not . . . if not). This is the deposit of many experiences of failure and temptation, as well as of liberation and assurance—experiences we must assume were shared by Jews who came to say: "We know that no one is justified by works of the law, but only by faith in Jesus Christ."

Why, finally, does Paul repeat the same thing once again in the form of a purpose clause? Something more is probably involved than a mere desire to emphasize the congruence between what motivated faith and what is actually attained through faith. Paul is obviously concerned to make it unambiguously clear that after the radical turning point of faith in Jesus Christ nothing remains as it was. The ἔργα νόμου (*erga nomou*, works of the law) are not restored as a basis for justification, only now in the name of faith in Jesus Christ. The passage might be paraphrased by saying: "We did not come to faith in Jesus Christ in order to fall back into being under the law, but in order to establish once and for all the principle: not by works of the law, but by faith alone." In this purpose clause Paul pushes to the ultimate limit of the formula of agreement, where in fact disagreement has already broken out, but *per nefas*, in contradiction to what every Jewish Christian must fundamentally concede.

The structure of vv. 15 and 16 is probably now clear. But in our efforts to understand what they mean we cannot be content with these observations. What is the actual significance of the great words Paul uses here: ἔργα νόμου (*erga nomou*, works of the law) and πίστις ᾿Ιησοῦ Χριστοῦ (*pistis Iēsou Christou*, faith in Jesus Christ), as well as δικαιοῦσθαι (*dikaiousthai*, be justified), what is the purpose of both, but is so resolutely denied the one and ascribed to the other? In the section under discussion (2:15–21), Paul merely states the *propositio* (thesis) for which he will give the *probatio* (proof) in the next two chapters. This not only allows but requires us to wait for Paul's own explanation of matters that have not yet been clarified. Although it demands patience, let us limit ourselves for now to the programmatic formulation Paul uses in this section. We shall follow the path already suggested, from the Jewish Christian agreement to the disagreement that arose from it.

The difficult vv. 17 and 18 share a common structure: each begins with a conditional clause, from which a conclusion is derived. And they both share another feature: their movement runs counter to that of vv. 15–16. The latter, reduced to their most stylized form, move from sin to justification; vv. 17–18, on the contrary, move *(cum grano salis)* from justification to sin. Nevertheless, the sentences in vv. 17–18 are not simply parallel. Verse 17 is a question, v. 18 a statement. Of course v. 17 could be read as a statement if the particle ἄρα *(āra)* had an acute accent (as in v. 21) instead of a circumflex, making it an inferential particle (ἄρα, *ăra*, therefore) instead of an interrogative word expecting a negative answer. Then the sentence would read: "But if, in our endeavor to be justified in Christ, we ourselves are [or: were] found to be sinners, then Christ is [or: would be] an agent of sin. Certainly not!" In this case the structure of v. 17 would resemble that of v. 21b: "For if righteousness is [or: were] through the law, then Christ died [or: would have died] in vain." Both statements agree in leading up to a conclusion that appears absurd in Paul's eyes. For Christ to be an agent of sin or for his death to have been meaningless amount to the same thing: the hope of justification through faith in him comes to nothing; he accomplished the opposite. In terms of what it means, it does not matter whether this conclusion is stated interrogatively or affirmatively; Paul rejects it out of hand as abhorrent. In either case Paul is confronted with the question that was crucial for his life and is now crucial for the lives of the Galatians and indeed of all people: is the crucified Jesus a kind of nonentity? Or does he bring to those who have faith in him the greatest gain imaginable, the chance to be totally clear with God?

If we are to follow Paul's train of thought, it is necessary to be fully cognizant of how serious the question is. For Paul everything is at stake, both with respect to Christ and with respect to us: was Christ a criminal or a fool, so that we are deceived and lost, or is he, in fact, the Son of God, who makes us likewise children of God? It is hard for us to follow Paul singlemindedly to this extreme limit, to find here the central question of life in which everything is at stake. But we must not be tempted into reading the text as though it were a complex intellectual riddle. The exegetical acumen that has been devoted to it stands in perplexing contrast to the elementary either/or that Paul intends.

The reference to v. 21b has not yet contributed much to our understanding of v. 17 and its relationship to v. 18. The nub of the problem in v. 17 is not the conclusion ("Is Christ then an agent of sin?") but the argument that leads up to it. Under what conditions would one be forced to conclude that Christ was an agent of sin, promoting and furthering it instead of freeing from it and making righteous? According to the text of v. 17—if read as a question, apparently, and if read as a statement, undoubtedly—this would be the conclusion if embracing Christ brought about a result contrary to expectations. It would run counter to the desire to be righteous in Christ if sin instead were the outcome, if one were to end up not righteous, but a sinner. How is this meant?

If we search for further clues in the context, two points attract our attention. First, the catchword ἁμαρτωλοί (*hamartōloi*, sinners) clearly echoes v. 15. This allusion is underlined by the added καὶ αὐτοί (*kai autoi*, even ourselves). To be found to be sinners is not an abstraction but refers to a specific point of comparison: we (the Jewish Christians) are like them (the Gentiles). Second, the antithetical activities of building up and tearing down in v. 18 clearly allude to the contradictory conduct of Cephas at Antioch. Here is Paul's verdict on the attempt to undo what had already been done. Therefore not just this verse but both verses should be read in the context of Cephas' censured conduct. These two points on which we can build our interpretation are in complete harmony. If the word "sinners" in v. 17 is taken as an allusion to the "gentile sinners" of v. 15, it is interchangeable with ἐθνικῶς ζῆν (*ethnikōs zēn*, live like a Gentile: v. 14). Then we are reminded how Cephas must have appeared to the Jews and the Jewish Christians devoted to the law when he refused to base his conduct on the law: as a gentile sinner. Thus v. 17 would refer to the first phase at Antioch and v. 18 to the second, to Cephas' retreat and separation.

Now we come to a further observation. Both verses speak of the appearance of sin, but they use different words: ἁμαρτωλός (*hamartolos*, sinner: v. 17) and παραβάτης (*parabatēs*, transgressor). A transgressor is a sinner who has transgressed particular requirements of the law. The only other occurrence of παραβάτης in Paul (Rom. 2:25) underlines this point: addressing the Jew, Paul says: "If you are a transgressor of the law, your circumcision becomes uncircumcision." The verb παραβαίνειν (*parabainein*, transgress) is not used at all by Paul, but the scattered occurrences of παράβασις (*parabasis*, transgression) confirm the relationship to the law of this term for sin (Rom. 2:23; 4:15; 5:14; Gal. 3:19).

Paul's use of words based on the root ἁμαρτάνειν (*hamartanein*, go astray, sin) is clearly very different, even on the quantitative level. He uses the noun ἁμαρτία (*hamartia*, sin) and the verb ἁμαρτάνειν especially frequently; less common are the nominalized adjective ἁμαρτωλός (*hamartolos*, sinful, sinner) and the noun ἁμάρτημα (*hamartēma*, lapse, sin), which appears only twice alongside the preferred term ἁμαρτία. All in all, this group of words represents the authentically Pauline term for sin. In addition, the statistical distribution in Paul corresponds to the usage of the Septuagint, where the occurrences of ἁμαρτάνειν (hamartanein, sin) and its derivatives far outweigh the occurrences of παραβαίνειν (parabainein, transgress) and its derivatives.

Now assuming that the juxtaposition of the two words in vv. 17 and 18 represents a deliberate distinction, and taking into account the allusions previously identified, we may state the following: v. 18 with its reference to Cephas casts a terrible light on his initial disregard for the law at Antioch. He is now admitting that his conduct was a transgression of the law and not freedom based on faith. The notion of sin here is therefore based entirely on the Jewish understanding of the law: freedom from the law was in fact transgression of the law. Now if the word ἁμαρτωλός (hamartolos) in v. 17 is interpreted on the basis of v. 15 ("gentile sinner"), it is likewise being used in a sense derived from the Jewish understanding of the law. And it is clearly being applied to this same conduct free of the law, which is now censured in even stronger terms. The devout observer of the law knows that the Gentiles are ipso facto sinners. From this perspective, conduct that is free of the law represents sinful gentile conduct. Therefore a Jew will not merely call another Jew who acts in this manner a transgressor of the law. Of course he is. But because of his clear break with the law as such he is fundamentally no longer a Jew but to all intents and purposes a Gentile.

For the time being we shall avoid the question of whether Paul does not have something more in mind here with the word ἁμαρτωλός (hamartolos, sinner) and above all with the word ἁμαρτία (hamartia, sin) in the statement about Christ as a possible agent of sin, whether he is not departing here from the Jewish understanding of sin and radicalizing the meaning of these words ἁμαρτωλός and ἁμαρτία in accordance with his own theological views. If, for the moment, we restrict ourselves to what we have so far observed, the result is a surprisingly simple and obvious meaning, in contrast to the variety of disputed exegetical interpretations that have been given for these two verses.

In vv. 15 and 16 Paul answered the question of why Jews had come to faith in Christ: they had come to realize that no one is justified by works of the law, but only through faith in Jesus Christ. Every Jewish Christian would have to agree. But now, as events at Antioch show, dissension has arisen that casts doubt on everything once more. It focuses on the verdict of the Jewish world concerning the Jewish Christians. It would not be hard to see here the actual words of the charge leveled against them. If they have table fellowship with the gentile Christians, they are open to the accusation that they are themselves nothing more than Gentiles. And since it is their desire to be justified in Christ that has brought them to this pass, Christ himself must be held responsible. He does not bring righteousness but grossly encourages sin. He turns Jews into Gentiles. Paul presents this argument in the form of a question in order to suggest that it is not merely his Jewish and Judaizing opponents who reason thus. Even enlightened Jewish Christians who support the Jerusalem agreement are tempted by this question and can be led astray in critical situations.

The "No!" with which Paul dismisses the accusation and silences the temptation undoubtedly refers primarily to the blasphemous conclusion that Jesus Christ is an agent of sin, which comes close to ’Ανάθεμα ’Ιησοῦς (*anathema Iēsous*, Jesus be cursed: 1 Cor. 12:3). In the conditional clause of v. 17 the term ἁμαρτωλοί (*hamartōloi*, sinners) may actually be understood as being in quotation marks: this is the general Jewish verdict on the Gentiles; it is now applied wholesale to the Jewish Christians, who have become one body with the gentile Christians. In the conclusion, however, the word "sin" in the description of Christ as an agent of sin takes on for Paul the full weight of his own understanding of sin. This is what makes the charge so absurd. Possibly, however, this in turn influences the word "sinners" in the conditional clause, so that it ceases to be a mere quotation. The blunt "No!" with which Paul expresses his own position would then refer already to this part of the argument.

We might offer the following paraphrase: Our desire for righteousness in Christ has led us to live as Gentiles with gentile Christians. This does not, however, make us sinners. On the contrary, it is an expression of the freedom which all Christians have, even those of Jewish descent, thanks to the righteousness of faith. In any case, Paul rejects the verdict that the freedom given by faith is sin. Quite the contrary!

And now in v. 18 Paul takes the opposite approach, showing that it is wrong to charge expressions of freedom from the law with being sinful. He argues on the basis of a countercharge. It is not freedom from the law—which is the fruit of righteousness through faith—but rather the abrogation of this freedom that makes one a sinner. By such a reversal those who had made use of this freedom declare themselves to be transgressors of the law. One could also go back to v. 17 and make an even stronger statement: those who thus pass judgment upon their own previous conduct accept the verdict that the Jewish Christians are nothing other than Gentiles. This then leads to the absurd conclusion that Christ is an agent of sin. What took place at Antioch is tantamount to a denial of Christ, indeed to a blasphemous condemnation of Christ.

So far the text is clear. But there is further cause for reflection. What is the object of the "building up" and "tearing down" in v. 18? The law? If so, the text would flatly contradict Matt. 5:17, which states that Jesus came not to tear down (καταλῦσαι, *katalysai*) but to fulfill (πληρῶσαι, *plērōsai*) the law. Even if this latter text is seen as a Jewish Christian formula placed in the mouth of Jesus for apologetic purposes—which is far from being undisputed—the contrary notion that the Torah should be torn down and abrogated is certainly not Paul's opinion. In Rom. 3:31 he cites the accusation brought against him that asks whether he wants to overthrow the law through faith. The verb καταργεῖν (*katargein*, overthrow) is here almost synonymous with καταλύειν (*katalyein*, tear down). This question in Romans misinterprets Paul's theology of the law; he responds to it with the same μὴ γένοιτο (*mē genoito*, certainly not) with which he rejects the accusation in Gal. 2:17. On the contrary, says Paul, he is in fact establishing the law, for the first time giving it its true weight. From this perspective it cannot be correct that in Gal. 2:18 Paul is calling freedom from the law a tearing down of the law and surrender of this freedom a building up of the law.

The antithesis stated in Rom. 3:31 by means of the verbs καταργεῖν (*katargein*, overthrow) and ἱστάνειν (*histanein*, establish) is repeated once again in a different context: Rom. 6:6 and 6:13. There we read: "Our old self has been crucified with Christ. The power of sin over our body has thus been destroyed, so that we are no longer enslaved to sin." This must not be reversed: "Do not yield your members to sin as instruments of unrighteousness, but yield yourselves to God as those who, having been raised from the dead, are alive, and your members to God as instruments of righteousness."

The context in Romans 6 exhibits a close connection with Gal. 2:19 in the notion of being crucified with Christ, which is common to both. In Gal. 2:19, however, this notion is connected with our relationship to the law, whereas in Rom. 6 it is connected with our relationship to sin. The consequence of being crucified with Christ is that sin loses its power over our body; this is probably the sense in which v. 6 is to be taken: ἵνα καταργηθῇ τὸ σῶμα τῆς ἁμαρτίας (*hina katargēthē to sōma tēs hamartias*, literally: in order that the body of sin be destroyed). In v. 13, as a counterpart to καταργεῖν (*katargein*, destroy) Paul uses not the simple verb ἱστάνειν (*histanein*, establish), but the compound παριστάνειν (*paristanein*), which likewise means "establish, provide." The members of the body are no longer to be yielded to sin as weapons of unrighteousness, but to God as weapons of righteousness.

Recalling this antithesis between "destroy" and "establish" as applied to sin, Luther arrives at a surprising interpretation of Gal. 2:18.[26] Here, too, he says, the object of καταλύειν (*katalyein*, tear down) and πάλιν οἰκοδομεῖν (*palin oikodomein*, build up again) is sin. Through the gospel, sin has been destroyed. When one accepts the gospel, therefore, sin is torn down; but when one abandons the gospel, sin is built up again. By Luther's interpretation, this affects one's relationship to the law. In Pauline usage, however, the effect would be the very opposite of what is stated here. If sin is destroyed through the gospel, the law is thereby in fact fulfilled. It is then truly established. If, however, sin is built up again through rejection of the gospel, then the law is abrogated and scorned; for sin is disdain for the law. There is, moreover, no conflict at all between this disdain for the law and the preaching of the law alone. It is preached as something that demands fulfillment, but a fulfillment that cannot be attained simply by virtue of the demand. The sinner is therefore ipso facto someone who has illusory expectations of the law.

This interpretation seems highly forced and can hardly be defended. Its intention, however, is indisputably correct. If we are to grasp Paul's real meaning in v. 18, we must dig deeper than the words of the text seem to require. If the verse is read as referring to events at Antioch and from a Jewish or Jewish Christian perspective, it is reasonable to assume that "tearing down" and "building up again" refer to the law—if not the Torah as a whole, at least sections of it. Certain ceremonial regulations had been considered abrogated and were then reestablished. This is Jerome's interpretation.[27] But this reading sets us on a path that takes us far away from Paul. It would be a total misunderstanding to interpret freedom from the law as an abrogation of the law even in part, as a revision that simply annulled the ritual regulations in particular. If this were in fact the case, there would be no problem in regulating the relationship between Jews and Gentiles: all that would be necessary would be to repeal those sections of the Torah that establish the division between them.

If, however, we try cautiously to define what it really was that was first torn down and then built up again at Antioch, it must appear superficial and unsatisfactory simply to say: the laws governing ritual purity. Even if we argue that they were actually abrogated and then later enforced, the question still remains: how? Surely not by some kind of formal act of legislation, but by a changed balance of power in the hearts and consciences of those involved. The delusion that righteousness in the eyes of God depends on such works of the law as observance or nonobservance of the regulations governing purity had been torn down by the power Christ had won over the hearts of those who had faith in him. Then the shattered illusions had been built up again and Jesus Christ had been unwittingly dismissed.

The depths of the situation are not grasped if "works of the law" are limited merely to observance of the ceremonial regulations—as though the delusion of self-justification depended on them alone, and as though they alone were affected when people were freed from this delusion! A limited interpretation focusing on the ceremonial law would be tantamount to saying that the gospel had merely brought about a revision of the law and itself represented a new law. Jesus Christ would then be a lawgiver, a new Moses. Not the least important source of confusion in what took place at Antioch was the fact that to the superficial eye everything really did seem to hinge on observance of the ceremonial law.

But freedom from the law through faith in Jesus Christ can be understood correctly in this context only in relationship to ἔργα νόμου (*erga nomou*, works of the law) in general, not the ceremonial law alone, with reference to everything that fulfillment of the law might be expected to gain in terms of one's standing in the eyes of God. Only when the νόμος (*nomos*, law) as such is the subject can we see what it means to say that righteousness before God comes not through it but through faith in Jesus Christ. For this very reason it would be wrong to say that the law has simply been abrogated. Instead our relationship to the law, the way we deal with it, the power assigned to it and the impotence ascribed to it—all have been redefined through faith in Jesus Christ.

Our further reflections on v. 18 have led to the discovery that the text reveals deeper problems even though its immediate meaning remains. Could the same hold true for v. 17? So far we have looked at the text from without: people are found to be sinners in spite of, nay because of their acceptance of Christ, in that the manifestation of freedom from the law makes them appear as gentile sinners. Now in such a complex situation we must remember that, as we change the perspective from which we view the statements, our understanding of them will change and they will take on an element of ambiguity. Paul cannot speak of so-called sinners from the Jewish perspective without overtones and undertones of his own understanding of sin, which may not be immediately perceptible to everyone. We have already noted that the word ἁμαρτία (*hamartia*, sin) in v. 17 differs somewhat in its connotations from the word ἁμαρτωλός (*hamartōlos*, sinner) in the same verse, which takes its basic meaning from "gentile sinners" in v. 15. But we have already surmised that the end of the sentence has exerted some influence, so that Paul's μὴ γένοιτο (*mē genoito*, certainly not) rejects not only the conclusion that Christ is an agent of sin, but possibly also the assumption that those who are free of the law are ostensibly sinners.

If we take v. 17 in isolation, apart from the train of the argument in which it is embedded, other interpretations are possible.

For example: If we seek righteousness in Christ, we show that we know ourselves to be sinners, both Jews and Gentiles (Rom. 3:9). Is Christ an agent of sin because he makes Jews and Gentiles equal?

Or: If we seek righteousness in Christ but then—like Cephas at Antioch and the Judaizers in Galatia—once more find justifying significance in works of the law, then we demonstrate thereby that we are sinners. We are admitting that faith in Christ does not suffice; for justification we still must rely on the law. Is Christ not then in fact an agent of sin, if he is not recognized without any limitations as the διάκονος τῆς δικαιοσύνης (diakonos tēs dikaiosynēs, agent of righteousness)? He is the one who accepts sinners, who is (to risk the play on words), though not ἁμαρτίας διάκονος (hamartias diakonos), nevertheless διάκονος τῶν ἁμαρτωλῶν (diakonos tōn hamartōlōn), not an agent of sin but an agent of sinners, one who is present on behalf of sinners, but not the righteous.

Or finally: If it turns out that in spite of belonging to Christ we are still sinners, not perfectly righteous in and of ourselves, *iusti in spe* (righteous in hope) though still *peccatores in re* (sinners in fact), *simul iusti et peccatores* (both righteous and sinners at the same time), is Christ then an agent of sin because he conceals, in a sense, our sin, which is still present, instead of removing it?

None of these associated exegetical possibilities, in my opinion, can hold the field against the interpretation already developed out of the immediate context on the basis of the perspective of Paul's opponents. But this does not mean that these same words could not take on a more radical meaning from the perspective of Paul. For those who accept Christ, to be sinners in the strict sense would mean to reject the gift of Christ and instead seek righteousness from the law. If we wished to understand the words in this sense, it would be best to read the sentence as a contrary-to-fact condition and the conclusion not as a question but as a statement, as though it contained ἄρα (*ăra*, consequently), as in v. 21b. For to Paul this is an impossible possibility, as the equivalent statement in v. 21b makes clear: "If justification were through the law, then Christ would have died to no purpose."

Although this interpretation claims our attention only as a secondary notion on the part of Paul, reflecting on it makes us aware of an important point: for Paul, a sinner in the strict sense is not someone who publicly transgresses the law but someone who claims to fulfill the law, someone who is not willing to rely on Christ but seeks instead to achieve righteousness through the law as something to boast of. That this idea lies just below the surface here is shown by Paul's explicit mention of it in v. 19.

The beginning of v. 19 marks a break. Our initial look at vv. 15–21 with their frequent change of grammatical subject showed that the emphatic ἐγώ (*egō*, I) at the beginning of v. 19 signals a new stage in the train of thought. This is not contradicted by the appearance of the particle γάρ (*gar*, for). In this case the particle does not establish a close causal relationship with the immediately preceding verse; it can simply bring out the continuation of a train of thought. If Paul, nevertheless, did intend a causal relationship, it refers back to everything that has been said from v. 15 on. Having posited the Jewish Christian agreement without further explication (vv. 15–16) and having taken his stand against objections and divergent conduct (vv. 17–18), Paul now adopts a confessional tone and tips the scales with the full weight of his understanding of the gospel. By doing so he explicates the formula stated so forcefully in v. 16: righteousness not through works of the law but solely through faith in Christ Jesus. At the same time, he shows why the freedom from the law that comes through faith is not sin, as many charge, but rather is in harmony with the righteousness of God. He now develops the positive statement of this position, but only in the briefest outline, which will be fleshed out in the chapters that follow.

But v. 19 marks a turning point in another way as well. The reference of vv. 15–18 to what happened at Antioch drew attention to the situation of the Jewish Christians. This does not mean that these statements are irrelevant to gentile Christians, who are in fact clearly affected. Paul's whole struggle against Jewish Christian errors and on behalf of a correct self-understanding on the part of the Jewish Christians is a struggle for the message of the gospel to those who are not Jews—not just to establish an apologetic and tactical advantage, but for the truth of the gospel. In this respect, Jewish and gentile Christians are mutually dependent, being, as it were, in the same boat. Without the mission to Gentiles, free of the law, Jewish Christians would have no clear vision of the truth of the gospel. But the converse is also true: without the problems caused for Jewish Christians by the gospel free of the law, gentile Christians would likewise never see the truth of the gospel. It would therefore be wrong to say that statements about the law—for Paul the Torah, at least primarily—are irrelevant to gentile Christians. And it would also be wrong to say that Jewish Christians can keep a safe distance from a gentile Christianity that is developing separately. The very distress that grows out of the shared experience bears witness to the miracle that Jews and Gentiles have thus become one. Mutual communication is indispensable; it is of the essence. Nevertheless, it may become necessary to shift the emphasis in a particular direction. Conflicts like those in Antioch and Galatia demand that the Jewish Christians be addressed specifically: ἡμεῖς φύσει Ἰουδαῖοι (*hēmeis physei Ioudaioi*, we ourselves who are Jews by birth). But if the gospel free of the law is to be not merely declared but also explained, at least in part, this must be done in such a way as to include gentile Christian readers directly.

In vv. 19 and 20, without speaking explicitly of righteousness or justification, Paul states what it really means to say that people are made righteous through faith in Jesus Christ. The reference back to v. 16 and the repetition of the catchword δικαιοσύνη (*dikaiosynē*, righteousness) at the conclusion in v. 21 confirm this: this is the topic when life and death are discussed, the most immediate concerns of all. In v. 19 the notion of death is dominant, although not without mention of the implicit prospect of life (ἵνα θεῷ ζήσω, *hina theō zēsō*, that I might live to God). Verse 20, on the other hand, is dominated primarily by the theme of life. This life, however, might appear debatable if not actually cloven asunder. And what is said about life begins and ends with references to death: the death of the self (ζῶ δὲ οὐκέτι ἐγώ, *zō de ouketi egō*, it is no longer I who live) and the death of the Son of God (παραδόντος ἑαυτὸν ὑπὲρ ἐμοῦ, *paradontos heauton hyper emou*, who gave himself for me).

Let us sum up these structural observations concerning v. 19. The human self and the Son of God are here strangely interwoven in a pattern of death and life. The death of the one determines the life of the other and the life of the one the death of the other. In this *communicatio moriendi et vivendi* (sharing of death and life) true life comes to pass, and the life of God prevails.

Before going on to detailed exegesis, we shall make one more observation about the language we find Paul using, both here and elsewhere. The content is always theologically determined, but the linguistic forms are also noteworthy with respect to their formal ontology. The various ways in which it is possible to speak of life and death give rise to characteristic syntactic structures that force us to take note of something frequently overlooked.

We use the intransitive verbs "live" and "die" for the most part absolutely, to state a fact that is in itself immediate and observable: we say that someone is still living or has died. Of course these verbs can be circumstantially qualified by a large variety of expressions referring to the nature and duration of living and dying: we may say that someone lives a long life in comfortable circumstances or dies a painful or sudden death. Other information about the place where someone lives or dies can be added, the means or cause of life or death, its purpose and meaning: we may say, for example, that someone lives in the city or the country, or—speaking metaphorically—in the past or in a different world. We may say that someone dies abroad or in the bosom of the family. We may state what someone lives on or dies of. We may say what someone lives for or why someone had to die. In a variety of ways we draw attention to the contexts in which living and dying take place. In comparison with Paul, however, we are linguistically impoverished when it comes to grasping living and dying in their contextuality.

The first thing we note in v. 19 is the unusual construction with a dative: "die to the law" (also Rom. 7:4) and "live to God" (also Rom. 6:10–11, in contrast to "die to sin"; Rom. 6:2, 10–11). Both expressions introduce an outside object. It is not dying per se that is under discussion, but the fact that dying is made relevant in a particular relationship. Living per se is not a clearly defined notion. It becomes clearly defined through the meaning that is imposed on it. Living and dying are defined with reference to an outside object totally external to the subject.

Now this formal similarity shared by the two phrases seems to confront an immediate restriction. The logical meaning of the dative in the phrase "die to the law" or "die to sin" differs from that in the phrase "live to God." This is connected with the difference between the two verbs. When I die "to" someone, I am no longer present for that person. The force of the dative might be suggested by the colloquial statement "My father died on me," expressing the fact that I am personally affected by this death. In Paul, however, the relationship is reversed. He does not say, "The law died to me" or "Sin died to me," but, "I died to the law and to sin." Of course, this also affects me but by a kind of detour via an outside object. This object no longer has any claim on me; it has lost all rights to me and I am free of it. No force in the world has power over someone who is dead. In death something definitive has taken place.

In the phrase "live to God" the situation appears to be simpler. We might be tempted to speak in this case of a "dative of advantage." To live to God would then mean to live one's life for God and for God's benefit. But this is not really what Paul means. Although the sense of devoting one's life to God may be included, more is involved. To live to God means more than to have this or that action determined by a desire to serve God. Instead, life itself is so intimately related to the power of God, so surrendered to his sovereignty, that it receives itself from God as a life absolutely dependent on God.

Thus the phrases "die to the law or to sin" and "live to God" are placed once more on the same footing: both speak of something that has an absolute claim on life, except that "dying" represents the negation of everything implied by "living." But Paul can go even further and equate what appear to be opposites. Living and dying are both equally claimed and determined by what they center on, whether the actual subject who lives and dies—a possibility Paul rejects vigorously: "None of us lives to himself, and none of us dies to himself" (Rom. 14:7)—or the external object that confronts both living and dying, so that Paul can say, "If we live, we live to the Lord, and if we die, we die to the Lord. In living and in dying we belong to the Lord" (Rom. 14:8).

The relationship expressed by the dative means therefore that living and dying are in a sense centered outside themselves. They are subject in one way or another to a power to which they belong and which they serve. In this sense what seems to us an odd syntactic construction is similar to the common prepositional constructions "live for . . . " and "die for. . . ." It is characteristic that the common language of today makes much greater use of "live for . . . " than "die for. . . ." There are many and complex reasons why the emotion with which people used to boast of dying for one's country seems rather threadbare today. It is true that we are profoundly moved by the rare occasion when one person freely dies in place of another, like Maximilian Kolbe at Auschwitz. Nevertheless (or perhaps therefore), this strikes us as so extreme an exception that it can hardly shape our understanding of dying to any great extent. On the other hand, we are well aware what it means to live for something. We could construct a lengthy scale of purposes for which people live, from self-sacrificing service on behalf of others to parasitic existence for oneself. Between the extremes lies a wide range of ambiguity: whether that for which people live truly transcends them or only hides the fact that they are twisted in upon themselves.

Surprisingly, Paul never uses the preposition ὑπέρ (*hyper*, for, on behalf of) with the verb "live," but only with "die" and its synonyms. The reference is always to Christ's dying for us (Rom. 5:6–8; 14:15; 1 Cor. 15:3; 2 Cor. 5:14–15). Only once does he cite the general possibility of one person's dying for another (Rom. 5:7), and then only to reject it. Our text also speaks of Christ's giving himself "for me" (2:20; cf. 1:4). It would be misleading, however, to insist that "live for . . ." and "die for . . ." are opposites. The statement that Christ died for us represents for Paul the crucial statement about Christ's life as a life for us. This dying for others is the extreme expression of living for others. Just as in the dative construction living and dying were finally equated in relation to God, so here they coincide in the construction with the preposition "for." Life—at least the life of Jesus Christ—is meant to be lived for others, not consumed by the one who lives it, and is therefore also meant to be surrendered in death for others as its most extreme fulfillment.

But there is a nuance to observe. The dative construction emphasizes that living and dying are totally caught up in our relationship with God. But although Paul uses the preposition ὑπέρ (*hyper*, for) in the sense that God is for us (Rom. 8:31), he never uses it in the opposite way to indicate that God is the end to which we devote our lives. Precisely when living and dying are totally devoted to God, life can become death on behalf of what is totally ungodly: sinners (Rom. 5:8) or even sins (1 Cor. 15:3; Gal. 1:4). This is how Paul uses ὑπέρ to express purpose. It is in harmony with the fact that we occasionally find the phrase ὑπὲρ Χριστοῦ (*hyper Christou*, for Christ; 2 Cor. 5:20; 12:10; Phil. 1:29). Whoever takes the part of Christ is included in the purpose of Christ's life. But this purpose is to die for the ungodly (cf. Rom. 5:6) that they may live to God (cf. Rom. 6:11). Therefore what takes place when Christ is for us is the prototypical instance of what is meant by the dative construction: "The death he died he died to sin, once for all, but the life he lives he lives to God" (Rom. 6:10). And this then holds true for us as well. Paul therefore concludes: "So you also must consider yourselves dead in relation to sin, but alive in relation to God in Christ Jesus" (Rom. 6:11).

Therefore the various syntactical constructions with the verbs "live" and "die" also are associated with the use of the preposition σύν (*syn*, with). In our text it is represented by the verb συσταυροῦσθαι (*systaurousthai*, be crucified with). It would seem that we today are exceptionally well prepared to understand this perspective of "togetherness." Life is in fact shared life together and must be so perceived and lived if we are not all to perish together. These sentiments are on everyone's lips, albeit not in everyone's conscience. Both the mutual interdependence of our destinies on a grand scale and the necessities of life for the individual have turned the notion of "loving one's neighbor" into a tired commonplace. It could easily be argued that shared life forfeits its humanity and gives rise to destructive forces when those who share a common life do not learn how to be themselves as individuals and how to live alone. Total absorption into a common life would give to an unchallenged "togetherness" the status of a false soteriology. This can even take the form of mass delusion leading to a shared death, as we have recently seen in the religious excesses of the People's Temple.

What Paul says about "dying with" and "living with" differs from all this in a variety of respects. Here, too, Christ is the focus of everything. As he is "for" us, so are we "with" him. In one passage, it is true, Paul can make συναποθνῄσκειν (*synapothnēskein*, die with) and συζῆν (*syzēn*, live with) refer to interpersonal relations and say to the Corinthians: "You are so much in our hearts that we can only die together and live together" (2 Cor. 7:3). But this is true only in the context of "dying together" and "living together" in relationship to Christ. It is in this relationship that they are linked in an indissoluble unity.

This brings us to the following observation: today we perceive an element of conflict between "being with others" and "being oneself." The relationship between society and the individual is repeatedly and tiresomely stated as a simple alternative. By contrast, the "together with" that Paul injects as a fundamental aspect of living and dying is firmly rooted in individuality. This is so in two respects.

First, the "together with" has its basis and focus in Jesus Christ, who through his crucifixion and resurrection has become the individual *par excellence*. Second, the "together with" takes place as involvement in the death and life of Christ only through incorporation of each individual into this being "with" Christ. Whether Paul is alluding to baptism in Gal. 2:19, as in Romans 6, may remain an open question. The act of baptism certainly demonstrates impressively that every person is incorporated as an individual into being "with" Christ. But the fact that this is so is not due to baptism; instead, baptism is what it is because of the Christ event, in which the "for" thus lays the foundation for a "with."

The Pauline understanding of what it means to be "with" others also differs from our interpretation in being based on an irreversible initial event. Dying with Christ and living with Christ are not matters for us to decide, as we can contemplate the natural given of human sociality and draw appropriate conclusions. Dying with Christ, being crucified together with Christ in the death of Jesus Christ on the cross—this has taken place in a single unique event. All we can do is hear the call to think of ourselves in these terms (Rom. 6:11).

Above all it is not in our power to bring into being life with Christ. This is the life of resurrection; it belongs to the future. Dying with Christ can be expressed in the aorist or perfect tense (Rom. 6:6, 8, 11; Gal. 2:19; cf. 6:14); living with Christ requires the future tense (Rom. 6:8; 2 Cor. 13:4; 1 Thess. 5:10). This, too, differs from our accustomed idiom. We know what living together means because the contextuality of life comes to us as a given, based upon the past, although it also presents us with tasks for the future. To the extent that the notion of dying suggests anything more than absolute isolation and the cessation of all relationships, we can only think of "dying together" as a future event, like the apocalyptic vision of a nuclear catastrophe.

This brings to light a further peculiarity in Paul's use of the expressions "die with" and "live with." This sequence is fixed. Within the limits of our experience, "dying with" can follow by chance after "living with"; at the most, it could be the deliberate consequence of a life together shaped in a particular way. In any case, there is a one-way street from the common life we all share—however we shape it, whether for or against or regardless of our neighbors—to the death that is equally common to us all. But because death is something we have in common, we are absolutely isolated from each other—or (it would be equally true to say) we are absolutely united. In saying this we are not limited to the hopes of a religious eschatology. We can also be expressing profound resignation in the face of death the leveler, which consumes us all.

Paul, too, sees a one-way street, but it goes in the opposite direction. Living with Christ is the result of dying with Christ. Only after the fact of bodily death do we find what it truly means to be with Christ (Phil. 1:23). This makes it clear that our relationship with Christ has fundamentally transformed the meaning of life. Life before death has been replaced by life out of death. Again we find a convergence of death and life in consequence of relationship with Christ. In common usage, living and dying are antithetical. In Christ, they constitute a single whole. Strictly speaking, no sequence is involved at all. One does not follow upon the other; each refers to a particular situation from its own perspective.

This differentiation among various aspects of the same situation is expressed in our text by different expressions indicating where this life is found: ζῆν ἐν σαρκί – ζῆν ἐν πίστει (zēn en sarki — zēn en pistei, life in the flesh, life in faith). We are also accustomed to qualify life as being "in" something—in the world, in hope, in fear. This is not an added factor, but something that encompasses and permeates life as a kind of atmosphere, something that is necessary for life but can also poison it.

What strikes us as unusual, however, is the way Paul uses such qualifications describing the "place" of life to bring home ultimate decisions about life. Life and death, as such, can be defined for Paul from the perspective of where they are found. Life is not something that can be transplanted to this or that place, remaining the same in substance even though undergoing necessary modification. The distinctions Paul is concerned with extend not merely to a new quality of life but to a new life in the strict sense. In this eschatological perspective he confronts what it means to be in Adam and what it means to be in Christ. He could easily distinguish between the life we have in Adam and the life we have in Christ, but instead he describes this Adamic life as death and life in Christ as life from death: "For as in Adam all die, so also in Christ shall all be made alive" (1 Cor. 15:22).

These qualifications of "place" transcend all that is merely accidental and penetrate to the very root of death and life, setting death and life themselves in motion in such a way that they cease to be a foregone conclusion and lose their clear identity. To die in Adam obviously means something different than to die in Christ. The former still awaits us, whereas the latter has already taken place. But this means that the life we have in Adam, as a life in sin, already belongs to the past (cf. Rom. 6:2).

Thus Paul also makes distinctions in his understanding of life. If, as life ἐν σαρκί (*en sarki*, in the flesh), it is life κατὰ σάρκα (*kata sarka*, according to the flesh: Rom. 8:12–13), it is a life that leads to death. But if, as life ἐν σαρκί (*en sarki*, in the flesh), it is life κατὰ πνεῦμα (*kata pneuma*, according to the spirit)—for which our text uses the apparently synonymous ἐν πίστει (*en pistei*, in faith)—it is a life that leads to the life arising from the δύναμις θεοῦ (*dynamis theou*, power of God: cf. 2 Cor. 13:4).

This remarkable ambiguity that the words "die" and "live" take on in Paul is obviously connected with his unusually intense grasp of their contextual relativity, which we find here. And this in turn is because life and death are seen in their relationship to God and thus in eschatological perspective. In other words: it is not life and death as they are that sets the terms within which all further statements must be made to fit. Instead, it is the all-inclusive relationship to Jesus Christ that sets the terms by which the decision is made as to the meaning of life and death. Christ is not given his place in the order of life and death, which seems so natural. Instead, life and death are given their decisive place in Christ. As a result, we have to reconsider not only our understanding of life and death, but also the question of who is really the subject of life.

Having made these general remarks about Paul's use of language, we shall now return to detailed exegesis.

In v. 16 a fundamental definition was given of what it means to turn to faith in Christ; in v. 17, this definition was guarded against misinterpretations. Now it is interpreted as a change of situation of the most radical kind. For this reason it must be expressed in the first person singular. Not as though a change were involved affecting only Paul himself, depicted solely on the basis of his own experience. Confessional as the words are, they do not constitute a private confession. The first person singular is necessary because the change being interpreted changes one's very self, not just the context of the self. It would, therefore, not be adequate to describe the change in situation as a change of religion or as a conversion with the self simply remaining the same, changing only its focus and thus its view of itself. Neither would it suffice to describe the change that has taken place here as a change of the locus where life is grounded, where it is fixed and makes its home. According to Paul, we need to use the terminology of the most radical change that can affect mortals: death and new life. In other words, it is not the self that remains while something else changes. Instead the self, which remains identical with itself as long as it lives, experiences the only change that can impinge on it directly: it dies.

Now it is not necessary to look ahead to the strangely ambiguous words of the next verse to learn that the self that is said to have died is in fact still alive. The very words "I have died" are paradoxical. Someone who has died is not heard making such statements. Does this imply that we are dealing only with figurative language? This would be true if it means that the self has not died the death usually intended when the word "die" is used: the end of physical life, which now belongs to the past and turns to decay. But it would not do justice to the demands of such a metaphor to stop with this understanding of death, refusing to go on to a sense that is meant not to becloud the issue but to define it more closely.

Paul's purpose is certainly not to use purely figurative, inauthentic language. This is clear from the fact that the death the self experiences is grounded in the death of Christ on the cross, which Paul would never consider treating docetically as mere appearance. Quite the contrary: this death was suffered in its full horror and was sealed by Christ's burial, as the tradition in 1 Cor. 15:4 expressly emphasizes. But even in this case it would trivialize what actually happened if one were to be content with what a random spectator could report. Not until 3:13 does Paul say more about what actually took place in this death of Christ. We shall not anticipate this discussion. But v. 20 already mentions the love that was at work in Christ's death, as the self-sacrifice of the Son of God for the self in question.

We see now that the self that is left to its own devices, without the love and sacrifice that comes to it, is in a hopeless situation, being ruled by an alien force. This force is here referred to as νόμος (*nomos*, law), in the parallel passage in Rom. 6:6ff. as sin. The latter passage also uses the word δουλεύειν (*douleuein*, be a slave, serve), confirming that the status of the self is enslavement. That the power of sin produces this hopeless situation, in which the self has no means of deliverance except for the sacrificial love of the Son of God, may be more evident than the statement in v. 19 that the enslaving power is the law.

The third chapter will also provide more information about Paul's understanding of the law. But it would be reasonable to assume from the outset that sin and law, which we are surprised to find playing similar roles in similar statements, cannot be understood independently of each other. That the law is present in sin is easy to accept, possibly easier than is good for a correct understanding of sin—at least as long as we have not got beyond the trivial understanding of the law as a mere norm. From this standpoint it is indeed hard to understand how sin can be present in the law, which Paul declares elsewhere to be holy (Rom. 7:12). Here we must be content with the statement that the "for me," the sign of the love of the crucified Christ, applies to what sinners are when under the law. It is not just that the law cannot help them. The hopelessness of their situation, their subjection to the power of sin, is made all the more hopeless by the law.

The way in which the self-sacrificing love that moves the Son of God to die for sinners, thereby communicating itself to those for whom it sacrifices itself, is expressed by Paul in the words "be crucified with." The "for me" must not be misunderstood as meaning that the self is simply spared the necessity of being crucified and dying. Paul uses the same word used by the Gospels for the criminals crucified with Jesus, who even in their crucifixion with him join the crowd in mocking him (Matt. 27:44; Mark 15:32). This makes it quite clear: the seriousness of the situation cannot be mitigated. The crucial point, however, is not reached through outward identification with Jesus. There is still an abyss separating those who are crucified with him and what is taking place for them in their very presence. The σύν (syn, with), the participation in the crucifixion of Jesus, is to take place after the manner of ὑπέρ (hyper, for), so that one shares in the love of this self-sacrifice of the Son of God—not in the literal sense, as though one merely received a piece of it, but in full, unlimited participation in this love.

It would be over-hasty to say that the σύν in the mode of ὑπέρ, participation in Christ's sacrifice, is accomplished by faith. Of course only faith can speak of it as something meaningful and real, for it consists in the realization on the part of those who have faith that in Jesus' crucifixion something took place for them, something in which they share, something in which they are included. But for this very reason those that have faith know that this σύν and this ὑπέρ come before themselves and their faith. Christ has preceded them. "While we were yet helpless, at the right time Christ died for the ungodly. . . . God has shown his love for us in that while we were yet sinners Christ died for us" (Rom. 5:6, 8). By virtue of the love in which the Son of God sacrificed himself, those for whom this took place are already included. The "for me" has already established the "with him"; it has spoken the verdict and anticipated my crucifixion with Christ.

Of course those involved must still undergo this crucifixion. Whether it takes place uniquely in baptism or throughout an entire lifetime, which as a whole also has its own uniqueness, may turn out to be a false disjunction when one reflects properly on baptism and its relationship to life. Nevertheless, even the uniqueness of baptism derives from the fact that in the crucifixion of Jesus something took place once and for all that is explicitly appropriated in each act of baptism and is consciously assimilated in each act of faith. My assurance of it is grounded in what I have experienced as a "with him" by virtue of the "for me." Therefore, Paul always speaks of being crucified with and having died with, being dead with, as something already accomplished. He does not speak of it as something that remains to be accomplished in the future, albeit the process may extend through all the rest of one's life in the flesh until bodily death.

The metaphor involved in saying that I have died to the law and have been crucified with Christ, therefore, does not lose its connection with bodily death—neither with Jesus' death on the cross nor with our own future physical death. Nevertheless, Paul declares the self to have died only with respect to a specific external entity, namely the law. According to Paul, however, this is the crucial dimension of those who are not in the right with God and therefore find themselves in a prison from which they cannot escape. They are, as it were, buried alive—a manner of life that stands in much sharper contradiction to the true nature of life than does the extinction of bodily life. Having died to this prison and having been raised from it to new life means that something has taken place far surpassing physical death in its significance for life.

Furthermore, this death and resurrection already has an effect with respect to the σῶμα τῆς ἁμαρτίας (sōma tēs hamartias, literally: body of sin), as Paul states: "The power of sin over our body has thereby been destroyed" (Rom. 6:6). This is, of course, an ongoing process. The members must not be yielded to sin as instruments of wickedness, but to God as instruments of righteousness (Rom. 6:13). The outer nature wastes away and the inner is renewed every day (2 Cor. 4:16). What is spoken of metaphorically as "having died" takes on the significance of a radical change that Paul likewise speaks of metaphorically as resurrection (Rom. 6:13).

Now for the first time we touch on the reason why the resurrection of the dead can be thought of as something glorious, something to be hoped for, and not (as would be all too reasonable) as something terrible, something to be more feared than death. There are two metaphors: death as dying to the law and restoration to life as life to God; but these two cannot be separated. They constitute a unity and focus our attention on what is ultimately at stake in both life and death. Their purpose is to free us from a superficial view of life and death and make us aware of the truly important element that lies hidden within.

Before examining the effect on life of this kind of death, we must devote some attention to the role that is here assigned to the law. We shall begin by recalling what has already been emphasized in our observations on Paul's language: it is not that the law is annulled in order to create freedom, although these are the only terms in which sinners can conceive the situation, whether as the dream of absolute emancipation or the nightmare of a total end to law and order. Instead, the self escapes from the law through death. For "the law is binding on someone only while alive" (Rom. 7:1). Therefore also "someone who has died is legally free from sin" (Rom. 6:7). Why this reversal? The most immediate approach would be to have done with the law by declaring the law itself a dead letter. Why choose, instead, the apparently strange idea of getting rid of the law through death, so that I am for the law a "dead issue"? It is important to Paul, especially in this context, that there not be the slightest hint of degradation of the law. That would contradict his understanding of sin as well as of the cross. The human situation cannot be changed on the basis of the law and certainly not by weakening or altering it.

Paul points to this in his apparently enigmatic statement that the law itself is responsible for my death to the law: διὰ νόμου νόμῳ ἀπέθανον (*dia nomou nomō apethanon*, through the law I died to the law). This idea does not come into conflict with the notion of dying with Christ, as though one's own experience with the law, with the impossibility of fulfilling it and the conscientious scruples it causes, showed that the law had, as it were, tortured its prisoner to death and thus done itself injury. Of course Paul can also say that the letter—that is, the law—kills (2 Cor. 3:6). But the result of this killing is more θεῷ ἀποθνήσκειν (*theō apothnēskein*, dying to God) than νόμῳ ἀποθνήσκειν (*nomō apothnēskein*, dying to the law). In this manner the law does not set anyone free.

Nevertheless, it plays a part in the death that sets us free, because it was the crucial factor that sent Christ to his cursed death on the cross (Gal. 3:13). Paul uses the paradoxical expression διὰ νόμου νόμῳ ἀπέθανον (*dia nomou nomō apethanon*, through the law I died to the law) to say that the law is not only affected by my death but also functions as its cause, thus linking this death of the self intimately with the death of Jesus Christ. Only thus does dying to the law take on soteriological meaning. This soteriological meaning is defined teleologically as θεῷ ζῆν (*theō zēn*, living to God), in sharp contrast to νόμῳ ἀποθνήσκειν (*nomō apothnēskein*, dying to the law). This must appear absurd to anyone who loves the law: living to the law means living to God, and consequently dying to the law must be tantamount to dying to God. Paul appears to turn all this upside down: living to the law is tantamount to being dead to God, and dying to the law is what makes it possible to live to God.

It is not only Jews, who love the Torah, who will take offense at this statement. Greeks as well, who, although not subject to the Torah, think very highly of the *nomos*, can only be puzzled by such an antithesis. That this reaction is shared by all shows that the theme of the law has a universal dimension. Although Paul is referring first and foremost to the Torah, non-Jews are also involved in this theme, and not just in the negative sense that the Torah must not be imposed on them. Mutatis mutandis, they are in the same situation as the Jews: freedom to live to God becomes possible only when they die to the law as an enslaving power.

Now what is involved in this life with God as its goal and purpose? The death of the self with respect to the law clearly does not bring life itself to an end; quite the contrary, it brings life to truth and to fulfillment. In v. 20, however, Paul is expressly concerned to counter any impression that the term "dying" in v. 19 is just rhetorical exaggeration. Life does in fact go on. The surrounding world may note certain changes, but will not doubt at all that the same self is involved. Paul is still Paul, even though later a kind of change of identity was posited in the interests of edification: Saul turned into Paul. But even if there actually had been a change of name, this would have been something totally different from what Paul is talking about here. The radical change of situation that eschatological language speaks of as the change from death to life effects a cleavage in the self, dividing the human subject.

The statement of v. 19: ἐγὼ . . . ἀπέθανον (*egō . . . apethanon*, I died) is first confirmed with reference to this self (ἐγώ, *egō*, I): ζῶ δὲ οὐκέτι ἐγώ (*zō de ouketi egō*, It is no longer I who live). The "I," the self, is no longer alive. It has been crucified with Christ and has therefore died to the law. This agrees with the explanation in Rom. 6:6, where "our old self" is the subject of "was crucified." There has been a change of subject. The place of the self that was prisoner to the law and is now dead to the law has been taken by Christ, crucified and now raised from the dead. It is no longer I but he that lives. Nevertheless, the old definition of what it is that constitutes personal individuality appears to be retained: the self can neither be communicated nor exchanged. Paul clearly avoids referring to the new subject as a new person. On the other hand, he cannot avoid speaking of a continuing self. The transformed situation therefore involves extreme tension, because two subjects are linked in a single life. Although the self was initially said to have died, to be alive no longer, now Christ is made the subject of the life of the self in such a way that he lives in the self—in me, still alive ἐν σαρκί (*en sarki*, in the flesh) even though dead to the law.

Clearly, these statements cannot be interpreted within the metaphysical schema of substance. Paul is dealing with the question of who has sovereignty over the human person. As long as the self (ἐγώ, *egō*, I) was left to its own devices, it was not its own master; it was slave to sin and prisoner to the law. When the self in this relationship died, thus being set free from all claims, it was not replaced by a new self, its own master and belonging to none. Instead, the new situation is defined by the fact that the continuing self is the locus of the life and sovereignty of Christ.

Contrary to initial appearances, Paul does not disregard the idea that the personal self is incommunicable. Neither does he lose himself in a schizophrenic image of the human person. He does not claim that Christ is fused with the continuing human self. He does not say that, after the self has died to the law, it is raised as Christ so that the new human person is identical with Christ. As in our relationship to the law, so too in our relationship to Christ the element of otherness is strictly preserved. Although Christ lives in me, I am not Christ. But as continuing self I am not master of myself; the ground of my life is external to me. Therefore, it amounts to the same thing whether Paul speaks, as he usually does, of my being in Christ or, as here, of Christ's being in me. Of course this language is permeated with mysticism; it is—we may safely say—enriched thereby. But the limit that is still observed here must not be overlooked. Even in the most intimate union with Christ, the difference is preserved. True love does indeed unite, but it does not sublate duality into an undifferentiated and inarticulate unity where language is left behind.

The restraint of Paul's statements can be seen from their refusal to overlook or pass over life in the flesh. The crucial confirmation of what it means that Christ lives in me does not take place in ecstatic flights of fancy transcending the earthly limitations of life and apart from the serving and suffering imposed on life. The interpretation that Paul places on the daring statement that it is no longer I that live but Christ that lives in me remains entirely within the framework of his *theologia crucis*. The Christ who lives in me is the crucified Christ. How could I be thus linked with him and still trivialize the life ἐν σαρκί (*en sarki*, in the flesh) that he himself endured to death on the cross!

It is also appropriate to this *theologia crucis* that Paul reunites the apparently divided self by understanding life ἐν σαρκί as life ἐν πίστει (*en pistei*, in faith). Paul could have spoken here of ζῆν κατὰ πνεῦμα (*zēn kata pneuma*, life according to the Spirit) or ἐν πνεύματι (*en pneumati*, in the Spirit) or simply πνεύματι (*pneumati*, by the Spirit: 5:25). But it is essential to his understanding of the Spirit that speaking of the Spirit should not be taken as something superior to faith. Because faith is faith in Jesus Christ,

149

nothing can surpass it; it points to the ground of the new life from which it cannot be separated without being extinguished. Therefore, when Paul speaks emphatically of life ἐν σαρκί (*en sarki*, in the flesh), with its subject correctly understood as the continuing self, then the life of Christ in me is most appropriately incorporated into the unity of the person as life in faith in Christ. The self has died and fallen victim to the law even while boasting in works of the law; what is now established as its antitype is not a spiritual self, boasting equally of its own self-sufficiency. The justification of the individual person, which is developed in vv. 19 and 20 with the notion of life substituting for the term "justification," thus remains fixed in the antithesis between works of the law and faith in Jesus Christ.

Faith does indeed lend an ecstatic aspect to life: it establishes the ground of life outside the human individual in Jesus Christ. But faith helps life achieve inner unity because the subject of faith, the one who has faith, can only be the subject who lives an earthly life. This does not silently contradict the climactic statement of our text: Christ lives in me. What is now made clear is that the life of Christ in me cannot dispense with my own personal identity. The life of Christ is, instead, integrated into my life through faith, so that all the life I have becomes a life of faith, and all the faith I have becomes a faith that shapes my life.

This section has finally taken us more deeply into the substantial meaning of the gospel. Paul concludes it with an emphatic protest. It has been suggested that Paul is referring here to an accusation made by his opponents, to the effect that he was nullifying the grace of God by opposing it to the law. This accusation could be understood in the sense of the critical catchword "cheap grace." But I see no convincing argument in favor of such an interpretation. It seems more appropriate to me, in the context of Paul's fundamental examination of the incident at Antioch, that he should here summarize all he has to say theologically against such surrender of the grace of God by avowing that nothing could bring him to surrender the grace of God. It must be steadfastly maintained, just as it would be impossible to annul what took place on the cross. If the grace of God were to be annulled, it would make the death of Christ meaningless. This is in fact what happens when one insists on expecting righteousness through the law.

In the discussion that follows, this will be theologically substantiated in detail.

Galatians 3—4
INSTRUCTION

How the Spirit is Received

3:1–5

1 O foolish Galatians, who has bewitched you, before whose eyes Jesus Christ was publicly portrayed as crucified?
2 Let me ask you only this: Did you receive the Spirit by works of the law, or by the message of faith?
3 Are you so foolish? Having begun with the Spirit, are you now ending with the flesh?
4 Did you experience such a powerful thing in vain? If it really is in vain!
5 The one who supplies the Spirit to you and works miracles among you, [does he do so] by works of the law or by the message of faith?

As is the rhetorical custom, and as is quite natural in the course of conversation or in a letter, a new term of address lends weight to what follows or draws attention to an important break in the train of thought. At the beginning of the argumentative central section of the letter, Paul addresses his audience by name, something he does very rarely (cf. 2 Cor. 6:11; Phil. 4:15). A marked caesura is thus combined with an intense personal approach to his addressees.

In 1:11, on the threshold of the narrative section, Paul had addressed the Galatians as "brethren" although he was deeply alienated and disturbed by their conduct. In the intervening discussion he has, of course, never lost sight of them. But now he has approached them once more by a kind of long detour. Had he simply continued his narrative, he would probably have introduced his missionary work in Galatia at this point. It is not chronology, however, in which Paul has no interest, that brings him back to the Galatians, but the increasing topicality of the narrative section. He concluded in 2:21 with the statement: "I do not nullify the grace of God; for if justification were through the law, then Christ died to no purpose." This was a clear allusion to the scene at Antioch. But the verse can also be understood as the spearhead of Paul's account that is aimed at the Galatians. They are on the point of deserting the one who called them into the grace of Christ (1:6). This is just what Paul totally rejects for himself: he will never surrender the grace of God (2:21). What he considers the worst possible consequence of a return to righteousness through the law, the fact that it makes vain the death of Christ (2:21), may already hold true for the Galatians. They have apparently lost sight of the crucified Christ, who had been portrayed so vividly before their eyes (3:1).

The emphatic caesura in 3:1, therefore, does not mark an interruption. It proves to be a major point of articulation in the uninterrupted train of thought. This must also be stressed from another perspective. In chapters 3 and 4, Paul expands his theological arguments. We would, therefore, expect a high degree of didactic generality and objective language that disregards personalities. And this is, in fact, the case in the major portions of what follows. But the introduction in 3:1–5, no less than the very personal section 4:12–20, appears to break this mold.

Now we might explain this as follows: The extremely tense situation makes it impossible to pursue a calm train of theological thought. It gives occasion instead for parenetic interruptions. Depending on personal taste, one might consider this beneficial or pernicious for theology. In a case like the present, of course, we are not dealing with artificial edifying passages but with matters of pressing concern. It is impossible to draw a line here between theology and proclamation, between intellectual reflection and aggressive struggle on behalf of others and life-or-death decisions. One must be well aware of the dangers involved in such situations. For theologians like you and me, who are not as filled with the Spirit as Paul, the opposite danger is more likely: at the very moment when a critical situation demands theological thought and adjudication, we theologize abstractly, ignoring the real temptations and decisions, instead of arguing theologically with the necessary courage and with truly illuminating insight. Such a tendency toward evasive abstraction seems to go hand in hand with an "application" that is merely formal or even invented out of whole cloth. Such an application often bears witness to a lack of patience that makes it impossible to sustain a justifiably abstract train of thought. But it may surely be taken as a sign that theology is being carried on in the power of the Spirit when high-level intellectual argument and vital direct address intermingle in a natural way that grows directly out of the case at hand.

It would not do justice to the stylistic interplay of parenesis and argumentation in these two chapters to rest content with this explanation. The sections that appear to stand outside the logical argument must also be examined for their function within the argument. This holds true now for the initial step, which is taken in 3:1–5. In contrast to the exegetical argument that follows, it represents an argument from experience. It is illuminating for the way Paul thinks theologically that an argument from experience and an argument from Scripture can stand side by side without coming into conflict, and that the argument from experience can provide the opening. Those to whom the argument is addressed are thus introduced as witnesses, so that there is a greater chance to convince them.

We may be surprised that Paul does not begin with a *captatio benevolentiae*. On the contrary, he accuses the Galatians quite unflatteringly of being fools. The repeated ἀνόητοι (*anoētoi*, foolish, fools: vv. 1 and 3) must not be interpreted as a term of opprobrium, denying the previously asserted "brotherhood" (1:11) or the spirit of gentleness (πνεῦμα πραΰτη-τος, *pneuma praÿtētos*) with which we who are spiritual are to restore others to the right way (6:1; cf. 1 Cor. 4:21). Even such a harsh word as ἀνόητος (*anoētos*, foolish) can sometimes be heard as an expression of love, even when it is translated even more harshly: you crazy Galatians.

Etymologically, the word means that they are without νοῦς (*nous*, mind, understanding), rational knowledge, the ability to judge a situation correctly. They are deficient in understanding and judgment with respect to the life-and-death implications of being Christians. The contrast is, therefore, more between wisdom and folly than between intelligence and deficient intellectual ability. Paul, in fact, assumes an extremely high intellectual acumen in his readers, as this letter shows.

We would, therefore, like to say that what is lacking is not so much νοῦς as πνεῦμα (*pneuma*, spirit), not so much the spirit of human intellect and the wisdom of this world (which cannot protect someone from being a fool in the eyes of God: 1 Cor. 12:3) as the Spirit of God without which no one can say κύριος Ἰησοῦς (*kyrios Iēsous*, Jesus is Lord: 1 Cor. 12:3). But in this very context Paul states explicitly that the Galatians have received the Spirit (v. 2) and are still supplied with the Spirit (v. 5). By deserting Christ for the law, it appears that they want to fall back from the Spirit to the flesh (v. 3). The struggle between flesh and Spirit is never over as long as one lives in the flesh (5:16–25). It is noteworthy, however, that Paul is not yet ready to deny the presence of the Spirit among the Galatians. Indeed, he refers to them explicitly as πνευματικοί (*pneumatikoi*, spiritual: 6:1). It is therefore reasonable for him here not to refer to them as unspiritual but as unmindful or foolish. The πνεῦμα (*pneuma*, spirit) cannot substitute for the νοῦς (*nous*, mind, understanding). Something is wrong when the two are out of phase, when manifestations of the Spirit appear without understanding, when πνεῦμα and νοῦς are not found together even in prayer and song (1 Cor. 14:14–19). But the discrepancy that Paul laments among the Galatians differs in this respect from that among the Corinthians. The lack of theological insight on the part of the Galatians stands in disquieting and dangerous contrast to their willingness to obey the dictates of the Spirit. This also indicates that the Spirit has not been sufficiently effective. Spirituality is defective when, as is so often the case, it lacks the capacity for clear and sober theological judgment.

Paul sees here something more than a lack of πνεῦμα expressing itself as a lack of understanding. His only explanation for such a failure is that it is the work of an evil spirit, which, even if it has not entered into them, at least exercises magical control over them. Something uncanny is afoot here; there is a demonic element at work, a fascination that literally deranges, so that the intellect and senses conjure up some illusion by which one is unconsciously taken in (cf. Vulgate: *quis vos fascinavit*). We do not have to discuss demonological theories to recognize that such circumstances are very real and far from rare. The Galatians themselves could hardly miss the objective irony in such a situation: they themselves, among whom the Spirit performs mighty acts such as exorcisms, are victims of demonic forces and therefore have need of an exorcist.

Paul seems to be aware of this: something more is needed here than recitation of theological orthodoxy. The gloss on τίς ὑμᾶς ἐβάσκανεν (*tis hymas ebaskanen*, who has bewitched you) that has crept into the text of v. 1 from Gal. 5:7: τῇ ἀληθείᾳ μὴ πείθεσθαι (*tē alētheia mē peithesthai*, so that you do not obey the truth), is very much to the point. The Galatians' lack of understanding is ultimately based on an unwillingness to understand, an inhibition and resistance in the face of so evident a truth.

According to Paul, this loss of clarity stands in incomprehensible contrast to the unambiguous clarity with which the point at issue has been presented before their very eyes: Jesus Christ crucified. Exegetically, the semantic nuances of the verb προγράφειν (*prographein*, write before) are and probably will always remain a matter of debate: are we to think of a publicly displayed notice, so that the watchword "Jesus Christ crucified" was like an inscription before their eyes, or of a vivid description, such as has always been an important instrument of rhetoric? If the latter, it is hardly likely that Paul depicted the details of Jesus' suffering and death in the garish colors of later passion spirituality.

A few textual witnesses insert the phrase ἐν ὑμῖν (*en hymin*, in you) between προεγράφη (*proegraphē*, it has been publicly portrayed) and ἐσταυρωμένος (*estaurōmenos*, crucified). This qualification is ambiguous. It may be meant to underline the idea of vivid portrayal: it is as though Christ was actually crucified in the midst of you. If, however, it is taken literally as "crucified in you" in contrast to the statement that Christ lives in us (2:20), the meaning of the entire sentence changes. Luther accordingly takes the statement not as a reminder of what Paul preached, but as a reference to the apostasy of the Galatians.[28] This apostasy, he claims, has been pointed out to them so clearly in the preceding discussion that they are crucifying Christ in themselves. The desire to live to the law cannot be reconciled with the desire to live to Christ. Therefore, the return to the law results in a fresh crucifixion of Christ (cf. Heb. 6:6).

Apart from the reading ἐν ὑμῖν (*en hymin*, in or among you) there is no need for such a forced albeit ingenious interpretation. Of course, Paul is referring here to his preaching of Christ in Galatia. The emphasis is on the fact that Jesus Christ was present to them forcibly and urgently as crucified, in the reality and specificity of this manner of execution, as was also the case at Corinth (1 Cor. 1:23; 2:2). And it is further emphasized that this is something they cannot overlook, because it was in whatever sense publicly portrayed to them. It is noteworthy that the apparently complex theme of justification and Paul's allegedly puzzling christology are both brought together in the figure of the crucified Jesus. In him the themes of both justification and christology find not only their visible anchor but also their decisive criterion. Some fascination has obviously blinded the Galatians to the vision of this figure and to this criterion, so that they are left theologically adrift.

The first clause is formulated not as a statement but as a question; a whole series of questions follows. This is appropriate to an argument from experience. If the Galatians are addressed with respect to what they have themselves experienced, they must also draw their own conclusions. Experience is remarkably ambivalent. It has the evidence of something that presents itself immediately but is dependent on an appropriate language for its interpretation. The Galatians certainly do not understand what they have experienced in the terms that Paul is now using. But his reference to their experience makes the claim that nothing new and different is being added to their own experience; instead, their eyes are being opened to it. Therefore, he asks them to pronounce their own verdict.

Although the opening question appears to be only a prelude, it already singles out an undeniable aspect of the Galatians' own experience. That Christ has been publicly portrayed to them in this fashion is a fact that they cannot deny. They must, therefore, consider whether it is even possible, with this as a starting point, to travel the road they wish to set out on. They are being provoked to ask themselves, if they really think so, whether they have not taken leave of their senses.

But Paul is unwilling to let the matter rest with this vague impetus. The argument from experience that he introduces is meant to bar the way so that the Galatians cannot evade the question. Therefore, he refers not just to an experience but to the interwoven complex of several experiences, including the experience of specific interpretative languages. To oversimplify, there

157

are two experiences that the Galatians must answer for: the gift of the Spirit and the dispute between two antithetical ways of proclaiming the gospel. Paul succeeds in reducing this complex constellation to a disjunctive formula by asking on what basis the Galatians received the Spirit. There are only two possibilities: did they receive the Spirit by works of the law or by the message of faith? This single question is all they need to answer. To anyone who knows what happened in Galatia the answer is self-evident: the Spirit was the gift bestowed when they accepted the first, the original proclamation of the gospel. The other teaching, meant to impose the law upon them, came later. Whatever its effect may be, it cannot be the gift of the Spirit. To anyone for whom the experience of the Spirit is crucial, the question is answered from experience without any qualification. The gift of the Spirit has come solely through the message of faith.

Convincing as this argument is, it creates—at least for us—a variety of problems. In the first place, we find it surprising that the Spirit can be identified so clearly as something experienced. The rest of the passage throws some light on this question.

To begin with, the gift of the Spirit is a process with a clear beginning, which can actually be dated. It is not limited, however, to this unique event, but remains effectual from then on. This polarity—a beginning limited to a specific point in time and an unlimited continuation—accounts for the difference in form between v. 2 (in the past tense) and v. 5 (in the present).

In addition, the Spirit can be recognized through certain specific signs, among which manifestations of power in miraculous cures are singled out (v. 5). Here Paul is probably referring to the same phenomenon he calls a "demonstration of the Spirit and power" ($\dot{\alpha}\pi\acute{o}\delta\varepsilon\iota\xi\iota\varsigma$ $\pi\nu\varepsilon\acute{\nu}\mu\alpha\tauο\varsigma$ $\varkappa\alpha\grave{\iota}$ $\delta\upsilon$-$\nu\acute{\alpha}\mu\varepsilon\omega\varsigma$, apodeixis pneumatos kai dynameōs) in 1 Cor. 2:4, in contrast to persuasive words of wisdom. The agent of such deeds of power remains an open question. According to the passage cited, Paul himself appears at first to have been the person in question at Corinth. But that was not the end of the matter; in his absence, such manifestations of the Spirit emerged from the local community (e.g., 1 Cor. 12:10). Gal. 3:5 suggests a similar experience.

The close association between $\pi\nu\varepsilon\tilde{\nu}\mu\alpha$ (pneuma, spirit) and $\delta\acute{\nu}\nu\alpha\mu\iota\varsigma$ (dynamis, power) here and in 1 Cor. 2:4 almost suggests a hendiadys with the meaning "powerful work of the Spirit." But despite the witness of so-called miracles as particularly evident "works of power," we must not forget the numerous other manifestations of the Spirit, which were especially plentiful in the Corinthian community. These included ecstatic states of various kinds. We may assume that a similar situation obtained in the Galatian communities, although perhaps not as fully developed as at Corinth. In any event, these phenomena and the problems arising from them play no perceptible role in the Epistle to the Galatians. The central problem here is the outgrowth not of a burgeoning pneumatomania but of the question whether these experiences of the Spirit do not imply acceptance of the Torah. But before examining this nexus more closely, we shall examine one final aspect of the question as to how the Spirit can be identified in experience.

As the language of our passage suggests, a distinction must be made between the Spirit and its manifestations. The much discussed relationship between the indicative and the imperative in Paul appears also as a statement concerning the Spirit: "If we live by the Spirit, let us also walk by the Spirit" (Gal. 5:25). This suggests a further distinction: when considering the manifestations of the Spirit, we must distinguish between spectacular deeds of power and ecstatic phenomena on the one hand and ordinary human conduct on the other, which Paul goes on to analyze under the general heading "fruit of the Spirit" (Gal. 5:22–23).

If we orient ourselves solely according to manifestations of the Spirit as they are experienced, we are faced with the inescapable need to distinguish between spirits (1 Cor. 12:10). The Spirit is not identical with the manifestations of the Spirit. It is self-evident that these manifestations, taken in isolation, are ambiguous. This is confirmed by what Paul says elsewhere. In our passage, the Spirit that has been received appears to be equated naively and without distinction with the phenomenon of manifestations of the Spirit, so that the Spirit can simply be identified as an experience. Paul's argument is compelling only if there is no doubt or ambiguity about the fact that the Spirit has clearly been received.

Paul nevertheless secures this premise against possible abuse by submitting his understanding of the Spirit to the criterion that emerges when the gift of the Spirit is traced back to its origin. If we have received the Spirit through the message of faith (and the Galatians' own experience makes this indisputable in their case), our understanding of the Spirit and our ability to distinguish between spirits must be grounded in what is fundamental for the ἀκοὴ πίστεως (*akoē pisteōs*, message of faith).

It is possible that Paul coined the term ἀκοὴ πίστεως deliberately as the antithesis to the phrase ἔργα νόμου (*erga nomou*, works of the law). The term itself suggests elements that are important for Paul's understanding of the Spirit: the centrality of faith—which precludes any alleged superiority of the Spirit to faith—and of the word as the source of faith (Rom. 10:17). The antithesis between mere words and manifestations of the Spirit is not intended to deny the connection between word and Spirit, nor is the antithesis itself contradicted by the connection. Faith, like the kerygma itself, is based not on human wisdom but on the power of God (1 Cor. 2:4–5). Once again, however, what is crucial is the content of the ἀκοὴ πίστεως, the gospel of Christ crucified. When Paul takes the undisputed fact that the Galatians have experienced the Spirit as the starting point for his argument from experience, by tracing it back to the ἀκοὴ πίστεως he also links it with the other undisputed fact, the proclamation of Christ crucified. In other words, the message of the cross is the absolute criterion for any understanding of the Spirit. In the case of Paul, it is impossible to play off a theology of the Spirit against the theology of the cross. The experience of the Spirit becomes theologically relevant only when it is understood and interpreted in the light of the *theologia crucis*.

Now how does the argument from experience look in the eyes of those who have now begun to win the ear of the Galatians? They certainly did not claim there was a fundamental antithesis between the Spirit and the law. It is, therefore, unlikely that they denied the fact of manifestations of the Spirit in consequence of Paul's preaching or that they refused to recognize these manifestations of the Spirit. They did not claim to be less devoted to Christ, but to be truly devoted to him. Their credentials included the eschatological gift of the Spirit. What they would absolutely refuse to accept would be the conclusion Paul draws from his disjunctive question, indeed even his right to set up such an antithesis between πίστις (*pistis*, faith) and νόμος (*nomos*, law).

For their part, they are unlikely to have claimed that acceptance of the Torah, especially through obedience to the requirement of circumcision, provided a new and better source for the gift of the Spirit. Their intentions can be deduced quite clearly from v. 3: they wanted to bring to perfection something that had only begun. The event of the Spirit must have seemed imperfect to them because it lacked, as it were, any *fundamentum in re*. It did not guarantee that one belonged to the lineage of Abraham and the chosen people. Therefore, the Spirit appeared to them to be merely the icing on the cake; it does not attain to its full value until it has a firm soteriological base. According to this view, this base consists in corporeal descent from Abraham, or at least in corporeal acceptance of the sign of circumcision associated with this descent.

Paul counters this notion through *reductio ad absurdum*. Alluding to the desired guarantee based on physical evidence, he sees a movement from σάρξ (*sarx*, flesh) to πνεῦμα (*pneuma*, spirit)—the only direction that would have soteriological significance—turned into a movement from πνεῦμα to σάρξ. This reversal means a total loss of what had been given in the experience of the Spirit. The experience of the Spirit would then have been in vain—a statement that recalls the idea that Paul's preaching might have been in vain (2:2) as well as the idea that Christ's death might be in vain (2:21). The cross is meaningless, Paul's preaching is meaningless, the Spirit is meaningless—that is the conclusion. Therefore, using the ambiguity of ἐπιτελεῖν *(epitelein)*, which can mean both "bring to an end" and "bring to perfection," Paul states his verdict: the claim that what has been begun is now being brought to perfection has as its deplorable outcome the transitoriness of what has been begun, so that it is brought to an end. But this would mean saying "No!" to God, for it is God who gives the Spirit and God who is at work in the event of the Spirit. Therefore, the very understanding of God stands or falls with the either/or of works of the law and the message of faith.

The Blessing of Abraham and the
Curse of the Law

3:6–14

6 Thus it was with Abraham: "He had faith in God, and that was reckoned to him as righteousness."
7 Understand therefore: It is those who live by faith that are children of Abraham.
8 But the Scripture, forseeing that God would justify the Gentiles by faith, preached the good news to Abraham beforehand: "In thee shall all the Gentiles be blessed."
9 Therefore: Those who live by faith are blessed with Abraham who had faith.
10 For all who have their being through works of the law are under a curse; for it is written: "Cursed is every one who does not abide by all things written in the book of the law and do them."
11 Now it is evident that when the law is sovereign no one is justified before God. For [it is written]: "The one who is just will live by faith."
12 But the law is not "by faith"; rather: "Whoever does them will live by them."
13 Christ redeemed us from the curse of the law by becoming a curse for us—for it is written: "Cursed be every one who hangs on a tree"—
14 that in Jesus Christ the blessing of Abraham might come upon the Gentiles, that we might receive the promise of the Spirit through faith.

The argument from experience (3:1–5) is followed by an argument from Scripture. At two other points in the main section of Galatians (chapters 3 and 4) we also find scriptural proof. The first is the immediately following section, vv. 15–18. It is therefore reasonable to ask whether those verses should not be included in the present section, both together constituting a single argument. There are, however, several reasons for keeping the two sections separate. In the first place, there is a clear caesura at the beginning of v. 15, itself emphasized by a vocative; there is also the observation that v. 14 answers the question introduced by vv. 5–6, bringing the section to an end. Further comments on the division will be postponed until our treatment of the next section. The third passage involving a proof from Scripture is 4:21–31; it concludes the entire demonstration.

163

These three arguments from Scripture in the main section of Galatians have one feature in common: they concentrate on Abraham. This is true even in the first passage, although it incorporates some other material that does not refer directly to Abraham. These contrastive quotations, however, have the subsidiary function of illuminating the primary quotation that Paul begins with in v. 6: Abraham was justified by faith. In the second passage (v. 16), where the argument from Scripture, as such, is clearly of secondary importance, the christological interpretation of the promises made to Abraham is emphasized. In the third passage (4:21–31), finally, Paul bases his argument on the two different ways of being a child of Abraham, represented by Ishmael and Isaac.

This concentration of the argument from Scripture on the figure of Abraham makes Paul's exegetical method appear in a different light than that in which it is usually seen. He is commonly said to tear isolated quotations arbitrarily out of their context, sometimes reinterpreting them violently and disregarding their historical meaning. Of course, it would be totally unhistorical to judge Paul's own first-century way of dealing with Scripture by the canons of historical-critical methodology. It would also betray a lack of self-critical perspective, which is badly needed by modern exegesis. But observation of the central role played by Abraham in the scriptural proof used by Galatians suggests that Paul's exegetical interest is here clearly concerned with a broad context: what it means to have the right to appeal to Abraham.

That Paul should take up this theme here should not surprise us when we consider the importance to devout Jews of being children of Abraham, as well as the importance of Abraham himself as a prototype, especially in relationship to the other nations. It was the election of Abraham and the promise given to him that set Israel apart from the Gentiles and constituted them the chosen people. At the same time, however, there is an element of universal hope connected with the story of Abraham, the expectation of a soteriology meant for all nations. Therefore the concept of being "children of Abraham" could not remain limited exclusively to his physical descendants. The potential inclusion of proselytes was based on the conviction that under certain circumstances and subject to certain restrictions it was possible to be a child of Abraham not only by inheritance but by desire. Even more radical were the words ascribed to John the Baptist, that God has the power to raise up children of Abraham from stones (Matt. 3:9). Here the association with Abraham takes on the nature of a pure miracle.

Paul's conflict with the Jewish Christians and especially with their Judaizing representatives over the gentile mission without the law was bound to address the problem of what it means to be children of Abraham. This was in fact the focus of the dispute. It would therefore be reasonable to assume that Paul's opponents forced him to deal with this theme and that these exegetical passages are primarily apologetical. Now of course we can no longer reconstruct the preceding discussions or say how Paul's use of Scripture might have developed in the absence of polemical influences. There can be no doubt, however, that it was Paul's own inner necessity that made him inquire into the scriptural basis of his understanding of the gospel. As a Jew, he could not avoid Abraham, the concrete expression of the problem.

Paul's opponents probably took the position that faith in Christ was not sufficient for gentile Christians; they must also become children of Abraham through circumcision. But Paul had probably long anticipated such ideas on his own. His unusual interpretation of Abraham also appears—in more extended form—in Romans 4. Its undeniable independence hardly gives the impression of arising from an apologetic dilemma. The discussion is tied seamlessly into the context of Galatians 3. This shows that we are not dealing with an ad hoc excursus but with the biblical unfolding of the heart of Paul's theology. The question of how the Gentiles can attain righteousness before God without works of the law coincides with the question of how the righteousness accorded Abraham is to be understood and how the promise given to Abraham extends to the Gentiles. If this question were answered in terms of the gospel without the law, a critical conflict would be inevitable with the understanding of the law that was determinative for the Jewish interpretation of Abraham. And the only satisfactory theological treatment of these problems would have to explain the sense in which Jesus Christ mediates the blessing of Abraham.

The basic thesis was stated in 2:16: people are not justified by works of the law but through faith in Christ Jesus. And in 3:2, 5 the gentile Christian Galatians were asked to remember that they did not receive the Spirit through works of the law but through the message of faith. Now comes the demonstration that applies to both statements as one: this is not only consonant with Scripture, but follows directly as its true import, which Paul summarizes at the end of this biblical argument in two purpose clauses introduced by ἵνα (*hina*, in order that): "that in Christ Jesus the blessing of Abraham might come upon the Gentiles, that we might receive the promise of the Spirit through faith" (v. 14).

As we have seen, the novelty of Paul's interpretation of the phenomenon of Abraham does not reside in his relaxing the requirement that people can be children of Abraham only through physical descent. Neither does it consist in the suggestion of new and different ways of finding solidarity with Abraham, in part through human conduct based on the prototype of Abraham, in part through an act of God that itself establishes the solidarity. The duality of these two foundations appears also, albeit profoundly transformed, in the emphatic concluding words of the two purpose clauses (v. 14): ἐν Χριστῷ Ἰησοῦ (en Christō Iēsou, in Christ Jesus)—that is, through an act of God—and διὰ τῆς πίστεως (dia tēs pisteōs, through faith)—that is, like Abraham. The extent to which Paul here plots an entirely new course will be shown briefly through comparison with the traditional interpretation of Abraham.

There is a variety of evidence for this interpretation. In the Old Testament Apocrypha, it is found in Sir. 44:19–21 and 1 Macc. 2:50–52; in the New Testament itself it appears in James 2:21–23 and Heb. 11:17. We could also cite Philo's *De Abraamo*. All these statements share a common feature: the central passage cited to illustrate that Abraham was a πιστὸς ἀνήρ (*pistos anēr*, trustworthy or faithful man: cf. v. 9) and that his πιστεύειν (*pisteuein*, having faith or trust) was reckoned by God as righteousness is the story of the sacrifice of Isaac (Gen. 22:1–19). In both Hebrew and Greek the root in question covers both meanings: being faithful or trustworthy and having faith. Therefore, the use of the sacrifice of Isaac as an example allowed the aspect of trustworthiness to dominate even in the face of the severest test. This was in full accord with obedience to God's law.

"Abraham, the father of many nations, had no stain upon his honor; he kept the law of the Most High and entered into covenant with him; on his own body he cut the established sign of the covenant, and in temptation he proved faithful. Therefore God assured him through an oath that he would bless the nations through his descendants . . . " (Sir. 44:19–21).

"Was not Abraham found faithful in temptation and was not that reckoned to him as righteousness?"—in these words the dying Mattathias reminds his sons of the patriarch; in the same breath, he admonishes them: "Now, my sons, be zealous for the law and pledge your lives for the covenant of our fathers" (1 Macc. 2:52, 50).

And the voice of the Jewish Christians in direct confrontation with Paul is heard in the Epistle of James (2:21–24): "Was not Abraham our father justified by works, when he offered his son Isaac upon the altar? You see that faith was active along with his works, and faith was completed by works, and the Scripture was fulfilled which says, 'Abraham had faith in God and it was reckoned to him as righteousness'; and he was called the friend of God. You see that one is justified by works and not by faith alone."

For Paul's divergent interpretation, it is significant that he does not deal with the story of the sacrifice of Isaac either here or elsewhere. He ignores it, not even reshaping it into a christological allegory as the human and therefore limited likeness of the heavenly Father's gift of his own Son. This silence is eloquent. Paul turns his back decisively on the exegetical tradition of the Abraham story. Not that he would prefer to eliminate the text about the sacrifice of Isaac, or that he found it an embarrassment. What would we not give to hear Paul interpret Genesis 22! But the extraordinary brevity and concentration of his scriptural proofs make it inappropriate for him to engage in detailed critical conflict with the exegetical tradition of such passages. He makes use instead of antithesis.

The faith of Abraham stands in sharp contrast to works of the law. According to the traditional view, the law itself includes both blessing and curse as its complementary aspects; now the blessing is associated exclusively with Abraham and the curse is connected exclusively with the law. Paul understands faith not as a demonstration of faithfulness through a human act but as faith in Jesus Christ and, therefore, as faith in the saving act of God that frees us from the curse. Here, Paul also dissociates himself from the notion that a pure creative miracle makes people children of Abraham, that Abraham's descendants can come from stones instead of from living seed. For a person to come to faith is a far greater and more appropriate miracle than the endowing of a lifeless stone with life. It involves death and resurrected life (2:19–20)—not in arbitrary separate acts, but on the basis of what took place once and for all through and in the crucified Christ (3:13): in explicit connection with the curse that had previously barred the way of Abraham's blessing to the Gentiles.

After these initial attempts to define the significance of Paul's scriptural proof through the context of Galatians and in contrast to the exegetical tradition, we must now turn to the inner flow of the argument. There is some evidence that vv. 6 and 7 contain the *propositio* and v. 14 the *conclusio*. In this case, vv. 8–13 would represent the several stages in the demonstration. But this does not exclude other structural analyses. If we look at the content of what is said, this dense and apparently convoluted section falls clearly into three sections. In vv. 6–9, the catchwords are "faith" and "blessing," in vv. 10–12, "works of the law" and "curse." The unifying theme is the question of righteousness before God. This question is answered positively in the first part and negatively in the second. The third division—and here we hit once more upon Paul's favorite figure of chiasmus—in a sense covers the same territory in reverse, showing how the curse is removed (v. 13) and the blessing fulfilled (v. 14).

This analysis is further supported by the way the scriptural citations are introduced into the text and structure it. There are six of them distributed through the whole passage. The first section contains two: Gen. 15:6 in v. 6

and a conflation of Gen. 12:3 and 18:18 in v. 8. The second section contains three: Deut. 27:26 in v. 10b, Hab. 2:4 in v. 11b, and Lev. 18:5 in v. 12b. The third section contains but a single quotation: Deut. 21:23 in v. 13b. It is noteworthy that except for Hab. 2:4 all the quotations are from the Torah. Of course Paul does not identify Scripture with the Torah; but the preponderance of Torah quotations cautions us against understanding Paul's verdict on the law, meaning primarily the Torah, as being undifferentiated rejection. We shall leave open the question to what extent his extremely critical remarks about reliance on works of the law and the desire to be under the law imply a "No!" to the law as such, whether they are not in fact based on the "Yes!" that Paul speaks of as "upholding the law" (Rom. 3:31; cf. Gal. 5:14; 6:2). In any case, he appeals to the Torah in his battle against a false understanding of the Torah, an understanding which may itself be grounded in the Torah. Abraham himself, although he lived before the Torah, is a figure recorded for us only in the Torah. The third scriptural demonstration (4:21–31) Paul introduces explicitly by pointing out to those who wish to be under the law what the law itself states concerning Abraham: that he had two different sons (4:21). Paul, accordingly, holds that the Torah itself contains both blessing and curse, albeit in a totally different sense from the traditional understanding, based on the catalogs of blessings and curses in Leviticus 26 and Deuteronomy 28. Initially, however, we shall not address the substance of the quotations but merely observe how they are formally introduced. As already suggested, such examination seems to me to support the division of the passage into three sections.

In the case of a writer like Paul, with a highly developed sense of language, it is probably not by accident that the passage exhibits the structure described here.[29]

In the first section (vv. 6–9) the quotation always comes first (vv. 6 and 8); it is followed in each case by a *conclusio*, which is introduced in v. 7 by γινώσκετε ὅτι (*ginōskete hoti*, understand that . . .) and in v. 9 by the logical connective ὥστε (*hōste*, therefore). These two *conclusiones* are identical in structure. Both have as subject οἱ ἐκ πίστεως (*hoi ek pisteōs*, those of faith). Two similar things are predicated of those who live by faith: οὗτοι υἱοί εἰσιν ᾿Αβραάμ (*houtoi hyioi eisin Abraam*, they are children [literally: sons] of Abraham), and εὐλογοῦνται σὺν τῷ πιστῷ ᾿Αβραάμ (*eulogountai syn tō pistō Abraam*, they are blessed with Abraham who had faith). Both quotations state fundamentally the same thing: those who have faith belong to Abraham; they are his children and share in his blessing.

In the second section (vv. 10–12) the structure is reversed. Here each verse starts with the thesis, the *propositio*, which is supported by the following quotation. Formally, then, the quotations do not appear as premises leading to a conclusion but as support for an assertion that has already been made. Therefore, the introductions to the quotations have causal rather than consecutive force: γέγραπται γὰρ ὅτι (*gegraptai gar hoti*, for it is written that: v. 10), δῆλον ὅτι (*dēlon hoti*, it is clear that: v. 11). The same is true in substance of the adversative ἀλλά (*alla*, but, rather: v. 12).

The three *propositiones* likewise exhibit the same structure. They all take the law as their starting point, using similar catchwords: ἐξ ἔργων νόμου (*ex ergōn nomou*, through works of the law: v. 10), ἐν νόμῳ (*en nomō*, in or under the law: v. 11), and ὁ νόμος (*ho nomos*, the law: v. 12). In each case there follows an assertion that is negative in meaning or form: ὑπὸ κατάραν εἰσίν (*hypo kataran eisin*, they are under the curse: v. 10), οὐδεὶς δικαιοῦται παρὰ τῷ θεῷ (*oudeis dikaioutai para tō theo*, no one is righteous before God: v. 11), οὐκ ἔστιν ἐκ πίστεως (*ouk estin ek pisteōs*, it does not rest on faith: v. 12). Here the three scriptural quotations argue, in part directly and in part *ex oppositio*, that those who rely on the law are under the curse because they are not righteous before God, because the law as such does not arise "from faith"; consequently, contrary to the first series of assertions, the law does not bestow blessing.

In the third section (vv. 13–14) the structure changes once more. Here the single quotation comes in the middle (v. 13b). It substantiates the preceding assertion (v. 13a) and leads up to the statement that follows (v. 14). This section clearly has Χριστός (*Christos*, Christ) as its superscription (v. 13), just as the first has Ἀβραάμ (*Abraam*, Abraham: v. 6). The second section, with its contrasting structure, does not explicitly state its theme of νόμος (*nomos*, law) until the beginning of v. 12, although it is already alluded to at the beginning of v. 10. The third section unites—one might almost say reconciles—the opposites of the first two. In contrast to them, it speaks first for the curse and only afterward of the blessing. By taking the curse upon himself Christ has abolished it, thus opening to the Gentiles the way of the blessing of Abraham.

These observations concerning the formal structure of the text make it perspicuous. We may well be astonished at such compositional art. There is nothing artificial about it. By virtue of an almost inconceivable intellectual concentration it exhibits a sovereign mastery comparable to the compositional art of Bach. But this must not divert us from the problem at hand. I am not referring here to the details of the logical relationship between quotation and *conclusio* or *propositio* and quotation. Our immediate concern is the logic of the argument as a whole. We must start once again with elementary considerations.

Paul brings the gospel to the Gentiles. They come to faith and receive the Spirit. The ancient promise to Abraham is here clearly fulfilled. The Gentiles have faith like Abraham. They are therefore children of Abraham. As a blessing given to Abraham they become partakers in salvation together with Abraham. How could this come to pass? Paul's answer is: through Jesus Christ. When the πλήρωμα τοῦ χρόνου (plērōma tou chronou, the fullness of time) came—whatever this may actually mean—when the appointed time was fulfilled, God sent his Son (Gal. 4:4). And because we ourselves thus became children of God—the notion of being children of Abraham merging thus into the notion of being children of God—God also sent his Spirit (Gal. 4:6). But Paul can also call this event, the sending of Christ and of the Spirit, the coming of faith (Gal. 3:23, 25). The coming of faith coincides with the point in time that is also called the coming of the πλήρωμα τοῦ χρόνου. Thus faith has come with the sending of Christ, and for Paul this means the faith of Abraham. Faith in Jesus Christ is essentially identical with the faith of Abraham. Now, however, it is the fulfillment of this faith, because this faith is now open to all. And thus righteousness before God is also opened to all who have faith.

Now this raises a question. Why could Paul in his demonstration from Scripture not pass directly from what is said about Abraham (vv. 6–9) to what is said about Jesus Christ (vv. 13–14, but reduced in this case to Christ's mediation of the blessing of Abraham)? Why do we have the interpolated complex of statements concerning the law (vv. 10–12)? If what is said about Christ came directly after what is said about Abraham, we would expect the following: Jesus Christ proclaimed faith in such a way that it could disregard the boundaries of Israel and come to the Gentiles. What had previously been a latent blessing was thus vouchsafed to the entire world, becoming manifest as the fulfillment of the promise to Abraham. In this direct line from Abraham, Jesus would then be the herald of the faith of Abraham in the figure of Christ bestowing a blessing. Some Hellenistic Jews and Jewish Christians may in fact have justified the mission to the Gentiles along these lines. Paul, however, points to the crucified Christ who bears the curse. There is no other way he can account for the fact that only now does the blessing of Abraham come to the Gentiles.

The detour Paul takes in his demonstration from Scripture is clearly for him the only possible way. It explains why the blessing of Abraham remained latent for so long. The way of the promise was barred by the law, the blessing by the curse. This explanation is central to Pauline christology and therefore to any understanding of what is meant by the faith, the blessing, and the righteousness associated with the figure of Abraham, now made manifest through Jesus Christ. The faith that justifies comes only through deliverance from the curse. Those who know nothing of the curse also know nothing of the blessing. Only the Christ who bears the curse can be the bearer of the blessing.

How is this to be understood? Paul describes the situation in terms of sacred history. The demonstration from Scripture follows the history of Israel. It begins with Abraham and moves on to Moses as the personification of the law; here as elsewhere in Galatians he is not explicitly mentioned, but Paul has him in mind. This history ends with Christ. Paul thus keeps entirely within the compass of the Jewish question as to how the promise to Abraham is to be fulfilled. Within this compass, however, he undertakes a radical change of course. As understood by Judaism, the way to the Gentiles had to be the way of law, by which the Gentiles were brought into the blessing of Abraham, which is tied to Israel. For Jewish thought, the law was not opposed to faith, but rather nourished faith by making demands of it; similarly, the law was not opposed to the blessing, but was considered the vehicle and mediator of the blessing of Abraham.

In opposition to this view Paul does not espouse evasion of the law; he does not seek to annul the law and replace it with Christ. This would only amend the law and change legislators; in substance, the status quo would remain. For Paul, too, the way of the blessing of Abraham to the Gentiles is via the law—not, however, as a potential vehicle of blessing but as the actual source of the curse. We will not yet ask how Paul arrived at this verdict and what it actually means. First, we must examine the implications of the fact that, although in this verdict Paul breaks with the self-understanding of Judaism, he does not, in any sense, go beyond the boundaries of sacred history. Quite the contrary. The tension between blessing and curse is no longer limited to a juxtaposition of the two ways which the law presents for decision; blessing and curse are instead placed in historical sequence and do battle within the arena of history. Therefore, only now does the idea of sacred history take on transcendent, eschatological moment.

One could, therefore, claim that Paul imposes the Torah on the Gentiles not as a condition for salvation but as an indispensable element of sacred history. They are not made subject to the law but are, nevertheless, drawn into sacred history and in a sense made subject to it. There is ambivalence here. What could sound more positive than to be drawn into God's sacred history with Israel? Although the Gentiles do not have the Torah imposed on them as law, do they not have the entire horizon of sacred history imposed on them as law, to which they must adapt themselves, their thought, their faith? What concern is Abraham to them? What concern is Moses to them, even if he is considered only in terms of the curse that comes with being under the law? What concern is Christ to them, if he can be understood only through a tradition that belongs to the history of Judaism, if Paul so involves him in the saving—or should we say damning?—historical function of the Torah that it is impossible to understand the salvific significance of Christ without taking into consideration a law to which Gentiles, not to mention gentile Christians, are not subject?

The aporia we confront here must be faced squarely. Gentile Christians are asked to consider what it means to be under the law, what is problematic about the law. And Jewish Christians are required to consider as a personal problem the question of how the blessing of Abraham comes to the Gentiles in spite of the law. Jews and Gentiles agree to being lumped together in an inclusive "us," of whom v. 13 says: "Christ redeemed us from the curse of the law by becoming a curse for us." It is accordingly clear that Paul is not referring to Jews alone when he speaks of works of the law and of the curse. And he is not thinking only of the Gentiles when he asks how anyone can come to share in the blessing of Abraham. The Gentile must enter totally into the mind of the Jew and the Jew into the mind of the Gentile, so that they bear each other's burdens. Only thus can sacred history be fulfilled.

But even if this does not leave the idea of sacred history totally behind, does it not transform it profoundly? Is not a radical departure from the Jewish interpretation of the Old Testament required if one is to understand what Paul really means by the sequence Abraham—Moses—Christ?

Let us illustrate the problem by comparing this schema of sacred history with the familiar theological schema of creation, fall, and redemption. The latter, too, involves a kind of sacred history, or at least did so when traditional thought interpreted the primal events of creation and fall quasihistorically, and accordingly associated redemption with the Christ event at the midpoint of history and with the events of the eschaton. At least this much still obtains: the meaning of "salvation" must be grasped through the medium of time and history. Being in the world is temporal and human life is historical. It would be a docetic sublimation of how the question of salvation arises and what makes access to salvation possible to ignore everything that determines and drives humanity in its temporal being-in-the-world and in its history.

Now the long trajectory from the primal age to the eschatological age clearly expresses something in a certain sense atemporal. Creation is always present; it is never a datum of the past. The fall, too, is an ever-present reality. The primal history of Genesis uses a narrative form to describe something that determines reality now and always: the interweaving and opposition of God's creative work and human rebellion against it. None of this has been altered by the Christ event, which intervenes precisely in this disordered reality to set it right. Therefore, those who have faith combine these different elements simultaneously: as human beings caught in the opposition of creation and fall—and only as such—they share in the reconciliation brought by Christ. But despite this simultaneity, the historical difference is not irrelevant, above all because the event of redemption is linked to a historical datum. Therefore, history is divided by the birth of Christ. And this is not all. The event of salvation itself is dependent on a specific historical mediation: the preaching of Jesus Christ together with its necessary context of narrative and tradition.

There is an unmistakable parallel between this theologically structured schema of sacred history and the theologicohistorical perspective that informs Paul's demonstration from Scripture. The function of the creation account in the former corresponds to the promise to Abraham in the latter. The common element is the universal call to God through God with its attendant blessing. Then the curse intervenes: in the former through the fall, in the latter in connection with the law. The twin paths then converge in Christ. The notion of deliverance as redemption from the curse, however, points to the specific background of the second. It cannot be applied in a parallelism, not even when differentiated in this fashion.

Both schemata exhibit a tendency toward mutual integration. The story of Abraham at the beginning raises the question of what has preceded that makes it necessary to speak of faith and righteousness, of promise and blessing. In contrast to classical dogmatics, we are not beginning here with a *status integritatis* of creation. Instead, the background of the Abraham story is the reality of a godless world: in the terminology of dogmatics, creation and fall. When Paul speaks next of the episode of the law and the curse that arises from it, he is not shifting the fall in the soteriological sense to the period after Abraham. What had always burdened humanity is now interpreted in its full extent and with utter precision: even—and in a sense above all—the people of the law are under the curse. Although this is stated initially with reference to Moses and his people, it is a universal human situation that is revealed. The law and works of the law and the consequent curse involve not just the Jews, but everyone. And not just because they block the way of the blessing of Abraham to the Gentiles, but also and above all because here the darkness of humanity as a whole is confronted by an uncommonly illuminating power.

Initially, then, the story of Abraham and the episode of the law received their full weight by being seen against the background of creation and fall

—or, if the themes are concentrated in a single name, with reference to Adam. Now the reverse is true. If one were to attempt to interpret the relationship between creation and fall and what took place in Jesus Christ while ignoring the history of Israel, without reference to it, without Abraham and Moses, the attempt would lead to a *reductio ad absurdum*. The intervening experiences and their explication in language are needed to give the necessary depth to our understanding of both the universal human condition and the singular phenomenon of Jesus Christ, so that they can illuminate each other.

These reflections on the thread of Paul's argument lead us to the following result: the two primary distinctions that dominate this demonstration from Scripture—Jews and Gentiles, curse and blessing—turn out to coalesce in their mutual relationship. This was already clear with respect to the curse/blessing dyad: their juxtaposition in the Jewish understanding of the law is transformed by Paul into a sequential relationship in sacred history. But as we can now see this really means an interpenetration: the obscure union of curse and blessing among the Jews and Gentiles, as well as the endurance of the curse on the part of the one who is truly blessed so as to separate the curse definitively from the blessing.

Furthermore, we have frequently noted in our exegesis of Galatians that the distinction between Jews and Gentiles must neither be interpreted as a definitive opposition nor reduced to a neutral juxtaposition. Here, too, we now find an interpenetration that both intensifies and clarifies the problem. "Salvation comes from the Jews"—this Johannine statement (John 4:22) could just as well come from Paul. But there is also the reverse statement that Israel is saved by the ingathering of the Gentiles (Rom. 11:25–26; Romans 9—11 as a whole). The Gentiles must deal with the Old Testament tradition and the specifically Jewish problems that grow out of it; the Jews must likewise draw on the example of the Gentiles to comprehend what the gospel free of the law implies. In Christ both have grown together into a single body so as to serve each other. The fact that here there is neither Jew nor Greek (Gal. 3:28) does not dispense us from reflecting on this difference; indeed, it makes this difference and its resolution the key to the gospel. One could emphasize the point by saying that in Christ everyone who has faith is both Jew and Greek, and yet—or therefore—neither the one nor the other, but a true child of Abraham. In Christ everyone who has faith shares in the movement from curse to blessing: involved in both, and yet through Christ freed from the curse and incorporated in the blessing to which alone the future belongs.

So far our interpretation of vv. 6–14 has dealt with the passage as a whole. This does not make exegesis in detail unnecessary but does free us from the need to examine each detail in order to pave the way for a general interpretation. Therefore, we shall be content with a few remarks focusing on specific points of the three component sections.

Does the reference to Abraham help us understand what faith means? Or does the quotation merely support an understanding of faith that is already presupposed? One could argue that faith is determined by its object; therefore only from Jesus Christ as the ground and object of faith can we expect information about faith, not from a reference back to Abraham—especially when nothing is said of any concrete details such as the promise of descendants or of the land, those objects of Abraham's faith that say so little to us religiously. Paul deliberately reduces what he says about the faith of Abraham to this core: its relationship to God. This concentration is extraordinarily helpful: whatever concrete form it takes, faith must be defined and judged as faith in God. Luther was therefore right in his exegesis of Gal. 3:6[30] to engage in a surprisingly intense discussion of what faith is and what it does. This led him to something one would not necessarily expect on the basis of the Pauline text: some extraordinarily critical statements concerning the relationship between faith and reason: reason kills faith, faith kills reason.[31] It also led him to the no less shocking praise of faith as *creatrix divinitatis in nobis* (creator of the deity within us).[32] What Luther is right about in his exegesis—assuming of course that these extreme statements are themselves interpreted appropriately in their context—is this: the πιστεύειν τῷ θεῷ (*pisteuein tō theō*, having faith in God) for which Abraham is invoked as a witness is not to be understood as a human virtue. Rather, in it, God imposes his own will on believers, contrary to their abilities and achievements but for their benefit.

Therefore, faith is comprehended in its purity only when it is not understood and judged on the basis of the concrete forms of human conduct it may assume from time to time, but rather when it is grasped in a kind of abstraction, with reference in each instance to the fundamental prior encounter between God and the believer. This is what lies behind Paul's distinction between πίστις (*pistis*, faith) and ἔργα (*erga*, works). Of course, faith must take concrete form in human actions in specific situations and tasks. It does so quite of itself when it is true, living faith. But what faith actually accomplishes, what it can do, is not measurable in terms of human consequences and achievements. Here one finds oneself in the realm of what is humanly impressive, whatever criteria are chosen. This forum is concerned with earthly righteousness. It is not to be despised, to the extent that it deserves recognition. But under no circumstances may it be confused with righteousness before God.

Therefore, both clauses of Gen. 15:6 are so important to Paul ("Abraham had faith in God, and it was reckoned to him as righteousness"). What matters to God is not anything Abraham does but the faith, as such, with which he hears the divine promise. We do not find here an open-and-shut demonstration of righteousness, as though God had no choice but to observe Abraham's righteousness and record it. Instead, what is reckoned as righteousness is Abraham's listening to God and finding God in the right, contrary to all self-assessment and the verdict of human probability. Abraham is not presented as the model of righteousness and sinlessness for what he does; it is, rather, for his faith that he is presented as being righteous before God by virtue of God's justifying verdict, despite everything about him that speaks against him. When Paul interprets what it means to be children of Abraham in these terms, he admits that he takes what is said about the blessing of the Gentiles as a kind of *vaticinium ex eventu*. Scripture looked into the future and formulated the promise to Abraham in consequence of what is now happening among the Gentiles through the gospel (v. 8). But this very fact gives Paul the right to say that the difference between the age of Abraham and the age of Jesus Christ has been resolved. Both then and now we face the same situation of faith and justification through God.

How does Paul come to make a sharp antithesis where Jewish thought —and in fact not just Jewish thought!—had found total harmony: between faith and works, faith and the law? What does Paul mean by works of the law? In the first place, it should be noted that Paul declares neither faith and works nor faith and the law to be antithetical, so that one excludes the other. He does not compare them as separate substances but speaks of them relationally. The contrast is not between πίστις (*pistis*, faith) and ἔργα νόμου (*erga nomou*, works of the law), but between οἱ ἐκ πίστεως (*hoi ek pisteōs*, those who live by faith: vv. 7, 9) and ὅσοι ἐξ ἔργων νόμου εἰσίν (*hosoi ex ergōn nomou eisin*, those who have their being through works of the law: v. 10). Similarly, there is no contrast between πίστις (*pistis*, faith) and νόμος (*nomos*, law), but between two relational expressions: πίστις ἐξ ἀκοῆς (*pistis ex akoēs*, faith through preaching), as one might here cite the phrase ἀκοὴ πίστεως (*akoē pisteōs*, message of faith) found in Gal. 3:2, 5 in its Rom. 10:17 form, and ὁ νόμος οὐκ ἔστιν ἐκ πίστεως (*ho nomos ouk estin ek pisteōs*, the law is not by faith: v. 12).

In other words, what matters is what I live by, what I rely upon, what I take as the ground of my existence, what I understand to be my purpose with respect to God: is it faith and therefore God himself in his grace, or is it my own demonstrable reality and therefore I myself in what I achieve and represent? The same situation obtains with respect to faith and the law: the real difference lies in their different sources. Faith is entirely dependent on what God promises in the ἀκοὴ πίστεως (*akoē pisteōs*, message of faith) and how he thus determines our inmost purpose—one might almost say makes us his ears. The law, by contrast, is in its essence not ἀκοὴ πίστεως. Its principle, if one may put it thus, is not πίστις (*pistis*, faith) but works.

Now the triple evidence of Scripture that Paul cites to support his position is not without its problems. His appeal to Hab. 2:4 in v. 11 ("The one who is righteous will live by faith") could be considered an *argumentum ex opposito*. If righteousness comes through faith, then it does not come through the principle of the law, which is works. It could be objected, however, that both here and in Rom. 1:17 Paul robs the noun πίστις (*pistis*, faith, fidelity) of its possessive pronoun. The Masoretic Text reads: "The one who is righteous will live through *his* fidelity," and the Septuagint: "The one who is righteous will live through *my* fidelity" (ἐκ πίστεώς μου, *ek pisteōs mou*). This omission of the possessive pronoun is connected with Paul's decision to take πίστις here in the sense of πίστις Ἰησοῦ Χριστοῦ (*pistis Iēsou Christou*, faith in Jesus Christ: cf. 2:16), that is, faith in the strict sense, rendering both possessive pronouns superfluous. The appropriateness of the quotation depends on this interpretation, which is itself determined already by the antithesis of righteousness through faith versus righteousness through the law.

What about the quotation from Lev. 18:5 in v. 12: "Whoever does them [the requirements of the law] will live by them"? It does provide evidence that the principle of the law is works rather than faith. But this positive statement about the life that arises from these works seems at odds with the idea of righteousness through faith and the life that is associated with it. One possibility is to strip the verb ζήσεται (*zēsetai*, will live) of its soteriological overtones (which is also a possible reading of Hab. 2:4). Then the passage would be speaking only of the different principles on which life can be based: in the case of someone who is (truly) righteous it is faith, in the case of someone who does what the law requires it is these very requirements. Another possibility is to interpret the statement as a hypothetical contrary-to-fact condition: someone who really did what the law requires, someone whose works truly fulfilled the law, would have life thereby—but where is such a person to be found?

Thus, our understanding of this quotation is connected with our understanding of the first (v. 10): "Cursed is every one who does not abide by all things written in the book of the law and do them." This quotation from Deut. 27:26 bears the burden of the argument. But here, too, we face a similar difficulty. It is not the person who does the works of the law that is cursed, but rather the person who transgresses the law. Does it not follow that those who do the works of the law are blessed?

Everything depends on our interpretation of ἔργα νόμου (*erga nomou*, works of the law) and what it means to have one's being ἐξ ἔρων νόμου (*ex ergōn nomou*, through works of the law). It would be stating the obvious to point out that works of the law are not transgressions of the law but acts in accord with the commandments or prohibitions of the law. The notion that the curse attaches to such acts is indeed a hard saying. The catalog of curses in Deut. 27:15ff. argues otherwise. Here the curse is upon specific transgressions. Only at the end, in the demand for total fulfillment (v. 26) might one see a different intention. Paul at least emphasizes this point. Fulfillment of specific requirements is useless if the law is not absolutely fulfilled in its totality (cf. Gal. 5:3). It is therefore also impossible to limit ἔργα νόμου to the fulfillment of the ritual requirements alone, in the sense that those who set their trust in such fulfillment are not made righteous thereby and consequently come under the curse. For Paul's doctrine of the law it is fundamental that the law is indivisible. Therefore, the curse of which he speaks also applies to the moral law. It is, therefore, impossible to get at the concept of ἔργα νόμου from the perspective of content.

If works that fulfill what is written in the law do not justify but rather bring the curse, this is in the first instance because they merely fulfill individual commandments. They are still in the realm of what can be reckoned to one's account and therefore lie totally apart from anything that might make the individual person righteous before God. By the criterion of a positive understanding of what it means to fulfill the law truly and completely, one could therefore easily say that those who have their being through works of the law are under the curse of the radical demand of the law, which can never be silenced. Despite all their individual good works they never achieve real fulfillment of the law. They are under the curse of a hopeless labor of Sisyphus.

The other perspective is closely related. Those who live by works of the law and build on them act against the spirit of the law because they place their faith in something that, as is true of the law, is not determined by the principle of faith and therefore cannot engender faith. Works of the law are works devoid of faith. As such they lead to the false faith of self-justification. All who live by works of the law are under the curse because they have themselves as the object of a pseudo-faith, whether in the form of *superbia* (pride) or *desperatio* (despair) or in a self-deception and hypocrisy made up of both, while refusing to have faith in God.

Speaking of the curse, which means separation from the blessing given to Abraham and to be vouchsafed through him to all the world, Paul says in terse confessional style: "Christ has redeemed us from the curse of the law by becoming a curse for us" (v. 13). He does not go on to explain this formula. The appended quotation does not explain anything; it merely confirms that a person who is crucified is cursed.

Strictly speaking, Deut. 21:23 does not discuss crucifixion—a Roman style of execution foreign to the Old Testament—but the impaling of the corpse of someone already executed so as to expose it to disgrace. Being unclean to the highest degree, it must not remain overnight. This slight discrepancy does not bother Paul. What he is concerned with is the catchword ἐπικατάρατος (*epikataratos*, cursed). The Septuagint adds ὑπὸ θεοῦ (*hypo theou*, by God). Whether Paul omitted this phrase deliberately or did not have it in his text or considered it obviously included in the term "cursed" is hard to decide. The full form of this quotation, "Cursed by God is anyone who hangs on a tree," may have been current as a Jewish battle-cry against Jesus Christ. Paul adopted it, possibly with the nuance of leaving the nature of this curse up in the air, whether it really was God's curse.

In any case, it is the same curse Paul speaks of here, in equally ambiguous terms, as the curse of the law. Of course something more is meant than that the cited Torah verse pronounces a curse upon an impaled corpse. But also something more is meant than the curse threatened by the law. It is, in fact, the curse brought by the law itself upon those who live by works of the law under the conditions of the law.

It would be wrong to conclude that the law as such is a curse. Since, however, it is incapable of imparting righteousness, true life, faith, or participation in the blessing of Abraham, its effect *rebus sic stantibus* on human beings as they are is that of a curse upon both Jews and, mutatis mutandis, Gentiles. All are in a state of subjection, which is not merely the subjection of being under the law but the subjection of being under the curse of the law. This curse of the law made Jesus Christ accursed because, although himself free and sinless (cf. 2 Cor. 5:21), he sacrificed himself for subject sinners. The turning point that became the source of blessing was brought about not through works of the law but by virtue of the suffering of faith. Those who are under the law necessarily find God against them. But those who are in Christ and therefore under faith have God on their side. In this clash between the law and Christ, the curse that issued from the law for all was broken for all, because a single person, indeed the only truly righteous and blessed person, did not flee from the curse but willingly bore it. He thus fulfilled God's salvific will, described in v. 14 as *causa finalis*, summing up the demonstration from Scripture.

The Inheritance of Abraham and the Function of the Law

3:15–25

15 To give a human example, brethren: A legally ratified testament, although made by someone who is only a human being, cannot be annulled or added to by someone else.

16 Now the promises were made to Abraham and to his "seed." It does not say "seeds," referring to many; but, referring to one, "and to your seed," which is Christ.

17 This is what I mean: a testament previously ratified by God cannot be annulled by the law, which came 430 years afterward, so as to make the promise void.

18 For if the inheritance is by the law, it is no longer by promise; but God graciously gave it to Abraham by a promise.

19 Why then the law? It was added because of transgressions, limited to the time until the seed should come to whom the promise had been made; and it was ordained by angels through an intermediary.

20 Now there is no such thing as an intermediary of one; but God is one.

21 Is the law then against the promises? Certainly not! For if a law had been given which could make alive, then righteousness would indeed be by the law.

22 But Scripture included all things under the power of sin, that the promise based on faith in Jesus Christ might be given to those who have faith.

23 Now before faith came, we were confined under the law, kept under restraint until faith should be revealed.

24 Thus the law was our custodian until Christ, that we might be justified by faith.

25 But now that faith has come, we are no longer under a custodian.

So far Paul has used two modes of argument: the first based on the experience of the Galatians (3:1–5), the second on Scripture (3:6–14). The next section follows directly upon what has preceded, continuing to speak of Abraham, the law, and Christ, but with greater emphasis on the phases of sacred history. Paul's method, however, changes. Instead of a scriptural proof based on a sequence of individual texts, now—with the single exception of v. 16, which appears somewhat peripheral—he does not quote and exegete but rather examines the logic by which these great biblical themes cohere. In addition to individual biblical allusions, he cites γραφή (*graphē*, Scripture) as a whole (v. 22). But the question that introduces this appeal to Scripture is raised by an extrabiblical argument: likewise an argument from experience, but this time secular rather than religious. As everyone knows, once a will or testament is in force, others cannot subsequently annul it or alter it by the addition of a codicil. On the basis of this juristic principle, Paul once more addresses the problem of how the promise to Abraham and the law are related. This makes it clear that a new argument begins here.

But how far does it extend? On this point there is a substantial difference of opinion. One difficulty is that the model Paul draws on for his argument undergoes a kind of shift. It is only natural that the phenomenon of a testament should suggest associations with an inheritance (κληρονομία, *klēronomia*: v. 18). Later, however, this idea reappears from a different perspective, transformed into personal terms in the figure of the heir (κληρονόμος, *klēronomos*: 4:1ff.). This shift is prepared for in 3:29: "If you are Christ's, then you are Abraham's seed, heirs according to the promise." Only with this verse does the description of the blessing of Abraham as a testament involving an inheritance seem to be completed. To this point the problem involves the question of whether the κληρονομία (*klēronomia*, inheritance) is affected by the law, which comes later.

Starting with 4:1, however, Paul turns to a question involving the κληρονόμος (*klēronomos*, heir). Although legally the heir, he cannot inherit until he comes of age. Here it is not some other document that affects the testament; the question is rather when the legal testament takes effect. Of course, this shift of interest to the changing situation of the recipient of the inheritance has been prepared for by 3:24–25. There the question as to the function of the law with respect to the promise to Abraham was answered in personal terms: the νόμος (*nomos*, law) is the παιδαγωγός (*paidagōgos*, custodian) under whose power the child is until maturity. The transition to the personal plane brings the argument to two rival conclusions. The first (3:29) has already been cited: "If you are Christ's, then you are Abraham's seed, heirs according to promise." The other conclusion appears in 4:7: "You are no longer a slave but a child [lit.: son], and if a child then an heir through God." But even at this point we do not appear to have reached the break where a new argument begins. Gal. 4:8–11 still stands under the sign of the change from slaves to children, although now in the threatened reversal of a return to slavery. The phrases ἀλλὰ τότε (*alla tote*, but formerly: v. 8) and νῦν δέ (*nyn de*, but now: v. 9) clearly repeat the development already presented in vv. 1ff. Nothing new appears until 4:12, where Paul introduces into the discussion the argument of his own relationship to the Galatians, the history of his involvement with them (4:12–20).

And so we are confronted with the problem of how to subdivide the long section from 3:15 to 4:11. Within this passage the argument clearly shifts from the legal status of the testament to that of its recipient. The turning-point is obviously the transition from 3:25 to 3:26. It is, therefore, not sufficient merely to identify a sequence of themes within the total complex, for example, promise (3:15–18), law (3:19–22), faith (3:23–29), inheritance of Abraham (4:1–7), and finally, beginning with 4:8, a personal appeal to the Galatians. If we focus instead on the turning-point in the argumentation, we shall find besides the shift already mentioned from the problem of the κληρονομία (klēronomia) to the problem of the κληρονόμος (klēronomos) other perspectives that point up the close relationship as well as the differences between the two sections 3:15–25 and 3:26—4:11.

One striking feature shared by both is the important role played by history. That the διαθήκη (diathēkē, last will, testament) of the promise to Abraham is not touched by the law is demonstrated by Paul on the basis of their temporal relationship (3:17). The question of "when" is also decisive for the legal ability of an heir to inherit. With respect to the coming of Christ, this is described in terms of the πλήρωμα τοῦ χρόνου (plērōma tou chronou, fullness of time: 4:4) as the counterpart to the προθεσμία τοῦ πατρός (prothesmia tou patros, the date set by the father: 4:2). In the former case, the time when the law was given was critical; in the latter, the time when we were freed from the law to become children of Abraham.

This is the most striking evidence that we are dealing with two different arguments from history. The details of the vocabulary used in the two sections confirm this observation. They exhibit striking differences, although they share a common vocabulary when speaking of time and history. Even the words common to both sections are distributed quite differently. The concepts that dominate the first section reappear in the second, but with much lower frequency.

First, a statistical summary. When we compare the first section (3:15–25) to the second (3:26—4:11), we find the following ratios: ἐπαγγελία (epangelia, promise), 6:1; νόμος (nomos, law), 7:2; πίστις (pistis, faith), 5:1; but for θεός (theos, God), 3:8. Apart from the word "God," the emphasis in the second section is on words that do not occur at all in the first, such as υἱός (hyios, son: six times) and δοῦλος (doulos, slave: likewise six times, including the cognate verb). Even more evidence could be cited for the difference in vocabulary, which reinforces the suggested division.

The emphasis, however, is not on the differences but on the similarities. Not only is the subject matter of each dominated by the notion of time, so are the actual words employed. This would seem obvious in the case of the verbs. What we are concerned with, however, is not their tense but a temporal element in their meaning. An example is the verb ἔρχεσθαι (*erchesthai*, come: 3:19, 23, 25; 4:4), which expresses a movement in which time is fulfilled. The numerous verbs from the legal sphere in the first section, such as κυροῦν (*kyroun*, make legally valid), προκυροῦν (*prokyroun*, make legally valid previously), ἀθετεῖν (*athetein*, declare invalid), καταργεῖν (*katargein*, annul), ἐπιδιατάσσεσθαι (*epidiatassesthai*, append a codicil), and so forth, refer to the future or the past, stating that something is made valid for the future or something coming from the past is made invalid. In the second section, one can point to the temporal meaning of verbs like ἐξαποστέλλειν (*exapostellein*, send), ἐξαγοράζειν (*exagorazein*, redeem), γίγνεσθαι (*gignesthai*, be born), ἐπιστρέφειν (*epistrephein*, turn, return), and so on.

Among the nouns we find explicit words for periods of time such as ἔτος (*etos*, year) in the first section and with particular frequency in the second: προθεσμία (*prothesmia*, date), χρόνος (*chronos*, time), ἡμέρα (*hēmera*, day), μήν (*mēn*, month), καιρός (*kairos*, specific time), and ἐνιαυτός (*eniautos*, year). But other nouns also have a temporal dimension. In the case of ἐπαγγελία (*epangelia*, promise) and κληρονομία (*klēronomia*, inheritance) this is immediately obvious. But it is also true for διαθήκη (*diathēkē*, testament) and νόμος (*nomos*, law): the instructions or enactments represent a kind of anticipation of the future on the part of the past. In addition to further nouns, this highly developed temporality could be illustrated through the prepositions, conjunctions, and temporal particles in both sections.

If we now try to define the specific differences between these two sections, we can begin with the observation that they exhibit contrary movement. In the first section the train of thought is historical: from Abraham through the giving of the law at Sinai to the coming of faith. In the second section the direction of movement is reversed. Here the presentation begins with the fulfillment of the promise to Abraham (3:26–29), goes back to the turning-point at which slaves become children (4:1–7), and finally ends with the threatened reversion to the point of departure, here described as slavery to the στοιχεῖα τοῦ κόσμου (*stoicheia tou kosmou*, elemental powers of the universe: 4:8–11; cf. 4:3).

This immediately suggests a further difference. This second section (3:26 —4:11) focuses on the gentile Christian situation, whereas the first (3:15–

25) describes the problem of Jewish Christians. Both are concerned at bottom with the same event: liberation from slavery, a liberation conceived as marking an epoch. But there is a striking difference in emphasis. In the first section, the primary historical statement concerns the era of the νόμος (*nomos*, law), as an ambiguous regulation: unlike the promise to Abraham and the coming of faith, it does not have the nature of something ordained by God (*ordinatio divina*). In the second section, however, the primary historical statement is concerned explicitly with just this *ordinatio divina*: the sending of the Son and the Spirit (4:4, 6). This not only abolishes slavery to the στοιχεῖα τοῦ κόσμου (*stoicheia tou kosmou*, elemental powers of the universe) but also the social divisions between human beings that are the result of human ordinance (*ordinatio humana*: cf. 3:28).

In the demonstration from Scripture (3:6–14), promise and law were not presented as antithetical. Their relationship was expressed in terms of those affected. Οἱ ἐκ πίστεως (*hoi ek pisteōs*, those who live by faith: v. 7) and ὅσοι ἐξ ἔργων νόμου εἰσίν (*hosoi ex ergōn nomou eisin*, all who have their being through works of the law: v. 10) were contrasted as those on whom the blessing rests and those weighed down by the curse. On the basis of these effects, the meaning of Christ was then explained as liberation from the curse of the law (v. 13) and participation in the blessing of Abraham (v. 14). The law as such is not termed a curse, nor did Christ set us free from the law itself. But it is easy to suspect that this is what Paul means. Therefore, the question now leads to a direct confrontation between the promise to Abraham and the Torah. Are they mutually contradictory? Supplementary? Does one abolish the other? Here the primary question is not about the consequences of these ordinances but about the documents themselves. They are examined to determine their validity and their function, as in a secular legal case like the model introduced in v. 15. In vv. 16–19, then, the indisputable primacy of the promise over the law is demonstrated on the basis of its immutable priority. But this in turn complicates the problem of what the function of the law actually is. This question is raised in v. 19; it is answered briefly, and then the answer is expanded upon in vv. 20–25.

Paul is well aware that in using an example from the legal realm he has shifted to a mode of argumentation that is no longer that of theology. He focuses on the difference between human beings and God not only to point up the difference between an ordinary testament and God's promise but also for the following reason: in the realm he intends the comparison to illustrate, an important role is also played by the contrast between what comes from God (the promise) and what cannot be attributed immediately to God: the νόμος (*nomos*, law). And so the double emphasis in v. 15 on the human element (κατὰ ἄνθρωπον λέγω· ὅμως ἀνθρώπου κεκυρωμένην διαθήκην, *kata anthrōpon legō: homōs anthrōpou kekyrōmenēn diathēkēn*, to give a human example: a legally ratified testament, although made by someone who is only a human being. . .) indicates more than an argument *a minore ad maius*. There is already in the background the notion that the law, as something lesser, differs from the unlimited divinity of the promise.

Initially, of course, Paul is pointing out that the example is only an analogy. Here κατὰ ἄνθρωπον (*kata anthrōpon*, after human fashion) does not have the same negative sense as in 1:11 (cf. also 1 Cor. 3:3; 15:32). If the gospel were κατὰ ἄνθρωπον, it would no longer be gospel. But here, when the promise is illustrated by an example κατὰ ἄνθρωπον, the example can serve in a sense as an explanation. But the difference between a human testament and the διαθήκη (*diathēkē*, last will, testament: v. 17) established by God must be taken into account. A similar neutralization of the phrase κατὰ ἄνθρωπον in the expression κατὰ ἄνθρωπον λέγειν (*kata anthrōpon legein*, speak in human fashion) appears elsewhere in Paul (Rom. 3:5; cf. Rom. 6:19), although the negative overtones are sometimes also heard (1 Cor. 9:8).

We are dealing here with specifically Pauline language not found elsewhere. This striking observation requires us to take seriously the theological considerations behind the expression κατὰ ἄνθρωπον λέγειν. It may therefore not suffice to speak of "neutralization." It is noteworthy that an argument based on a legal principle, that is, something from the realm of the law, can be cited to justify the primacy of the promise over the law. It would distort the difference between human beings and God to understand it merely as contradiction and not also as analogy. The separation caused by sin is in no way reduced by the fact that human beings still remain God's creatures; it is rather intensified. The fact that law, righteousness, and justice are found within the human race does not make us righteous before God but enables us to experience what comes from God. The law of inheritance itself may exhibit highly problematic developments and consequences, so that it is indeed κατὰ ἄνθρωπον (*kata anthrōpon*, after human fashion) in the negative sense; nevertheless, a legal principle like that which Paul cites is a true blessing. Where would we be if a testament were not inviolable, in some sense sacred?

When Paul shifts to the application of the principle, one may ask why he immediately burdens the clear and—one might say—noble beginning of his argument with a petty and hairsplitting exegesis. To reduce the christological intent of the promise to the use of the singular τῷ σπέρματί σου (*tō spermati sou*, to your seed) strikes us as a conjuring trick. But for the rabbinical hermeneutics Paul was trained in such an approach was legitimate. It was more illustrative than demonstrative. It need not detain us. The important question is why Paul was concerned to introduce the christological reference at this particular point.

The shift from διαθήκη *(diathēkē)* in the general legal sense of (last will and) testament to διαθήκη in the biblical sense of *b^erith* (covenant) was no problem, because the Septuagint uniformly translates *b^erith* as διαθήκη; the latter word therefore has a semantic range that includes both testament and covenant. Our English word "covenant" is of course no less problematic with reference to God than is the term "testament." What is involved is neither a contract between equal parties nor a last will and testament to be in force at death. Following the Septuagint, Paul can speak of several διαθῆκαι *(diathēkai*, testaments) in the Old Testament (Rom. 9:4). But he clearly intends so to concentrate linguistic usage that the καινὴ διαθήκη *(kainē diathēkē*, new covenant) replaces the παλαιὰ διαθήκη *(palaia diathēkē*, old covenant).

But Paul does not maintain a strict temporal sequence. In Gal. 4:24 he speaks of two διαθῆκαι already prefigured in the Old Testament era through the two sons of Abraham. The Sinai event, that is, the law, is also termed a διαθήκη, and in 2 Cor. 3:14 the law is called παλαιὰ διαθήκη *(palaia diathēkē*, old covenant). In our passage (Gal. 3:16–17), however, Paul reserves the word διαθήκη for the promise to Abraham and avoids using διαθήκη as a general term for both the promise and the law. As we can see, the definitive terminology is still taking shape. The basic meaning must therefore be taken to be "legal disposition." For Paul, the theologically positive content is not associated primarily with the term διαθήκη but with the term ἐπαγγελία *(epangelia*, promise). The restriction of the term διαθήκη in this passage to the promise to Abraham is determined by the course of the argument, which could not speak of the law as another διαθήκη. In addition, the term διαθήκη is firmly rooted in the story of Abraham itself (Gen. 15:18 and Genesis 17 passim). Paul is concerned here to claim the theologically important concept of διαθήκη exclusively for that which was fulfilled in Christ. He not only has to keep it strictly separate from the law, he also has to effect a radical concentration of the different promises to Abraham and their earthly goals (many offspring and possession of an enormous land), reducing them to a single eschatological end, namely Christ. This also means that this διαθήκη is final and is valid for all eternity.

Only in this context does the primary argument, presented in v. 17, take on sharp contours. Greater antiquity per se does not of course demonstrate priority. Neither does it provide proof of authenticity. The historical distance of the Torah, given in round figures as the duration of Israel's sojourn in Egypt (Exod. 12:40), serves, in the first instance, only to show that by virtue of this legal principle the law, coming so much later than the διαθήκη of God with Abraham, cannot annul it and render the promise void. A more precise dating is not needed. Paul also has the secondary purpose of representing the Torah to be a relatively late historical phenomenon. The Torah also has a historical termination analogous to its beginning, in contrast to the eschatological status enjoyed by the promise, which leads up to Christ. This represents an outrageous affront to the Jewish understanding of the law, according to which the Torah is preexistent, created before the world; it was also valid for Abraham and is therefore not subject to temporal limitation.

When confronted with this contradiction, we are also alerted to another idea implicit in the Pauline argument that must appear totally blasphemous to any Jew. The force of the argument depends on the two legal dispositions having different authors. Obviously, someone who has written a last will and testament can also change it. When Paul asserts that the promise to Abraham cannot be changed by the Torah, the Torah is denied divine authorship equivalent to that of the promise. He presents them as competing alternatives. Verse 18 accordingly forces a decision whether the inheritance, that is, the announced salvation, comes by the law or by the promise. It must be the one or the other. This puts promise and law in a position where they are mutually irreconcilable—absurd from the Jewish perspective. Paul for his part reaches his decision by appealing to grace, which belongs by nature not to the law but to the promise. And it is grace that is constitutive of the promise to Abraham.

It is impossible to evade the question in v. 19: τί οὖν ὁ νόμος (ti oun ho nomos, why then the law?). It is noteworthy that Paul does not find himself having to face this question because others have driven him into a corner. It is he himself who has pursued the argument unhesitatingly to this point. The enormous implications of this question and its answer help account for the force with which Paul practically flings out the four statements that follow, each shorter than the preceding: "It [the law] was added because of transgressions; limited in time until the seed should come to whom the promise had been made; ordained by angels; through an intermediary." Here we feel an inner sense of overwhelming constraint that is the reverse side of a freedom whose eschatological character produces effects of historic dimensions.

The four components of v. 19 can be grouped into two double statements. The two concluding phrases describing the source of the law most clearly go together, although they appear most obscure: διαταγεὶς δι' ἀγγέλων (diatageis di' angelōn, ordained by angels), ἐν χειρὶ μεσίτου (en cheiri me-

sitou, through an intermediary). But the two statements of purpose and goal also go together: τῶν παραβάσεων χάριν προσετέθη (*tōn parabaseōn charin prosetethē*, it was added because of transgressions), ἄχρις οὗ ἔλθη τὸ σπέρμα ᾧ ἐπήγγελται (*achris hou elthē to sperma hō epēngeltai*, until the seed should come to whom the promise had been made). The law is in fact an addition, not within the framework of the testament but outside it and limited in time until the promise is fulfilled. It was not added for the sake of the κληρονομία (*klēronomia*, inheritance) but because of transgressions —not to prevent them, but to give rise to them. In the verses that follow Paul gives his explanation of the two double statements in this reverse order, that is, once again chiastically. The comment in v. 20 about the source of the law refers to the last two sections of v. 19, to which it is merely a short gloss. The statement about the function of the law is somewhat more expansive: first a negative to counter a false conclusion (v. 21), then a positive statement to present Paul's own interpretation (vv. 22–25).

Concerning the source of the law, Paul says: "Ordained by angels, through an intermediary" (the phrase ἐν χειρί [*en cheiri*, through the hand of] is a Hebraism). The explanation follows immediately: "Now there is no such thing as an intermediary of one; but God is one." Much ink has been spilled over this obscure statement, but Paul's basic meaning is clear in outline. The participation of angels in the giving of the law at Sinai is suggested by the Septuagint of Deut. 33:2. At the beginning of the blessing of Moses, the Hebrew text reads: "The Lord came from Sinai . . . with flaming fire in his right hand." The Septuagint interprets this natural phenomenon as involving angels: ἐκ δεξιῶν αὐτοῦ ἄγγελοι μετ᾽ αὐτοῦ (*ek dexiōn autou angeloi met' autou*, at his right hand angels with him). There is an ambiguity about the appearance of heavenly intermediaries to bridge the gap between the world and the increasingly transcendent Lord. It can underscore the majesty of God. But it can also turn into a competitive notion, as the Gnostic idea of an inferior demiurge as the author of the law shows.

Stages in the development of this notion can be seen elsewhere in the New Testament. Besides Heb. 2:2 ("the word that went forth through the mediation of the angels"), we also find Acts 7:38 ("This is he who was in the congregation in the wilderness as a mediatior between the angel who spoke to him at Mount Sinai and our fathers") and 7:53 (" . . . you who received the law as delivered by angels but did not keep it"), all of which come close to Paul's words by including the mediating role of Moses. This role, already emphasized in Exod. 20:19, is now interpreted as mediating between the angels who give the law and the people. Paul shares this notion. Its appearance in the speech of Stephen shows that it was current in Hellenistic Jewish circles. It impugns the direct divine origin of the Torah. The explanation added by Paul appears merely to support the idea that angelic powers were responsible for authorship of the Torah, on the basis of Moses' undisputed function as a mediator. A being who is one, like God, says Paul, does not need an intermediary. Therefore, the existence of an intermediary proves that several authors—to wit, angels—were involved in the giving of the law. But the remarkable thing about Paul's argument is that he bases this understanding of the law on the fundamental confession of Israel, the Shema: "Hear, O Israel, Yahweh our God is the one Yahweh" (Deut. 6:4: *sh⁽e⁾ma yisrael yahweh elohenu yahweh echad*). The divinity of God will tolerate no intermediary for its revelation.

Only here does Paul use the word μεσίτης (*mesitēs*, intermediary), which is used christologically later in the New Testament (1 Tim. 2:5, and in explicit contrast to the mediation of Moses in Heb. 8:6; 9:15; 12:24). The theologically inferior significance of the mediator concept for Paul agrees with the Pauline valuation of the law. This does not exclude the possibility that even for Paul God is ultimately responsible for the law. He can call it holy and spiritual (Rom. 7:12, 14). It is fulfilled in love (Gal. 5:14; Rom. 13:8). And it can even enter into such phrases as ὁ νόμος τοῦ Χριστοῦ (*ho nomos tou Christou*, the law of Christ: Gal. 6:2), ὁ νόμος τοῦ πνεύματος τῆς ζωῆς ἐν Χριστῷ ᾽Ιησοῦ (*ho nomos tou pneumatos tēs zōēs en Christō Iēsou*, the law of life in Christ Jesus given with the Spirit: Rom. 8:2), and νόμος πίστεως (*nomos pisteōs*, the law of faith: Rom. 3:27), however they are to be interpreted in detail. But for Paul the mode of God's revelation does not fall within the category of mediation but rather reconciliation (2 Cor. 5:19). Reconciliation has nothing to do with the law. We would have to trace the broadest outlines of Pauline theology to test the conjecture arising out of Gal. 3:20, that the distinction between law and gospel illuminates Paul's understanding of revelation. The law is intimately bound up with mediation; it therefore derives from God only indirectly. The promise, however, the gospel—and that is nothing less than Jesus Christ in person— reveals the δόξα (*doxa*, glory) of God in the face of Jesus Christ.

More important than the statements about the source of the law and Paul's explanation of them is what he says about the purpose and goal of the law. He therefore comments upon it at some length (vv. 21–25). This is the heart of his answer to the question in v. 19: Τί οὖν ὁ νόμος (*Ti oun ho nomos*, What about the law?). Of course, the question does not concern the substance of the law or where it may be found. It is the Torah that is under discussion. Its identification raises no problems. Nor is there anything about a search for a compendium of the law in the form of a single statement—a question answered by Paul in Gal. 5:14 with the commandment "You shall love your neighbor as yourself." As the preceding confrontation with the promise would lead us to expect, the primary focus is on what function the law still has if it is antithetical to the promise. Has it not become irrelevant and meaningless? For this reason the double statement about the law in v. 19 already involves a comparison with the promise: the law was added because of transgressions, limited to the time until the seed should come to whom the promise had been made. The function of the law is bounded by fulfillment of the promise. The question of its goal is answered by the statement that, in accordance with its purpose, it comes to an end as soon as the promise achieves its goal. The question of its purpose can therefore be answered only in absolute contrast to the purpose of the promise: instead of opening the way to the inheritance of Abraham, it occasions transgressions and thus, in fact, leads away from sharing in the inheritance.

Paul, therefore, quite appropriately begins his explanation of what he has just said about the purpose and goal of the law with a new question (v. 21): "Is the law then against the promises?" This question could be seen as the consequence of what has already been said on the theme: *Tí οὖν ὁ νόμος* (*Ti oun ho nomos*, What about the law?). This initial question could well appear offensive. How is it possible for me to question the purpose of the law when it states so clearly and absolutely what I must do? Therefore the second question gives voice to the expected reaction. The Jew formulates it in what must appear to be absurd terms: can the law be against the promises?

At first glance we may be startled by Paul's answer: *μὴ γένοιτο* (*mē genoito*, certainly not), in which we hear overtones of his own shock at such a suggestion. But surprise at Paul's negative answer reveals a failure to understand what has gone before. The law would indeed be against the promise if it were in competition with the purpose of the promise. According to Paul, however, the profound difference between the law and the promise is precisely of such a nature as to eliminate all possibility of such a hostile competition. Establishment of righteousness before God is a function not of the law but of the promise. For *δικαιοσύνη* (*dikaiosynē*, righteousness) is not brought about by those who are faithful to the law; it is hoped for as a pure gift of grace on the basis of faith in the promise, just as an inheritance drops into my lap because someone else has disposed of it to my benefit in a testament.

Paul explains that righteousness cannot issue from the law because the law cannot make alive (v. 21). This argument is extremely enlightening. Initially, however, it may appear confusing. Paul himself insists that the commandment was given to me for the sake of life and not, as in the actual event, for death (Rom. 7:10). So far we have been very hesitant about comparing Galatians and Romans. To engage in such comparison would greatly expand our exegesis. There are substantial reasons not to interpret Galatians from the perspective of the later Epistle to the Romans with the intent of harmonizing them. Certain changes might well have taken place within Paul's theology. Such reservations notwithstanding, it is hardly possible to perceive any difference in this passage. We may leave open the question whether it is significant that in Rom. 7:10 Paul qualifies ἐντολή (*entolē*, commandment) rather than νόμος (*nomos*, law) with the phrase εἰς ζωήν (*eis zōēn*, for life). In any case, what is meant is that the commandment is not intended to bring about death but to preserve life.

Even here Paul does not state that the commandment can in fact create life. Only the power of ζῳοποιεῖν (*zōopoiein*, making alive), which belongs to God alone, can deal effectively with the human situation under the law. I am not a blank page. My situation is not that of a neutrality open to every possibility, so that I might still hope that my efforts would finally result in righteousness. As a person without righteousness I lack the most basic prerequisite for establishing righteousness, namely the life that constitutes the being of the righteous. This demands no less a power than the raising of the dead, ζῳοποιεῖν (*zōopoiein*, making alive) in the strict sense, which for Paul is a predicate of God (Rom. 4:17). It cannot be hoped for from the law, because God is not immediately present and revealed in the law.

We could also reverse cause and effect and say that the relationship of the law to God differs fundamentally from the way in which the promise belongs to God. This can be seen from the law's failure to bring about what we would have to demand of it if it were really to be in competition with the promise.

That ζῳοποιεῖν (*zōopoiein*, making alive) is necessary for attainment of righteousness is, according to Scripture, the consequence of sin. Here, as in 2:17–18, we find again the distinction between ἁμαρτία (*hamartia*, sin) and παράβασις (*parabasis*, transgression). The latter is associated with the law and presupposes ἁμαρτία. Rom. 4:15 reads: "Where there is no law there is no παράβασις"; "there is no ἁμαρτία" would be impossible. Similarly, it would be impossible to restate Gal. 3:19 to say that the law was added because of sin rather than because of transgressions.

In v. 22, Paul has deliberately chosen ἡ γραφή (*hē graphē*, Scripture) as the subject rather than ὁ νόμος (*ho nomos*, the law) in order to substantiate his statement about universal slavery to the power of sin: "Scripture included all things under the power of sin." As in 3:8 ("because Scripture foresaw"), Scripture here plays an active role with respect to sacred history, now in the sense that it not merely states but also ordains by virtue of its authoritative verdict. Rom. 11:32 says the same of God: God has consigned all to disobedience that he may have mercy upon all. Here, of course, this authority of God's will made known in Scripture is needed in order to validate so radical a verdict, which contradicts all human self-evaluation. Note that this verdict is not limited to itself. As the will of God and the verdict of Scripture, what Paul says about the universal power of sin can be maintained only in the light of the soteriological goal, God's plan of salvation. Just as in Rom. 11:32, the edict that all without exception are prisoners of sin merely constitutes the background against which God's salvific will is set forth in a clause beginning with ἵνα (*hina*, in order that): a mercy no less universal or, in the language of our text, the gift of the promise to those who have faith by virtue of their faith in Christ.

How else could one endure the incomprehensible fact that all find themselves guilty, trapped together in the constraints of a disastrous situation, if the primary emphasis were not already on the divine antithesis, the fact that the bars of the prison have already been broken? Thanks to this movement from darkness to light, even the main clause, which taken in isolation conveys no hope ("Scripture included all things under the power of sin"), already feels the pull of the purpose clause with its rising expectations ("that the promise based on faith in Jesus Christ might be given to those who have faith"). But the opposite is also true: how could the content of this purpose clause be valued properly apart from the untold burden imposed by the main clause?

Only from the perspective of Scripture as a whole can the question of the law's function be answered. The divine ordinance that the existence of sin establishes a universal imprisonment under the power of sin, so that sin becomes a prison, constitutes the framework within which the role of the law must be interpreted. The brief statement in v. 19: τῶν παραβάσεων χάριν προσετέθη (*tōn parabaseōn charin prosetethē*, it was added on account of transgressions) is not explained directly in vv. 23–24, where the question of what the law is receives its definitive answer. We would be groping in the dark in our attempts to understand these enigmatic words were it not for the light cast by Rom. 4:15 and 7:7–9. The naive and rationally convincing interpretation would of course be that the law was given to prohibit and, as much as possible, prevent transgressions. What would be the good of a law if it were not expected to improve matters? That transgressions should be the very purpose of the law seems perverse.

We see that Paul is looking at the theme of "law" from another perspective than that of ordinary legislation. His question about the function of the law is not juristic but theological. Of course, the latter does not exclude the former. Of course, Paul would never deny that in civil usage the law serves to specify and prohibit transgressions (cf. Rom. 13:1–7). Even though it cannot prevent them, at least it can limit them. The evil in the world is not fundamentally lessened, but the obvious damage it causes is reduced as much as possible. Paul is neither an antinomian nor an anarchist. He could not appeal to the law of inheritance if he thought nothing of civil law.

From the theological perspective, however, the situation is entirely different. Here the point is not to remove the worst consequences of ἁμαρτία (*hamartia*, sin), but to eliminate sin itself. Only then can one speak of righteousness before God. It is, nevertheless, difficult to overcome the constraints of rational thought, which incline us to think of a process analogous to the civil use of the law but incomparably greater in scale. By nature we all think of this positive function of the law, even in the religious realm. Constrained by this rational ideology, we try to quantify our relationship to God and adapt it to the human need for self-assertion.

The Jewish understanding of the Torah uses the metaphor of a fence to express this idea. The Torah is for Israel a protective fence. It prevents contact with everything unclean, which is kept outside, and it restrains the desire to break out and overstep the salutary boundary. It would almost be possible to say that Paul takes a polemical stance toward this image of the Torah as a beneficent fence by radicalizing it and thus transforming it into its opposite. It is not the law but the sin preceding the law that must be first taken into account. And it is no longer a protective fence but a prison from which there is no escape. Within this transformed metaphor the law does not have the function of partially breaking through the walls of sin, making a breach in them to open a way of escape. On the contrary, the law has the function of an additional attendant, a prison guard who makes those who live in the custody of sin fully aware of where they are. This φρουρεῖν (*phrourein*, confinement) is the function of the law: it watches over those imprisoned in sin and keeps them in custody. The purpose is stated in v. 19: τῶν παραβάσεων χάριν (*tōn parabaseōn charin*, because of transgressions). The law stimulates sin to take concrete form so that it is experienced in specific transgressions.

Even the disciplining and ameliorating effect of the law brings about only a kind of modification of sin. In the form of *opinio iustitiae*, imagined righteousness, sin becomes even more dangerous to our relationship with God. Therefore, works of the law do not overcome sin but transform it. From this perspective it must actually appear salutary that the law finds repeated occasion to register transgressions and even provides new occasion for them through the familiar attraction of what is forbidden.

Exegetical tradition has been misled by the catchword παιδαγωγός (*paidagōgos*, pedagogue) into finding here a statement that the law has a positive educational function with respect to Christ. More recent exegesis, however, is unanimous in emphasizing that the preposition εἰς (*eis*, until) serves here only to specify the terminus, not the inner goal, and that the occupation of a pedagogue in antiquity, which seems so ideal to us, was inferior, almost disreputable. Well-to-do families kept a slave who was usually incompetent for anything else as an attendant and companion for the children. The most popular pedagogical tool was the rod.

It is not without reason, however, that Paul shifts from the appropriate image of a prison guard in v. 23 to the concept of a παιδαγωγός in v. 24. The element common to both is undoubtedly the notion of a state imposed more or less by force until the time of liberation. Imprisonment does not contribute to this idea. It does not suggest a positive development leading up to liberation. Liberation must come from without. Paul's slight change in the metaphor may well be due to his intention of applying the inheritance model to the person of the heir and the heir's reaching majority. But it would be wrong to overlook the nuance introduced by the primitive and forbidding figure of the παιδαγωγός. It allows for the inclusion of what seems at least to be the positive effect of the law, the prevention of something worse and even the improvement and education of humanity. The παιδαγωγός had to protect his charges from being molested and see that they behaved properly. Not that we should fantasize about the word παιδαγωγός and exploit it to describe the function of the law in more cautious and as it were more humane terms. From the theological perspective, nothing fundamental would be changed. But this very fact demands consideration. Even if we abandon ourselves to the more recent meaning of "pedagogue" and interpret the law with reference to the highest aspirations and best possible results of modern pedagogy, there is not the slightest change in human imprisonment under the power of sin. This Paul insists on in the name of γραφή (*graphē*, Scripture).

The turning point is introduced as a unique, epochal event, dividing history into two eras: the era under the dominion of sin and the law, and the era of freedom, which dawns—which has dawned—with the coming of faith. The time of being under the παιδαγωγός is now past. When Paul speaks here of πίστις (*pistis*, faith) in the objective context of sacred history, he obviously means faith in Jesus Christ. His purpose is thus on the basis of the principle ὁ νόμος οὐκ ἔστιν ἐκ πίστεως (*ho nomos ouk estin ek pisteōs*, the law does not rest on faith) to emphasize the fundamental change that has taken place with the coming of Christ: the prison of sin has been opened, life in righteousness has been given. What was impossible through the law (ἐν νόμῳ οὐδεὶς δικαιοῦται παρὰ τῷ θεῷ [*en nomō oudeis dikaioutai para tō theō*, under the dominion of the law no one is justified before God: 3:11; cf. Rom. 8:3]) has become reality through the revelation of faith: δικαιοῦσθαι ἐκ πίστεως (*dikaiousthai ek pisteōs*, justification through faith).

Even though the law had no part in bringing this to pass, this justification is, nevertheless, the end and goal of the divine dispensation that willed imprisonment through sin and therefore also the function of the law, and made use of them for the purpose of salvation. A conflict between law and promise was rejected earlier on the grounds that the law was incapable of entering into competition with the promise (v. 21). Now, any suspicion of a conflict is eliminated by the fact that law and promise, despite the profound difference between them, are joined by the bond of the single salvific will of God. There are two sharply distinguished eras, but only one God. In this sense, too, it is true that ὁ δὲ θεὸς εἷς ἐστιν (*ho de theos heis estin*, God is one: v. 20). Paul is not a dualistic Gnostic.

Does this answer the question: τί οὖν ὁ νόμος (*ti oun ho nomos*, Why then the law?)? Probably it does so for Paul's train of thought, but the explanation is certainly not sufficient for our own understanding. On the contrary: the undertow of this question threatens to engulf all the concepts Paul draws on here. We are forced to ask not only: τί οὖν ὁ νόμος, but also τί οὖν ἡ ἁμαρτία (*ti oun hē hamartia*, Why then sin?), τί οὖν ἡ ἐπαγγελία (*ti oun hē epangelia*, Why then the promise?), τί οὖν ἡ δικαιοσύνη (*ti oun hē dikaiosynē*, Why righteousness?), τί οὖν ἡ πίστις (*ti oun hē pistis*, Why faith?). Paul's thought moves within a conceptuality that strikes us as a formulaic structure; we admire its inner consistency, but are somewhat perplexed as to how we might verify this language.

The most amazing thing about Paul's language is its antithetical reduction. This has two aspects. First, without qualifications or nuances, Paul sets up what appears to be a vastly oversimplified and forced black-and-white antithesis contrasting sin and righteousness, law and promise, works and faith, captivity and freedom, being under the one and being under the other, the era of one and the era of the other. Second, there is a related but not identical reduction to a handful of concepts, which, however, do not give the appearance of being a narrow ghettoization, but brim with life for Paul and are fraught with universal significance: sin, although a verdict of Scripture that is far from evident on the basis of experience, is nevertheless something that extends through the totality of life; righteousness, although referring to the relationship between human beings and God, is nevertheless crucial for what it means to be human; the law, although always in the first instance the Torah, is nevertheless something that has some analog among all human beings; the promise, although given to a single individual— Abraham—and fulfilled in a single individual—Christ, is nevertheless something that is meant for all and affects the ultimate future of all. Despite the sharp antitheses, this reduction is dominated by the notion of unity: ὁ δὲ θεὸς εἷς ἐστιν (*ho de theos heis estin*, but God is one), our section states (v. 20). The perspective in the next section is different, but unity is once again emphasized, and not by accident: πάντες γὰρ ὑμεῖς εἷς ἐστε ἐν Χριστῷ Ἰησοῦ (*pantes gar hymeis heis este in Christō Iēsou*, for you are all one in Christ Jesus: v. 28).

It would be inappropriate to try to do justice to this fundamental hermeneutical question in a short excursus. To examine it in more detail would be the job of a treatise on dogmatic theology, although even there the task could at best be addressed only fragmentarily. On the other hand, it would be a crucial omission if exegesis were to stop before understanding could lead to assent or a well-reasoned dissent.

Of course, we do not want to be guilty of the gross oversimplification of claiming that so far we have understood nothing of what Paul has been saying. What seems to be missing is primarily the ability to grasp what might be called the fundamental organizing principle of Paul's thought, the point of crystallization and the associated structure of this crystalline theology.

Do not take exception to this inadequate and only partially serviceable description of what is needed or to the apparently arrogant statement of the problem. What we are looking for is not a fixed schema like a crystal lattice, but an inner movement in which it is important to share. And of course exhaustive completeness is out of the question. It would be a great accomplishment just to find an encouraging incentive to think further and a suggestion as to the direction such thought should take. In the following discussion we shall focus on the concept of time, which according to our analysis determines the structure of Paul's argument in this section and the next.

Temporality leads to the phenomenon of life. We have already noted (in our interpretation of 2:10–20) that this concept appears the moment Paul describes in quite elementary terms what it means to say that faith in Jesus Christ makes people righteous.[33] The phenomenon of life, and thus also the antithesis of life and death, only seems to lead us away from Paul's focus on sacred history into narrow anthropology. The Pauline text itself gives us ample grounds for the association, as we have already noted in studying the relational language in 2:19–20.[34] Paul is concerned with the basis and end of life. These are questions we must also face, questions that confront us even though we are usually only vaguely aware of them or evade them completely. The clarity with which Paul grasps them is alien to us. But this need not prevent us from understanding them. It could actually turn out to be an enormously helpful resource for our understanding of our own life situation. The way we deal with the reality of life is usually the opposite of what we find so striking in Paul, his antithetical reduction and concentration. Usually life is diffuse and confused, a mixture of many factors both pleasant and unpleasant, complex and ambiguous. It rarely confronts us with authentic decisions, with an either/or.

This diffuseness can be illustrated by the way we encounter time. Everything under the sun presses its claim on us. We complain that time passes so quickly. Or we need some kind of distraction to kill time. It is quite normal that when we are engaged in our everyday business time crumbles into fragments, a rapid alternation of dates: burdensome times and enjoyable times, days we dread and days we look forward to, periods of boredom and periods of fulfillment. But even in the midst of this everyday experience of time we are aware of concentrations and antitheses, as can be seen even from our banal description. It does not require a long search to find analogs to what Paul speaks of as captivity and freedom, law and promise.

Life moves in a sequence of individual chunks of time, one hour after another, one day after another, one year after another. But the problem of time is not disposed of when time is broken down in this fashion, so that it comes and goes. Its course is irreversible and so life is irreversible. Every moment is unique and is of significance and import for life. Just as life is itself a single totality, so is the time allotted it. But not just in the sense of successive addition, but above all in the intertwining of temporal ecstasies. Time as it is lived is not merely—if at all—a continuous present in the flux of time; it is also a present realization of past and future. It is influenced by both, so that it is even possible to neglect the present in order to dwell in the past or to anticipate the future. Although this very fact shows how easy it is to lose the wholeness of time and the unity of life, they continue to draw attention to themselves. The death that awaits me reminds me of them. So does the recurring question of the meaning of the whole, who I really am, the fallible verdict others may reach concerning me or I may reach concerning myself, a verdict that comes infallibly and inescapably when time has run out and life is finished, even though it is now obscure to me whether any eye—and if so, what eye—beholds me from eternity. And so from time to time in the midst of time there is a concentration of time, when my gaze is not distracted by the variety of life but is directed instead at the single thing that ultimately demands decision.

This concentration is not amorphous but requires discrimination and decision. The features of ordinary life are blurred. Things that are accidental but momentarily near stand out with exaggerated clarity and intensity. But other things, matters of ultimate concern, are lost in a fog. On the other hand, the totality is revealed in all its coherence and the individual details are set in their proper context when such a concentration brings about a comprehensive discrimination that defines the outlines of life, so that an either/or, a yes/no imposes an ultimate order on apparent confusion.

Discrimination is of fundamental ontological relevance. Without discrimination there is no knowledge; without distinction there is no being. One must distinguish in order to unite. So it is with life. It attains clarity and authenticity only when one is able to distinguish those things that are confusingly confused. This is illustrated by language and by everything that shapes life through language, whether in the broad realm of what is possible or what is required, in short, the realm of technology or the realm of ethics. Religion is obviously concerned with ultimate distinctions. It therefore defines the coordinate system of life as a whole. But when religion vanishes, at least it leaves behind the problem of identifying the coordinates that determine life. It goes almost without saying that coordinate systems that impose ultimate distinctions on life and reality as a whole are not automatically desirable per se. Life can be terribly perverted and violated by antitheses that separate what belongs together instead of discriminating in a manner appropriate to human life, so that truth and falsehood, good and evil, what is salutary and what is pernicious may be distinguished for the benefit of life.

Once again we shall use time as an illustration. The question of discrimination and decision can be urgent even when the end is not involved. It is well known that the whole can suddenly make its demands felt in any part, the unconditional in the conditional, the ultimate in the transitory. This dimension of depth in time is what the word "eternity" means. But let us first keep to the question of how fundamental distinctions arise with respect to the temporality of life. It is impossible to ignore what no one can deny, that life is menaced and troubled. That which is hostile to life is a part of life itself. Death does not come just at the end of life; it is present in the midst of life; it is an instrument of life itself. Life is preserved by killing; in the act of living it can destroy not only other life but its own. What is intimated here points, on the one hand, to biological necessity but also and above all to the myriad manifestations of evil. Just as eternity can be understood as the depth dimension of time, so sin can be understood as the depth dimension of evil.

The wealth of phenomena that cry out to be illustrated will be exemplified by a single crucial phenomenon as it is presented in the Pauline text. It is a phenomenon that the secular world, too, is well aware of, to which the secular world may in fact be especially sensitive. We are prisoners of time and we would be free, as masters of time. This motif of captivity to time admits many variations. Consider our dependency on outward circumstances, on anonymous forces, on false consciousness, on social structures. The catalog denouncing such present-day enslavers is familiar, as is the corresponding plea for emancipation on every possible front by means of changes in the human situation.

But it is important also not to lose sight of the individual aspect of all this. This aspect demands our attention on the basis of common experience: how I use my time, how I waste it and squander its opportunities or overburden it with projects and expectations so that in either case I become slave to my time instead of being sovereign over it, devoting myself freely to the present and delighting in it. This individual aspect must be kept in mind when we consider the problems of time that affect humanity as a whole, which become problems of freedom. How does it happen that even where it is by no means inevitable we fall victim to time, to fashion, to the jargon of the moment, to intellectual fads? Even the watchwords and symbols of emancipation can prove to be mere variations on captivity and subservience to time. Why is freedom with respect to one's own time so rare, the courage to say and to do what the times do not expect, so that what the times demand may truly come to pass?

Our relationship to time gives us relatively easy access to the meaning of "law." We would not be true to our own experience if we were to think of "law" only in terms of specific statements instructing us what to do. Of course law always involves the articulation and possibly also the codification of what must be done. But the very inevitability with which we are required to do certain things makes us aware that we are at the mercy of an effectual and powerful law. Like an insatiable monster, time constantly demands that we do something but refuses to tell us clearly what we must do. And the mass of articulations that press upon us, stating what time requires us to do, makes it perfectly clear that the law is not just an intellectual construct; it is a reality, albeit a reality usually as confused and confusing as life itself.

We become fully sensible of one characteristic of the phenomenon "law" when we are confronted with its insatiability. Nothing that is done will completely silence its demands. One law always calls for new laws. We might say this is because time does not stand still. But we might also say it is because time is not fulfilled. Although the law is in some respects so powerful—for it subjects all without exception to its demands, representing the elemental spirits or powers of the universe, the στοιχεῖα τοῦ κόσμου (*stoicheia tou kosmou*: Gal. 4:3, 9; Col. 8, 20)—it is, nevertheless, remarkably powerless to make us masters of time. The law cannot make us truly free. It can ordain and establish the conditions of freedom, but to make free use of them is not in its power to give. This road does not lead to the root of what disorders and destroys human life. This is obviously connected with what Paul means when he denies works of the law the capacity to make us righteous, to justify us, to set us "right" in the full sense of the word.

On the other hand, our relationship to time does not appear to give us easy access to what "promise" means. Of course we know that no one can live without hope. Life imprisonment—that is almost the death penalty. Now there are probably many things that seem promising to us, that promise us some benefit. But first there is always something we must undertake and accomplish. Hard work pays off—that is the principle. Or else we set our hopes on good fortune in the form of something unexpected that will someday come to pass—a large inheritance or a happy human relationship. In either case what is promised depends on time; it comes with time and goes with time. Therefore, new objects of hope must constantly replace those that have been realized or discarded as unrealizable but in either case belong to the past. This kind of promise is therefore as insatiable as the law. Time passes over all our fulfilled wishes, if it does not in fact mostly bring disappointment. But even this trivial and short-lived experience of promise should not be despised. There is also this to say about life: along with all the demands it makes on us, all the labor it requires, it accords us infinitely much, far beyond what we can accomplish and independently of anything we do. Each piece of bread we are given to eat, each morning with which we begin a new day, each day past and what it brought us—do these not make us aware of something that brings courage and hope, something that holds a promise, because it reveals a ground of life that anticipates and far surpasses everything we do?

But if our eyes are to be opened to this vision, we need an explicit promise. Even here ordinary experience provides an analogy. Someone with a hopeful attitude, for whatever reason, looks at everything differently; many things look different to such a person and look upon such a person differently. But if there is to be more than a temporary attitude and perspective, if our concern is for a hope that transcends time and overcomes the world, we find that this hope is not simply available on demand. What is true of the law is even more true of the promise. Wherever there is life, the law is at work and is somehow already articulated. But it does not always attain an explication that corresponds to the will of God. Consider the decalog and the law of love—they are indispensable interpretations of the law, coming to us from a specific tradition. Above all, we do not always find a true understanding of the function of the law, what it can do and what its limitations are. For such an understanding of the law we are dependent on the New Testament. Nowhere else is there anything similar. This is connected with the special situation of the New Testament with respect to the phenomenon of promise. Traces of the promise are found everywhere; but to discover them and find hope in them and not fall victim to all the deceptive promises that are made on every side requires a ground of hope that does not depend on the presupposition that we still have time at our disposal and life left to live. All earthly hopes depend on this condition that there is still time remaining. A hope that transcends time and overcomes the world can be grounded only in a faith that knows of a radically liberating event, deliverance from the dominion of sin as the destroyer of true life, in other words, ζῳοποιεῖν (zōopoiein, making alive). Therefore, Paul's understanding of the promise is indissolubly linked with the *theologia crucis*. There is no other way to share in such a promise than the way of this promise itself, which leads from Abraham to Christ.

Does this not make not only the concentration but also the antithetical structure of Paul's thought accessible to us? The sharp distinction between law and promise creates problems for us, just as it did for Paul's Jewish contemporaries. Luther knew how difficult the distinction is that Paul demands here. He nevertheless thought that it was fundamentally the simplest thing imaginable: a horse could teach us that being fed oats is not the same thing as being harnessed.[35] A gift and a demand, a present and an obligation —everyone knows the difference. But to grasp this difference and maintain it when we must reach our verdict on life as a whole—this threatens to elude us and miscarry. In comparison the distinction between right and wrong, true and false, good and evil; the decision we are called on repeatedly to make under the most varied circumstances, is comparatively simple, however often it may fail in confused situations.

The distinction between law and promise and the corresponding distinction between works and faith presupposes the fundamental antithesis between the sinner and God, as well as the surprising transformation of this antithesis into the antithesis between sin and grace. Here the one contradicts and excludes the other. Not so, however, in the relationship between law and promise, works and faith. In this relationship there is a kind of both/and. They are intimately associated in our lives. Faith brings forth works. And the proper understanding of works demands faith. Only someone who has a personal experience of the law understands truly the meaning of the promise. And the law is rightly understood and used only by someone who knows the promise.

Nevertheless, making such distinctions involves more than the easy situation of having to distinguish between various aspects, realms, or perspectives in order to avoid confusion. We know this from experience: a financial transaction requires a different procedure than social welfare. In the scholarly world, too, there is an obvious distinction, for example, between literary analysis and chemical analysis. At first, therefore, nothing more seems to be involved than the separation of different aspects when the Reformers' interpretation of Paul distinguishes two types of righteousness: *iustitia operum* or *civilis* and *iustitia fidei* or *divina*, as well as a twofold use or function of the law—not, be it noted, two kinds of laws or two stages in the law, but a double use of the law,[36] the *usus civilis* or *politicus* and the *usus theologicus* or *elenchticus*. It is not necessary to pursue this matter further. But this much must be emphasized: the difficulty in making these distinctions is not intellectual. It is inherent in the very nature of life. This is the point at which everything keeps coming together. On the one hand, this is as it should be. The righteousness of faith is not meant to annul the righteousness or justice of civil life but to establish it in its right place. When one lives one's life, faith is not a separate entity alongside praxis. The totality of life constitutes a single nexus.

But alongside this legitimate interplay that comports with the nature of human life, there is the constant counterfeit interplay of law and promise, a confusion of works and faith, of *iustitia civilis* and *iustitia fidei*, that endangers and corrupts life, so that the divine grace is now indeed obscured by human accomplishment. In life these should be intimately linked, but they are instead usually catastrophically confused. Therefore, for the sake of life, there is need of preaching that can distinguish between law and gospel. And, therefore, there is need in turn for a theology that incorporates something of the intellectual comprehension of this distinction.

Is there here, too, a generally accessible indication of where this fundamental theological distinction has its roots in life itself? Our answer might run as follows: that we must distinguish between a person's utterances and the person is generally evident and relevant. It makes a difference whether we are dealing with specific acts of the human self in which this self is naturally presupposed but remains untouched in the protective shadow of this natural presupposition, or whether the very being of this self is called into question and challenged by the question of what constitutes its right and ground of life. Paul's way of discussing this difference and intervening in it may raise many problems for us. But that he touches here on a fundamental distinction within human existence—which could be symbolized by the terms *ratio* and *conscientia*—this should not be difficult for us to recognize and treat as a vital theme, since we live in an age of psychological and anthropological awareness. Who could deny that confusion in this area yields disastrous consequences?

During this last stage of our reflections we seem to have quite lost sight of the key notion of time. It seems that we might reintroduce it at this point by claiming that the distinction between the two kinds of *iustitia*, between works and faith, between law and promise, touches on the distinction between time and eternity. That is true. But the Pauline text raises a problem: although Paul does not deny the distinction between time and eternity, he speaks here of an epoch that distinguishes two times: the time of the law and the time of faith, the time of servitude and the time of freedom. The sequential relationship of these two phases of sacred history is strongly underlined by οὐκέτι (*ouketi*, no longer): ἐλθούσης δὲ τῆς πίστεως οὐκέτι ὑπὸ παιδαγωγόν ἐσμεν (*elthousēs de tēs pisteōs ouketi hypo paidagōgon esmen*, now that faith has come, we are no longer under a custodian: 3:25), ὥστε οὐκέτι εἶ δοῦλος ἀλλὰ υἱός (*hōste ouketi ei doulos alla hyios*, so you are no longer a slave but a son: 4:7). Does not this claim of temporal succession make nonsense of the distinction?

Let us for the moment ignore the pre-Christian era. In the Christian era it is clear that "being under the law" is still far from a dead issue. It ill behooves us to measure our vaunted maturity by the criterion of sonship as Paul understands it. At this point Luther seems to have deliberately ventured an interpretation contrary to the actual words of the text, seeing an unchronological both/and of two times in one and the same person: " . . . Christianus est divisus in 2 tempora: quatenus caro, est sub lege; quatenus spiritus, est sub Euangelio" (Christians are divided into two times: as flesh, they are under the law; as spirit, under the gospel).[37] This is not the place to go into the much-debated question of the relationship between Paul and Luther's exegesis of him. In any case Paul himself, despite the epoch he proclaims in sacred history, is aware of the struggle between flesh and spirit within every Christian (cf. 5:17). And Luther's speaking of two "tempora" (times) is probably more than a mere metaphorical accommodation to the Pauline text. First, the two times are not in equilibrium, and so he recognizes a movement: "Tempus legis non perpetuum . . . tempus gratiae sol aeternum sein" (The time of the law is not forever . . . the time of grace is to be eternal).[38] Second, like any pastor, he knows that it is not always appropriate to say the same thing. When law and when gospel—that is not a question of arbitrary prescription but of spiritual judgment. Ordinary experience confirms this. Although outwardly contemporaneous, in many ways we belong to very different times, especially with respect to our inmost being. Here, therefore, it is necessary to be especially conscientious in distinguishing what the times demand. Understanding of this task and sensitivity to its demands have never been more highly developed than under the influence of Pauline theology.

After this brief excursus, which has been able merely to suggest a few interpretive leads, let us return to an exegesis of the text.

Sons and Servants

3:26—4:11

26 For in Christ Jesus you are all sons of God through faith.

27 For all of you who were baptized into Christ have put on Christ.

28 There is neither Jew nor Greek, there is neither slave nor free, there is neither male nor female; for you are all one in Christ Jesus.

29 And if you are Christ's, then you are Abraham's seed, heirs according to promise.

4:1 I mean that the heir, as long as he is a minor, is no different from a slave, although he is lord of all;

2 but he is under guardians and trustees until the date set by the father.

3 So with us: when we were minors, we were slaves to the elemental spirits of the universe.

4 But when the fullness of time had come, God sent forth his Son, born of a woman, born under the law,

5 to redeem those who were under the law, that we might receive adoptive sonship.

6 And because you are sons, God has sent the Spirit of his Son into our hearts, crying, "Abba! Father!"

7 So you are no longer a slave but a son, and if a son then an heir through God.

8 Formerly, when you did not know God, you served gods that by nature are not gods.

9 But now that you have come to know God, or rather to be known by God, how can you turn back again to the weak and beggarly elemental spirits, whose slave you want to be once more?

10 You observe days, and months, and seasons, and years!

11 I fear for you, lest I have labored over you in vain.

Some light has already been cast on this section by the textual analysis with which the exegesis of the previous section began, as well as by the excursus with which it closed. The argument Paul now presents parallels the preceding, the reference to the epoch in sacred history that distinguishes being under the law from being in Christ. Now, however, instead of the Jewish Christian situation, Paul addresses primarily the gentile Christian situation. Therefore, the perspective is reversed. The new argument begins immediately where the previous one ended, with the fulfillment of the promise through the coming of faith (3:25). From there it returns via a new presentation of the epoch in sacred history (4:1–7) to the *status quo ante* and the danger of falling back into it (4:8–11), in order to demonstrate by this retrograde argument the absurdity of such a return.

This formal observation leads to an observation having to do with content. Although the inheritance promised to Abraham is still the theme, it is now treated on the personal rather than the institutional plane: not with reference to sacral history with a temporal sequence of διαϑήκη (*diathēkē*, testament), νόμος (*nomos*, law), and πίστις (*pistis*, faith) as transsubjective entities, but with reference to the biographical development of an heir who reaches majority and the absurdity of returning to minority.

This focuses attention on the notion of sonship. We have already met the expression υἱοὶ ’Αβραάμ (*hyioi Abraam*, sons of Abraham) in 3:7, and the notion of being children of Abraham, which also finds expression in the phrase σπέρμα ’Αβραάμ (*sperma Abraam*, seed of Abraham), controls the entire course of the argument in chapters 3 and 4. But the phrase υἱὸς τοῦ ϑεοῦ (*hyios tou theou*, son of God) has so far been used only with reference to Christ (1:16; 2:20). Now the two lines converge. The entire seed of Abraham is the Son of God (3:16). Therefore those who through faith in him have become sons of Abraham are sons of God, thanks to the Son of God. This sonship of those who have faith dominates the rest of the text.

Verse 26 begins thematically: πάντες γὰρ υἱοὶ ϑεοῦ ἐστε (*pantes gar hyioi theou este*, you are all sons of God). This is identified immediately with being sons of Abraham: ἄρα τοῦ ’Αβραὰμ σπέρμα ἐστέ (*ara tou Abraam sperma este*, therefore you are Abraham's seed: 3:29). The reason for υἱοϑεσία (*hyiothesia*, adoption as sons: 4:5) is then stated: God sent his Son (4:4). The consequence of this sharing in sonship is that God sent the Spirit of his Son (4:6). Therefore, the word υἱός (*hyios*, son) stands as a kind of middle term in the syllogistic summary of the argument (4:7).

The fact that the last subsection (4:8–11) forms part of the argument is clear when one notes the constituents of sonship as they are treated in 4:1ff. after the introductory description of sonship in 3:26–29: first by way of contrast the στοιχεῖα τοῦ κόσμου (*stoicheia tou kosmou*, elemental spirits of the universe) as the dominant created powers during the period of minority (4:3), then—incipiently trinitarian—the Son (4:4–5) and the Spirit (4:6), and finally—as the culmination of these last verses, which seem to speak only of imminent destruction (4:8–11)—God the Father (4:7 end and 4:9a).

The identification of "sons of Abraham" with "sons of God" and its derivation from the divine sonship of Christ are enlightening but also problematical. If to be a son of Abraham is to be a son of God, such sonship is not

208

genealogical. This makes it impossible for it to come about κατὰ σάρκα (*kata sarka*, according to the flesh); it cannot be understood or boasted of κατὰ σάρκα. Here everything can only be κατὰ πνεῦμα (*kata pneuma*, according to the Spirit: cf. 4:29). Just as Paul denies that the so-called gods are gods by nature (4:8), so it could also be said of us: we are οἱ φύσει μὴ ὄντες υἱοὶ θεοῦ (*hoi physei mē ontes hyioi theou*, those who by nature are not sons of God). We are sons only by adoption, by υἱοθεσία (4:5). Not, therefore, φύσει (*physei*, by nature) but θέσει (*thesei*, by decree), the Stoic distinction lurking in the background. With reference to the so-called gods, the qualification θέσει represents a human and therefore arbitrary and impotent decree—these gods are ciphers—but the θέσει of divine υἱοθεσία (*hyiothesia*, adoption) refers to an eternally valid and authoritative decree of the God who makes alive and calls into being that which is not (Rom. 4:17). This understanding of sonship κατὰ πνεῦμα (*kata pneuma*, according to the Spirit) is explained by Paul with reference to its basis in what is obviously a change that occurs within time: διὰ τῆς πίστεως ἐν Χριστῷ ᾿Ιησοῦ (*dia tēs pisteōs en Christō Iēsou*, through faith in Christ Jesus: v. 26).

The association with Jesus Christ is meant to indicate a double relationship. First, our sonship corresponds to his sonship, because it is brought about by his sonship. On the other hand, however, for this very reason our sonship differs from his. What it means to say that we are God's sons is defined in terms of Jesus Christ. In addition to 4:4–5, other christological formulas in Galatians also provide important evidence (1:4; 2:20; 3:13). Here all human fantasies about the meaning of divine sonship are scattered to the winds. But there is also an indirect warning against weakening the unprecedented statement that we are God's sons through a terminological distinction, to the effect that we are children of God, in contrast to the only Son of God. This could result in a failure to observe the internal relationship between the two expressions.

Observe Paul's deliberately nuanced language here. He speaks of the Galatians as his children (τέκνα, *tekna*: 4:19), but as God's sons (υἱοὶ θεοῦ, *hyioi theou*). It is true that Paul sometimes uses the expression τέκνα θεοῦ (*tekna theou*, children of God), as in Rom. 8:16–17, 21; 9:8. The distinction between the υἱός τοῦ θεοῦ (*hyios tou theou*, Son of God) and the τέκνα τοῦ θεοῦ (*tekna tou theou*, children of God) is primarily Johannine; but the truth it reflects is expressed in a different way by Paul in Galatians. While we are God's adopted sons, Jesus Christ is God's preexistent Son and therefore not θέσει (*thesei*, by decree) but φύσει (*physei*, by nature). Paul does not state the difference in these terms, but he could certainly do so in contrast to 4:8.

The explanation that divine sonship has come about through faith parallels its derivation from Jesus Christ. Thus, Paul takes up the immediately preceding statement about the coming of faith (vv. 23 and 25). The reference to faith can be taken as an interpretive gloss on the wholly appropriate κατὰ πνεῦμα (*kata pneuma*, according to the Spirit). Its purpose is not to shift divine sonship to the future—the present tense is emphasized!—but to protect against the misinterpretation that such sonship belongs only to a spiritual elite. "All of you" are God's sons, as Paul states emphatically (v. 26; cf. v. 28b). And ὅσοι (*hosoi*, all who: v. 27) takes up the same thought with reference to all the baptized. Whether the phrase διὰ τῆς πίστεως (*dia tēs pisteōs*, through faith) also applies here must be determined from how baptism is related to the argument.

This is the only explicit mention of baptism in Galatians. It must not be forced to contribute more than its appropriate share to the Pauline understanding of baptism. It would be risky simply to supplement it on the basis of the baptismal theology in Romans 6, but it would also be overly hasty to interpret negatively Paul's reserve with respect to his own baptizing of others (cf. 1 Cor. 1:14–17). There are some stylistic grounds for believing that Paul is drawing here on a formula from the baptismal liturgy. Verses 26–28 could be understood easily as a declaration addressed to the newly baptized, stating the meaning of their baptism and who they are thereafter: a statement of identity and in tenor a performative declaration. The structure of this liturgical formula would be even clearer if v. 26 were accommodated to v. 28b by taking the phrase διὰ τῆς πίστεως (*dia tēs pisteōs*, through faith: v. 26) as a Pauline addition. Then the original baptismal formula would exhibit the same structure twice: πάντες γὰρ υἱοὶ θεοῦ ἐστε ἐν Χριστῷ Ἰησοῦ (*pantes gar hyioi theou este en Christō Iēsou*, for you are all sons of God in Christ Jesus), and πάντες γὰρ ὑμεῖς εἷς ἐστε ἐν Χριστῷ Ἰησοῦ (*pantes gar hymeis heis este in Christō Iēsou*, for you are all one in Christ Jesus). These twin declarations frame the statement about baptism as a "putting on of Christ," through which all distinctions that separate people are removed.

Such a traditio-historical hypothesis could also be supported by the observation that only the first pair of opposites (Jew/Greek) has any meaning in the context of Galatians. In the following section of the letter, the contrast between slave and free is not considered sociologically but theologically; far from being declared void, it is in fact affirmed. And there is not only no occasion to mention the difference between the sexes, it even appears to disagree with other statements of Paul on the subject (e.g., 1 Cor. 11:3–12). The discrepancy is even more marked here than in the question of slavery.

But even if we are right in assuming that Paul is drawing on traditional language here, the borrowing must be taken as an affirmation of the formula on the part of the Apostle. It is even worth considering the possibility that Paul had a hand in shaping the liturgical formula. On the other side, there is also the real possibility—in addition to the recognizable insertion of διὰ τῆς πίστεως (*dia tēs pisteōs*, through faith) in v. 26—that differences of interpretation played a role in the use of the formula. On the basis of this hypothesis we can outline Paul's understanding of these verses as follows.

The reminder of baptism emphasizes that divine sonship is based on a unique event, the epoch marked by the sending of Jesus Christ and the coming of faith. The purpose is not to make the trivial point that all human beings are children of God; neither is it to cite the inner transformation of the individual and the personal decision to be baptized. Of course baptism is an act performed on an individual who has said "Yes!" to faith. But this individual act proclaims nothing less than what took place for all people and for all time. It would, therefore, be contrary to Paul's understanding of baptism to see a tension between baptism and faith or between baptism and the proclamation of the word. The emphatic and explicit statement διὰ τῆς πίστεως (*dia tēs pisteōs*, through faith) here means the same as ἐξ ἀκοῆς πίστεως (*ex akoēs pisteōs*, through the message of faith: 3:2, 5) and stands in contrast to ἐξ ἔργων νόμου (*ex ergōn nomou*, through works of the law: ibid.), and thus also to everything that might be hoped for from the νόμος (*nomos*, law).

Of course, it is only through our own faith that we share in the faith that came through Christ to free us from being under the law. The act of baptism is obviously not an isolated *opus operatum*. It cannot be performed without an accompanying declaration like this liturgical formula, bearing witness to and appropriating the Christ event. Performed once and yet extending throughout an entire individual life—this is a lemma to assist our understanding of the entire problem. It is implicit in the phrase διὰ τῆς πίστεως (*dia tēs pisteōs*, through faith)—a canon of interpretation that applies not only to the baptismal event itself but also to everything these verses say about the being of those who are baptized.

The baptismal event is described as "putting on Christ." The verb ἐνδύ-εσθαι (*endyesthai*, clothe oneself) with accusative object is in the middle voice. One generally puts on and takes off one's own clothing. In the present instance, however, it would be well to take the verb as being passive in meaning. One cannot baptize oneself; neither can one put on Christ in the sense of clothing oneself in Christ as a garment. This appears to contradict Rom. 13:14; but the latter passage speaks in an imperative of putting on Christ, and in contrast to our passage (Gal. 3:27) it refers not to a single act but to a continuing process. This merely reflects the πίστις (*pistis*, faith) structure of the Christ reality. Its perfective-indicative nature gives rise to the imperative in order to express this structure. The imperative thus presupposes the indicative, demanding an acknowledgment of the indicative and a constant return to it. The life of one who is baptized is thus a constant recollection of baptism, a repeated return to it that is always new. Its meaning transcends all earthly life. Although the act of baptism lies in the past, it is always far in advance of all of the life that lies before us.

The metaphor of putting on a garment requires further explanation. It suggests not just protection from the elements, but protection from the gaze of others. But even this does not touch the heart of the matter. The point is not the contrast between prudery and the joy of nakedness, which itself can take a variety of forms, as may be illustrated by comparing the Greek sense of beauty with the modern commercialization of sex. Closer to the mark are proverbs such as "Clothes make the man," the function of a disguise, or even ceremonial investiture. Our clothing ornaments and exalts us, it lends us honor and esteem. The symbolic sense of the Middle Ages had a highly developed appreciation of this function of costume. Therefore class-related sumptuary laws were the subject of perpetual political debate. We get a clearer picture of the phenomenon from noting the role played by a uniform or from observing how protests against the bourgeois establishment find expression in typical styles of dress.

Our text, however, deals with a more radical transformation than that effected outwardly by a change of clothes. It would take deep exploration of the symbolic language of religion and the ontological structure of being human to describe the full extent of the relationship between human beings and garments. The body itself can be thought of as a garment; fear of disembodied nakedness gives rise to the need for a new resurrected body, as we also read in Paul (2 Cor. 5:1–4). On this basis we could establish an analogous relationship to the incorporation of those who have faith into the body of Christ.

In any case, putting on Christ means more than a mere change of clothing, beneath which I remain the same and only appear to be someone else. Neither does it mean being clothed like Christ, in the sense that those who have faith wear a kind of Christian uniform. It means being clothed with Christ himself. This notion merges into the paradoxical-seeming idea of putting on a new humanity (Eph. 4:24; Col. 3:10). Putting on Christ does not merely change my outward appearance or something related to my own being. It affects something within me so deeply that Christ himself becomes my own self (2:20). Those who have put on Christ have put off their own selves, they are released and set free from themselves. They look upon themselves as being past and as being totally incorporated into the future that has already begun with being in Christ.

The unity established as a shared being in Christ through baptism into Christ is expressed not impersonally with a neuter but personally. Paul does not say: ἕν ἐστε (*hen este*, you are one [thing]), but: εἷς ἐστε ἐν Χριστῷ Ἰησοῦ (*heis este en Christō Iēsou*, you are one [person] in Christ Jesus: v. 28). This avoids the misunderstanding that would reduce human beings to the uniformity of mere functionaries, denying themselves (in a pejorative sense) and merely playing a role instead of following the example of Christ, acknowledging themselves openly and finding their true identity in Christ without role-playing. Unless our definition of "uniformity" is pushed in the direction suggested by the Aristotelian concept of form, then Christ could be considered the essential form of those who are baptized. This would agree in a way with the Pauline understanding of unity, which can be defined in terms of the Aristotelian understanding of *eidos* as a unity of spirit as well as a unity of body. Thus we read in 1 Cor. 12:13, a passage closely related to Gal. 3:27–28: "By one and the same Spirit we were all baptized into one body, Jews or Greeks, slaves or free."

What are we to make of this resolution of fundamental human opposites in the unity of being in Christ? Paul cites three examples. And they are in fact only examples. The series could be extended at will: black or white, Republican or Democrat, Capitalist or Communist, conservative or liberal. Or in other terms no less provocative: there are no longer the bright and the retarded, the educated and the uneducated, the depressed and the happy. Or again: clergy or laity, religious or secular, strong and self-sufficient or thin-skinned and assailed by doubts. Such extensions of the catalog are useful ways to internalize what Paul means, but they can also serve to blunt his real point.

For this very reason the pairs of opposites named by Paul are more than exemplary. They are especially well chosen to represent the tensions from which we suffer but from which we also draw our life. These are first of all religious tensions with their concomitant racial background, then social tensions with their material basis and biological tensions between the sexes. In all these instances there is a confusion of natural and historical causes. It is impossible simply to turn our backs on human differences as being unnatural, nothing more than human constructs. Even where this verdict is easiest to sustain, in the case of class differences between the oppressors and the oppressed, one must recognize that there are preexisting natural differences at work that cannot be eliminated. On the other hand, even the most natural and—if one may say so—wonderful human difference, the difference between male and female, expresses itself historically in forms that are offensive if not actually unnatural. All these opposites involve an element of hostility. In part they lead to pernicious and even inhuman results, in part they are necessary for the continuation of life.

The latter is true not only of sexuality, but also of ethnic differences —think of the importance of one's native language or the security of one's native land. It is true in a sense even of class distinctions, as a totally undifferentiated and atomized society demonstrates. But the positive aspect of such polar structures in human life is never free from problematic manifestations that tend toward inhumanity. Therefore, the human attitude toward them is inherently contradictory. Sometimes such differences, often even including their pernicious aspects, are affirmed and supported with a blind passion. Sometimes there is a utopian yearning to overcome them, to establish a state of universal peace, equality, and justice. But even the struggle for this goal can be highly contradictory, as can be seen from the gamut of reactions against the difference between the sexes: from extreme feminist ideas of women's liberation or homosexuality or transvestism to the ascetic ideal of virginity or even androgynous myths that dream of abolishing this difference totally.

The perspectives opened by the distinctions fit surprisingly well into Paul's overall theme. We see that this tense juxtaposition and hostility of fundamental human differences and polarities exemplifies the powers that control life and history. They illustrate vividly the reality of the στοιχεῖα τοῦ κόσμου (stoicheia tou kosmou, elemental spirits of the universe: 4:3, 9). At the same time they make clear what the νόμος (nomos, law) is about: it not only issues decrees but creates institutions to keep order among people threatened by chaos and self-destruction, although often the only result is legalization of violence and injustice. Paul characterizes the νόμος (nomos, law) as a prison guard and a disreputable παιδαγωγός (paidagōgos, attendant), then states that its time has come to an end with the appearance of Jesus Christ. He preaches deliverance from enslavement to the στοιχεῖα τοῦ κόσμου (stoicheia tou kosmou, elemental spirits of the universe), which he denigrates as being poor and contemptible. By so doing he issues a challenge to these vast dimensions and harsh realities of human history, thus also exposing himself to the question of what he is accomplishing by such a challenge and denigration based on the proclamation of a radical turning point in history. Is he not preaching a frivolous enthusiasm that sows chaos everywhere? Or is he gambling on a human yearning that cannot be fulfilled and is therefore disappointed all the more bitterly?

Paul's struggle is the same throughout. The gospel must not be falsified and turned into a new law; the body of Christ must not be transformed into political zealotry of whatever shade. That has always aroused false hopes, which have been shattered. How could something that is part of the form of this world be removed from the world? It is obvious that the difference between the sexes cannot be done away with. For primitive Christianity, considered in its historical context, a universal emancipation of all slaves was not a realistic possibility. When the emancipation finally did come about, as was proper, it did not mark a soteriological epoch but resulted in a historical change of scene that cloaked the ancient evil in other manifestations. Finally, the difference between Jews and Gentiles Paul was unable and unwilling to eliminate. The fact that later, under Christian auspices, it took on demonic dimensions is a terrible symptom of the constant threat that Christianity will be perverted by a return to slavery to the elemental spirits of the universe.

For in the body of Christ all these polarities are invalidated, not just in word but in fact. Paul attaches absolute priority to the definitive removal of what separates Jews from Gentiles before God. In Christ they are one with each other: the Israel of God (6:16). The difference that still remains between them does not contradict this fact. Instead, in the mutual relationship of the members of the body of Christ to each other it becomes the material for love. The situation is analogous for the outstanding social distinction of the period. In the ἐκκλησία (*ekklēsia*, church) a slave is not a slave; the freedom of one who is free is not measured by the criterion of social class. Both are free through Jesus Christ and for this very reason belong totally to him; they are his slaves and are therefore not in bondage to any worldly power. Even the difference between male and female, which imposes the maximum caution on the apostle lest the freedom of the Spirit degenerate into anarchy, is fundamentally invalidated by the fact that each sees in the other someone for whom Christ has died.

Out of caution, Paul undertook to preserve the distinction between a program of emancipation and a spiritual liberation that leads to a self-understanding and conduct toward others based on Christ. This very caution dramatizes the existence of a place in the world where things are different: Jews and Gentiles share the same table; slaves and free citizens are treated equally as brothers and sisters; women are accorded a respect that is more substantial than a merely outward and sometimes two-edged "equality."

The triumphant tone of the equality formula thus seems somewhat subdued, and rightly so, to the extent that it may be transformed unthinkingly into slogans of emancipation, losing its ties to the significance of having become sons of God. People attach great importance to these differences, allowing themselves to become captive to them so that they control their lives. For Paul, however, these differences have lost all their meaning through the coming of faith. To be set free from that madness through adoption as sons of God—that is indeed cause for a sense of triumphant ascendancy. Its emancipatory consequences in the circumstances of the world have no limit but do have a criterion by which they may be judged; it appears in the phrase διὰ τῆς πίστεως (dia tēs pisteōs, through faith: v. 26) and consists in the freedom to love that comes through faith. This is the primary subject of the last two chapters of Galatians.

We need not analyze in detail the new legal metaphor Paul uses to explain the dramatic change that makes us sons (4:1–2). Whether and where in the ancient world we can demonstrate that the underlying concepts of majority and inheritance were legally in force is irrelevant to Paul's purpose. We can also pass over the minor inconsistency between the metaphor of reaching majority and that of adoption. The former emphasizes the contrast between two stages set apart by a critical date. This leads in turn to the epoch marked by Christ and the increasingly important contrast between slavery and freedom. The latter metaphor serves to interpret sonship itself—not just the right of inheritance—as a gift deriving from the sending of the Son of God.

Now when we turn to the state of minority or enslavement, we note that Paul describes it primarily in terms of the pagan past of the Galatians, but also brings the Torah into the discussion, apparently deliberately. There are no concrete references to the earlier religion of the Galatians. Religious syncretism and exposure to a variety of cults are probably in the background. The few hints suggest a polytheism (v. 8) involving devotion to the στοιχεῖα τοῦ κόσμου (stoicheia tou kosmou, elemental spirits of the universe: vv. 3, 9) and the observation of cyclically recurring times with an astrological background (v. 10a). The concept of "elemental spirits of the universe" seems also to suggest a spirituality focused on nature and natural phenomena. But the modern distinction between nature and history cannot be applied to a religiosity involving the world as a whole. The central element was probably a feeling that life is dependent on personified universal powers; dread of what fate might have in store probably mingled with an attempt somehow to manipulate it, as in the use of horoscopes today.

These reminiscences of the Galatians' pagan past are now mixed with their relationship to Judaism. The first thing to notice is that the expected use of the second person plural is not consistent. The change of person in the preceding text is easy to explain. The use of the first person plural in 3:23–25 corresponds to the fact that the epoch described there has come for both

Jews and Christians. When Paul shifts to the second person plural in 3:26–29, it is because he is now addressing the gentile Christian situation of the Galatians. Even if this form of address derives from the embedded fragment of the traditional baptismal liturgy, the two explanations would still be compatible. To address the Galatians as they were addressed at the time of their baptism would be highly appropriate to the course of the argument. Paul also retains the second person plural in 4:8–11. What is striking is that in v. 3, which speaks explicitly of former cultic enslavement to the στοιχεῖα (*stoicheia*, elemental spirits), the first person plural reappears, while in v. 6 both forms of the pronoun are almost inextricably interwoven: because *you* are sons, therefore God has sent the Spirit of his Son into *our* hearts.

Particularly noteworthy is the use of the second person singular in v. 7: "So you are no longer a slave but a son, and if a son then an heir through God." Apart from the words addressed to Peter at Antioch quoted in 2:14 and the formulaic "Behold!" used as a particle in 5:2, the second person singular occurs only here and in 6:1. Its appearance in 4:7 may be due to the gnomic form of the statement, if the close approximation to the situation of prayer was not the influencing factor. But the significant point is this: Paul uses a single "we" to include both himself as a Jewish Christian, and therefore the Jewish Christians as a whole, with the gentile Christians, not only in the miracle of their oneness through the sending of the Spirit into their hearts (v. 6) but also in the time of their strictest separation, their past as Jews and Gentiles. Of course, he cannot do the same thing in v. 8. That the Jews were as ignorant of God as the Gentiles can be stated only with major restrictions; it is hardly possible to make the general claim that they served gods that by nature are no gods. Nevertheless, Paul does not seem to hesitate to find the common denominator of their antithetical pasts in the enslavement of all, Jews as well as Gentiles, to the elemental spirits of the universe.

This is met by a further striking conjunction from the opposite perspective. That v. 4 should speak of the νόμος (*nomos*, law) is a necessary implication of the christological statement. The Son of God was born as a Jew and was therefore under the Torah. Paul does not mention this as a chance biographical observation, but because it is the key to a soteriological understanding of the Christ event. For it to have happened in any other way—that the Son of God might have been born a Gentile!—would have seemed an absurd idea to Paul. Whether and how history might have been different is not even a matter for idle speculation. The soteriological nature of the Christ event depends on its being an integral part of God's sacred history with Israel. But it is by no means limited to a connection with the promise to Abraham. It is quite conceivable that the connection might have involved something other than the intervening period of the law. At least as important to Paul as the promise to Abraham is the situation of the Christ event within the period of sovereignty of the law, for otherwise the sovereignty of the law could not have been overcome.

According to this view, then, the soteriological event finds its more pressing occasion and stronger resistance not in the gentile world, where people did not know God and worshiped other so-called gods, but in Judaism, where God was known and worshiped under the sign of the law. Therefore, the law and the consequent crucifixion of Jesus are not accidental circumstances of the soteriological event but are of fundamental significance to it. Even though this is not stated explicitly, it is in the background when Paul speaks of the atonement (1:4; 2:20). But it is also emphasized *expressis verbis* when the curse of the cross, because decreed by the law, is understood as redeeming us from the law (3:13; cf. also 2:19). When Paul uses the first person plural here ("Christ redeemed us from the curse of the law"), he is thinking of the situation from the perspective of the law. But the statement refers not just to those who live under the Torah. Otherwise the christological principle previously stated would be untenable: there can be no christological statement that does not apply in some form to both Jews and Gentiles. Because all of us, Jews and non-Jews, have been redeemed from the curse of the law, this curse lay upon us all, albeit under different conditions.

This "we" comprising both Jews and Gentiles appears also in 4:5, explicitly in the second ἵνα (*hina*, so that) clause, where it refers to those who have been adopted as sons of God, but also implicitly in the first ἵνα (*hina*, so that) clause. For although οἱ ὑπὸ νόμον (*hoi hypo nomon*, those under the law) refers in the narrow sense to the Jews, who are under the Torah, it also includes the Gentiles as being likewise subject to the law. This is implicit in the logic of the argument, and is based on the concept of legal minority, which had the same effect among both Gentiles and Jews. In the earlier history of the gentile Christians, the role of the νόμος (*nomos*, law) as παιδαγωγός (*paidagōgos*, custodian: 3:24) was played by a variety of guardians and trustees (4:2). Standard legal practice requires only a single guardian in each case; it is reasonable to suppose that Paul deliberately introduced the plural here in order to express the plurality of enslaving powers that are the gentile counterparts to the one Torah. This does not, however, alter the fact that we are dealing here with an equivalent to the Torah that makes it possible to say that the Gentiles are also ὑπὸ νόμον (*hypo nomon*, under the law). And that is not all. The argument can be reversed. The Jews' being ὑπὸ νόμον appears likewise as a form of slavery under the στοιχεῖα τοῦ κόσμου (*stoicheia tou kosmou*, elemental spirits of the universe).

This shocking notion is rendered even more difficult by what follows. The Galatians have been urged to follow the Torah; it has been commended to them on the grounds that this is the way of further religious progress. Paul, however, declares it to be a return to the bondage of their earlier minority. Paul does not accuse them of wanting to worship once more the φύσει μὴ ὄντες θεοί (*physei mē ontes theoi*, beings that by nature are not gods). Outwardly there is nothing to suggest that they are thinking of returning to polytheism. But what else can be meant when Paul declares the alleged progress to be a hopeless return to enslavement under the στοιχεῖα (*stoicheia*, elemental spirits)? In a word, by subjecting themselves to the Torah they are returning to paganism.

This Pauline provocation may be understood more readily when one examines the mutual interpenetration of gentile and Jewish religion in the medium of Hellenistic syncretism and finds points of contact between speculative Jewish angelology and some variety of teaching concerning elemental spirits of the universe. What Paul says in 3:19 about the origin of the law also bears on this question. But nothing can ameliorate the harshness of Paul's verdict. He is not trying to prevent a paganization of Judaism. On the contrary: because in Christ the distinction between Jew and Gentile has been overcome by faith, the inherently fundamental difference is not so much abrogated as retrospectively relativized. With respect to bondage the difference vanishes and becomes identity. The verdict "one in Christ" (3:28) implies as a kind of mirror image that Jews and Gentiles, separated before and apart from Christ, are nevertheless fundamentally the same. Only an examination of Romans would show how Paul carries this idea to its logical conclusion in his doctrine of the law, paving the way for a generalized version of the law as a theological concept.

We have already dealt proleptically with vv. 4–5. Beyond what has already been said, the following points may be made concerning the sending of the Son of God.

First, Paul presents the two eras of bondage and sonship as a sharply defined temporal succession without any transitional stages. Nothing is said of preparation or development, of spiritual progress to achieve divine sonship. The turning point—like the date set by the father—depends only on God's determination to send his Son.

Second, in contrast to enslavement to the spirits of the universe and their temporal cycle, the strict distinction here between God and the world leads to liberation through the sending of God's Son into the world. Time is not understood as a wheel, recurring in a merciless cycle of eternal return, but as leading up to a unique and crucial epochal event.

Third, the sending of the Son of God does not take place as human desires would have it. What 4:1 says about the minor could apply as well to Jesus Christ: οὐδὲν διαφέρει δούλου κύριος πάντων ὤν (*ouden diapherei doulou kyrios pantōn ōn*, he is no better than a slave, although he is the lord over all). He appeared in the form of a slave (Phil. 2:7) as an ordinary human being, born of a woman (an expression that must not be taken as referring to the Virgin birth simply because the father is not mentioned) and subject to the law. His appearance, therefore, although he is Lord over all, expresses the situation of a minor or a slave. Instead of demonstrating deliverance from enslavement under the law, he takes the curse of the law upon himself, submitting utterly to its dominion.

Finally, this is in fact how the Son achieves deliverance of those who are subject to the law. Deliverance comes not through abrogation of the law but through its fulfillment, not through instruction in how to find freedom for oneself but through vicarious suffering on behalf of others who are thereby set free. Freedom in the sense meant here exists only in the form of being set free. But this deliverance is brought about not through transformation of the world around us—which can only be a result—but through transformation of our relationship to God, and not as a consequence of an inward transformation—this, too, is one of the results—but as a consequence of God's transformation of the situation, through God's adoption, which is mediated only through our being pronounced his sons.

Thus, at the very moment the promise is fulfilled all still remains under the sign of the promise. The εὐαγγέλιον (*euangelion*, gospel) does not bring the ἐπαγγελία (*epangelia*, promise) to an end. It is fulfilled initially by being grasped as a pure ἐπαγγελία. Therefore the era of mere faith is not past once the Son of God has appeared, and our adoption as sons of God has been proclaimed. On the contrary, only now has the era of faith come. Fulfillment of the promise does not render faith unnecessary by virtue of secure possession, as though faith were merely the symptom that fulfillment of the promise is yet to come, as though those who have faith were "have-nots." Faith is itself the fulfillment of the promise. As Luther says, "Glaubst du, so hast du" (if you have faith, you have everything).[39] Faith is the fullness and fulfillment of promise. Those who know they are accepted as God's sons because they have accepted the Son sent by God are filled totally with the knowledge that only this sonship is truly promising. They therefore know only the promise and know the law only as fulfilled by Christ. This christological basis of freedom determines not only how freedom is realized but above all how it is understood. Paul's text fills in the details later when it speaks at more length of Christian freedom.

Alongside the statement about the sending of the Son we find the parallel statement about the sending of the Spirit (v. 6). Here, too, we shall merely note a few points.

First, the parallelism does not indicate an alternative to the sending of the Son but something that belongs inseparably to the sending of the Son while, nevertheless, being a consequence of that sending, remaining distinct. So Paul establishes a causal relationship: "Because you are sons, God sent the Spirit. . . ." Receiving the Spirit does not make us sons; it is our being made sons that enables us to receive the Spirit.

This might seem to contradict Rom. 8:14–17, which is closely related to our present text: "For all who are led by the Spirit of God are sons of God. For you did not receive the spirit of slavery to fall back into fear, but you have received the spirit of sonship, through which we cry, 'Abba! Father!' And it is the Spirit himself bearing witness with our spirit that we are children of God. But if we are his children, then we are also heirs, heirs of God as fellow heirs with Christ, who [now] suffer with him in order that [later] we may also be glorified with him." Even here, however, being filled with the Spirit does not constitute the ground of our being God's sons, but rather the ground of our knowing that we are God's sons. It is not what takes place within and issues forth from our hearts—important as it is—that makes us sons of God. Our sonship is brought about instead by what issues from the heart of God and comes to us in the appearance of Jesus Christ: the υἱοθεσία (*hyiothesia*, adoption) that is proclaimed through the spoken word of the ἀκοὴ πίστεως (*akoē pisteōs*, message of faith), but is then testified to through the voice of the Spirit in the hearts of those who have faith.

Second, going beyond this inner causal relationship between the sending of the Son and the sending of the Spirit, Paul emphasizes the close connection between sonship and the Spirit. He calls the Spirit (and not just here) the Spirit of the Son of God. From the perspective of later trinitarian theology, one might venture to find support here for the *filioque*, the procession of the Spirit from the Father and the Son. Strictly speaking, however, this ἐκπόρευσις (*ekporeusis*, procession) refers to something that takes place within the Trinity. Only in this sense does the Eastern Church reject the *filioque*; it has no quarrel with the christological association of the historical sending of the Spirit. This is undoubtedly the crucial point: the Spirit must not become an independent soteriological principle. Pneumatology must not compete with Christology.

221

The crucified Christ is the criterion by which the Spirit is rightly understood and spirits are distinguished. No spirit that does not meet this criterion is Holy Spirit. Here and in Rom. 8:15 Paul accordingly cites something quite unspectacular as the true and definitive manifestation of the Spirit: the Spirit causes us to address God as "Father." The Spirit is the Spirit of sonship and hence the Spirit of prayer. The Spirit responds to υἱοθεσία (*hyiothesia*, adoption) by calling God "Abba!" That is the unsurpassable sign of sonship and the Spirit. Words expressing absolute dependence on God express absolute freedom. There is no direct evidence in Galatians for polemic against spiritual enthusiasm. In any case, however, Paul gives us here an important commentary on the Galatians' experience of the Spirit, the experience he refers to at the beginning of his argument (3:1–5). The Galatians received the Spirit ἐξ ἀκοῆς πίστεως (*ex akoēs pisteōs*, through the message of faith) and not ἐξ ἔργων νόμου (*ex ergōn nomou*, through works of the law); they comprehend the Spirit as the Spirit of the Son of God only when they see, in their ability to cry out "Abba!" vouchsafed by the Spirit, the infallible and sufficient sign that they are sons of God—here, not in any extraordinary ecstatic manifestations nor in an allegedly more trustworthy guarantee of divine sonship through acceptance of circumcision.

Here it is the Spirit who cries or even shouts out; in Rom. 8:15 it is we ourselves, moved by the Spirit, who cry and shout. This, too, is not a contradiction. One must remember that according to Rom. 8:26–27 the Spirit helps us in our weakness, interceding for us with wordless sighs far beyond our comprehension; but God, who searches human hearts, understands them well. There is no need to resort to extravagant phenomena like glossolalia in order to describe experiences of the Spirit and even share such experiences. The sighs of our prayer express more than we are able to articulate. The use of "Abba!" as a form of address in prayer goes back to the earliest Christian community; this is why it was preserved in its original Aramaic. It is highly probable that the usage goes back to Jesus himself. For Paul, "Abba!" is a fundamental sound in the language of the Spirit. In it our weakness and the power of the Spirit come together in a manner paralleling the christological polarity of ἀσθένεια (*astheneia*, weakness) and δύναμις (*dynamis*, power) (cf. 2 Cor. 12:9; 13:3–4).

Sonship by nature implies an originating father. Paul accordingly describes divine sonship in the sending of the Son and of the Spirit as originating with the Father. But divine sonship manifests itself in a return to the Father, so that it also concludes with the Father. The entire Pauline teaching about the law and justification, apparently so complicated, is reduced to the simplest possible terms, so that at this point we hear in Paul the voice of Jesus himself. What took place through Jesus Christ and what was accomplished by the coming of faith can be reduced to our ability to address God as "Father" with all our heart. Therefore, in the structure of these verses all statements about the Spirit are not only grounded in statements about God but also evolve into such statements. The apostrophe ἀββὰ ὁ πατήρ (*abba ho patēr*, Abba! Father!) in v. 6 and the concluding assurance διὰ θεοῦ (*dia theou*, through God) at the end of v. 7 together define the theological scope of the entire argument.

Therefore, Paul can simply define the content of the change from paganism to Christ as knowledge of God (vv. 8–9). It would be a mistake, however, to treat the implied acceptance of monotheism as a theoretical enlightenment in the realm of metaphysics. Just as one must learn a new meaning for the word "God," so, too, the meaning of "knowledge" must be redefined. It refers to an encounter that claims the human self totally. That such an encounter can be called "knowledge" stems from the Hebrew verb *yada* (know), which can also be used as a term for sexual intercourse. Here the subject-object relationship is overturned, the relationship that determines our "scientific" concept of knowledge, making it incapable of conveying the meaning of "knowing" God. The sublation of the subject-object relationship already has its counterpart in the realm of interpersonal understanding. With respect to knowledge of God, our grammar, based as it is on a metaphysics of substance, proves totally inadequate and begins to come apart. Knowledge of God is grounded in God's active desire to be known. Otherwise the human search for God degenerates into a game of blindman's buff.[40] But even more important: to know God cannot mean anything other than to be known by God. This reversal is not a sudden insight on the part of Paul. It represents a fundamental theme of his theology (cf. 1 Cor. 8:2–3; 13:12). Those who know God are aware that they stand in God's presence, that God's eyes are upon them and that God is far in advance of them. The Septuagint of Ps. 139(138):16 reads: τὸ ἀκατέργαστόν μου εἴδοσαν οἱ ὀφθαλμοί σου (*to akatergaston mou eidosan hoi ophthalmoi sou*), "Thy eyes beheld me when I was yet unready" (Luther's translation). The literal meaning is: "when I was still in my native state"—the sense in which the rare adjective ἀκατέργαστος (*akatergastos*) is used—like a fallow field, like an unbaked loaf.

Measured against such knowledge of God, which takes seriously the nature of God as creator, what meaning can the gods have that one makes for oneself and are therefore impotent? They represent nothing more than the power of the creature and therefore have only the power that those who fall into their power ascribe to them. To attempt to influence God by works of the law instead of trusting in what he does and being oneself a work of God is pure paganism, even when it appeals to the Torah. Not only is an article of faith imperiled, but faith itself is cast away. Not only is the outcome of Paul's missionary labors changed, but all his labors have been made in vain. My concern is "over you," Paul emphasizes, sounding the note of love.

The History Shared by the Apostle and the Galatians

4:12–20

12 Brethren, I beseech you, be as I am, for I also am as you are. You did me no wrong.
13 You know that I preached the gospel to you at first in bodily infirmity.
14 For although my condition was a trial to you, you did not scorn me or spit in my presence, but received me as an angel of God, as Christ Jesus.
15 What has become of the satisfaction you felt? For I bear you witness that, if possible, you would have plucked out your eyes and given them to me.
16 Have I become your enemy by telling you the truth?
17 They make much of you, but for no good purpose; they want to shut you out, that you may make much of them.
18 For a good purpose it is always good to be made much of, and not only when I am present with you,
19 my little children, with whom I am again in travail until Christ be formed in you!
20 I could wish to be present with you now and speak movingly to you, for I am perplexed about you.

These verses appear to interrupt the course of the argument, which is taken up for the last time in 4:21–31 and concluded with another scriptural proof. But is the personal element that suddenly takes over here really irrelevant to what Paul is about? His concern for the gospel and his concern for others are two sides of the same coin. And this is true not just with respect to his general intent but with concrete reference to these very people who are so close to him, whose fate is interwoven with his own like that of a mother and her children. Even if one were to emphasize one-sidedly the emotional element, which does indeed run high here, and speak of an argument from the heart, this would still not be inappropriate. When others have been won to grace and are then lost to it once more, the one who knows he is responsible suffers a heartbreak that can be likened only to the tears and devotion of a mother. Commenting on v. 11, Luther already says: "Lachrymas Pauli haec verba spirant" (In these words one hears Paul's tears).[41] But Paul does not merely give vent to such emotions as disappointment and bitterness, as we might expect. He charges the Galatians to remember what they have shared. Could anything carry more weight than what people have gone through together?

When this observation suggested the title "The History Shared by the Apostle and the Galatians" for 4:12–20, it is true that I was already thinking of the next section (4:21–31). At first glance it seems so different from the present section that many exegetes are only able to interpret the transition from the one to the other as an interruption, a break in dictation. Of course, we must reckon with the possibility of such a break and even with the eventuality that it might have influenced Paul's train of thought. But the general character of Paul's epistolary style makes it difficult to accuse him of being so distracted as to forget where he had left off. The juxtaposition of this warm personal passage and the somewhat contrived allegory of the two sons of Abraham (4:21–31), which breathes an atmosphere of intellectual chill, is quite abrupt. For the moment we shall put aside the question of how to understand this juxtaposition. But it does not appear accidental that the subject discussed in each case is the problem of a shared history of conflict, involving in the first section the apostle and the Galatians, in the second the slaves and the free. But let us not anticipate by suggesting further parallels.

The structure of vv. 12–20 creates difficulties. It is easy to see that v. 12 is an introduction, followed by a recollection of the past (vv. 13–15). To this moving picture of solidarity is contrasted the sad present fraught with dissension (vv. 16–17). Finally, Paul turns an anxious gaze to the future (vv. 18–20). Beyond this, we would be open to the suspicion of pedantry if we were to examine such a text looking for the logical connection between each sentence and the next. I suspect that a different organizing principle is at work here, a kind of chaining in which some associations are antithetical and others are based on direct repetition of the same catchword. Thus, the catchword $\dot{\alpha}\delta\iota\varkappa\epsilon\tilde{\iota}\nu$ (adikein, do wrong: v. 12) is followed by a reference to acts of love (vv. 13ff.); $\dot{\alpha}\lambda\eta\vartheta\epsilon\dot{\upsilon}\epsilon\iota\nu$ (aletheuein, tell the truth: v. 16) is contrasted with manipulative zeal ($\zeta\eta\lambda o\tilde{\upsilon}\nu$, zeloun, make much of: v. 17). Or as contrary examples: the $\zeta\eta\lambda o\tilde{\upsilon}\nu$ that has no good purpose (v. 17) is followed by zeal for a good purpose (v. 18), and the idea of separation—both physical and spiritual—is followed by the desire to be present (v. 20). But no further importance will be attached to this approach; it would have to be tested by more detailed analysis and by critical stylistic comparison with similar texts. With respect to content, its major contribution would be to prevent us from looking for associations that are not present.

Neither is it possible to treat the individual exegetical problems that make it so difficult to translate this text with the thoroughness they deserve. I shall only cite a few examples and without discussing in each case the entire range of problems and possibilities.

The very first sentence (v. 12) presents a problem. In my opinion, there is no reference to some particular act. Paul is appealing to the existing bond of solidarity, which he expects the Galatians to enter into just as he has done. In such general imperatives, the verb γίγνεσθαι (*gignesthai*, become) can simply have the meaning "be," as many passages attest (e.g., Matt. 10:16: "Be wise as serpents and innocent as doves"). It must be noted, of course, that the equation established by this sentence does not involve equal parties. The idea of mimesis indicates that the apostle is the controlling factor.

In v. 13, δι' ἀσθένειαν (*di' astheneian*, in or on account of weakness) has given rise to much analysis. According to Attic usage, this use of διά (*dia*) would have to indicate the reason why Paul first preached the gospel to the Galatians. Bodily infirmity or sickness might be involved if Paul stayed in the region for some time instead of journeying on as planned. More likely to me seems the hypothesis of colloquial usage in which διά (*dia*) with the accusative introduces the circumstances under which the apostle carried out his missionary work among the Galatians. At least this is what is stressed in the discussion that follows.

The question as to what kind of sickness may have been involved has given rise to much speculation, but there is no evidence to suggest a convincing answer. It is possible, but by no means certain, that Paul's eyes were affected. The "eyes" may simply be a proverbial expression for the most precious possession anyone can have, which the Galatians were ready to sacrifice for Paul.

Interpretation of the metaphor in v. 19 is very complex; closer examination reveals its extraordinarily broad implications. Have two ideas been telescoped here—the notion that Paul is giving birth to the Galatians a second time as his spiritual children and the notion that there is also a birth going on within them, namely that of Christ himself? Is the dominant idea a Christ mysticism, or is Paul speaking quite soberly of didactic instruction in the proper understanding of Christ? In any case, the two poles appear together here: the suffering of the apostle in his devotion to his communities, which is crucial to his very existence, and the necessity that the spiritual life of the communities not be surrendered to whim, but be patterned after the model of Christ.

Finally, the expression ἀλλάξαι τὴν φωνήν μου (*allaxai tēn phōnēn mou*, literally: change my voice) seems to be hard to find an English equivalent for rather than presenting a true problem of interpretation. The attempt to see Paul as saying he would like to impress the Galatians by speaking in tongues I do not find convincing. I interpret the phrase in strictly human terms and therefore render it freely as "speak movingly to you."

In fact Paul is already doing just this. In this passage he shows what a range the instrument of his language has and how skillfully he knows how to employ it. We are not dealing simply with a series of unconnected statements. There is a constant interplay between the addressees and the writer. Or to shift to an optical metaphor: Paul displays himself to the Galatians in the shifting colors of this mutual relationship. The play of light and shadow that they cast on him he reflects back in strange refractions and transformations as he receives and returns it. Paul's own features are reflected in what he says here about the Galatians. The result is an uncommonly vivid picture, which reveals him to us more clearly than if we had a portrait of him or had him as a contemporary before our eyes.

Perhaps in direct confrontation we would react to his appearance κατὰ σάρκα (kata sarka, according to the flesh) quite the opposite of the way the Galatians reacted, to the astonishment of Paul himself. We would probably not spit as an apotropaic gesture in the presence of this sinister man, whose sickness has something demonic about it. But we would probably find his mere outward appearance highly unappealing. But the distance created through the medium of the written word, the process of filtering and spiritualization, make it easier to see the essential point.

Let us illustrate what we mean through the example of the various roles in which Paul appears. First, he appears as supplicant (v. 12). He does not feel injured or aggrieved, as though deserving an apology. He does not level charges and does not presume on his authority. He beseeches the Galatians as their brother not to be untrue to themselves but to hold fast to what they have become through their encounter with him. He presents himself to them in his weakness, just as he appeared among them initially afflicted with weakness (v. 13). But he became their debtor for what they gave him. This was anything but a matter of course. And he still has a sense of indebtedness and gratitude to them. After all that has happened, this is certainly not a matter of course. But has love on the part of the Galatians turned into hate (v. 15)? He comes to them in the guise of an enemy, although his intentions toward them are unexceptionable (v. 16). Here, of course, we come face to face with the role that one takes on in the eyes of others. The Galatians may well have seen a threat—"Now let me tell you the real truth!"—in the refusal to compromise that is itself an act of love.

And so Paul now appears in the role of a rejected suitor (vv. 17–18). His opponents have outstripped him through their zeal, and the Galatians have been unable to tell the difference between selfishness and love. He is back where he started (v. 19). As their spiritual mother he must suffer their birth pangs once more if they are indeed to be born to the life that Christ lives in them (cf. 2:20).

It is in this spirit that Paul writes his letter. It is natural for someone writing a letter to think of those addressed as a mother thinks of her children, to long to be with them in person and speak with them directly (v. 20a), and for this very reason to try to use the written word to bridge the gap. But a letter perforce suffers a disadvantage: it cannot evoke an immediate reaction. It requires the writer to wait for an answer, sometimes at great length and occasionally in vain. In such a situation, therefore, the writer's perplexity is evident (v. 20b).

The History Shared by the Slaves and the Free

4:21-31

21 Tell me, you who desire to be under the law, do you not hear the law?
22 For it is written that Abraham had two sons, one by a slave and one by a free woman.
23 But the son of the slave was born according to the flesh, the son of the free woman through promise.
24 Now this is an allegory: these women are two covenants. One is from Mount Sinai, bearing children for slavery; she is Hagar.
25 For the word Hagar in Arabia refers to Mount Sinai. This corresponds to the present Jerusalem, for she is in slavery with her children.
26 But the Jerusalem above is free, and she is our mother.
27 For it is written: "Rejoice, O barren one that dost not bear; break forth and shout, thou who art not in travail. For the children from the desolate are many, far more than the children of her who hath a husband."
28 But you, brethren, like Isaac, are children of promise.
29 But as at that time he who was born according to the flesh persecuted the one who was born according to the Spirit, so it is now.
30 But what does the Scripture say? "Cast out the slave and her son. For the son of the slave shall not inherit with the son of the free woman."
31 So, brethren, we are not children of the slave, but of the free woman.

The desire to be present instead of just writing a letter, coupled with the confession of total perplexity, signals that the body of the letter is drawing to its close. But it would not chime with Paul's sense of faith and mission to close with an expression of resignation. Quite the contrary. In order to conclude his argument he brings it to a new height from which the parenetic conclusion opens a broad and liberating perspective on Christian life. Awkward as this second approach may appear, it has much in common with what has gone before.

It would not be hard to establish a connection with the abrupt conclusion of the preceding section (v. 20): you have left me so perplexed that I do not know what to think or say; now you tell me (Λέγετέ μοι, legete moi: v. 21) how things stand. And be guided entirely by the Torah, to which you want to be subject. In his perplexity, the apostle asks the Galatians for their own verdict on the basis of their own principles. This approach is perfectly adapted to the previously established tone of motherly love. He does not want to give the impression of wanting to run roughshod over them and seeking to force his views on them in an authoritarian manner. In their answer they should not go beyond what seems clear to them. Thus, the argument returns formally to its point of departure. In 3:1–5, Paul began with the evidence of the Galatians' experience of the Spirit; now once again he challenges them to realize the consequences of what anyone who recognizes the Torah should easily be able to accept.

The new demonstration from Scripture likewise returns to the beginning. Like 3:6ff., it speaks once again of Abraham. Now, however, even the outward form of the argument is different. In contrast to the extremely abstruse and demanding interpretation in 3:6–14, we find here an unusually clear and vivid picture, capable of impressing even the simplest soul. The earlier passage dealt with the highly abstract relationship between God and Abraham, between promise and law, between the curse decreed for failure to fulfill the law and the curse on him who hangs on a tree; here a handful of individuals appear as characters in a familiar narrative: two women of entirely different social status and two sons who differ not only in their inherited social status but in their human individuality. And the outcome of the ensuing dramatic narrative is a clear separation that illustrates a definitive decision.

This climax is marked not only by simplicity of form but also by clarity of scope. The banner of freedom is unfurled as a symbol summarizing the whole. Up to this point the catchword ἐλευθερία (*eleutheria*, freedom) has appeared only once: in the account of the apostle's second journey to Jerusalem (2:4), where it stands programmatically for what he had to defend against the hostile and suspicious gaze of his opponents: "our freedom which we have in Christ Jesus." In the central argument, however, although the contrasting concept of slavery already spoken of in 2:4 is mentioned several times (δοῦλος, *doulous*: 4:1, 7; δουλοῦσθαι, *doulousthai*: 4:3; δουλεύειν, *douleuein*: 4:8–9), the concept of freedom is not mentioned. Of course both had to be involved, but the image of subjection dominated, characterized above all by the frequent use of the preposition ὑπό (*hypo*, under) with various accusative objects: the curse, sin, the law, the παιδαγωγός (*paidagōgos*), the guardians and trustees, and the στοιχεῖα τοῦ κόσμου (*stoicheia tou kosmou*, elemental spirits of the universe). But there were also several suggestions of liberation: in the catchword "redeem" (ἐξαγοράζειν, *exagorazein*: 3:13; 4:5), in the concept of being sons and heirs (especially in 3:26 and 4:5, 7), in the emphasis on the definitive epoch marked by the coming of faith, the sending of the Son, and the sending of the Spirit, and finally by the focus on the role of the deliverer marked by the adverbial particle οὐϰέτι (*ouketi*: 3:25, "no longer under a custodian"; 4:7, "no longer a slave"). No longer—one might almost say, to emphasize the sense of release, never again!

The basic theme of chapters 3 and 4 is not yet fully conceptualized. The abstract noun ἐλευϑερία (*eleutheria*, freedom) makes its appearance like a comet in 5:1. It is preceded, however, by the concrete antonyms παιδίσϰη (*paidiskē*, [female] slave) and ἐλευϑέρα (*eleuthera*, free woman) in vv. 22 and 31. Not as in 3:28, though, where the antithesis between slave and free is overcome in Christ. The immediate reference of the two words here is likewise to social status, but they immediately take on transcendent spiritual meaning. Here, therefore, the antithetical concepts of slavery and freedom are represented as being definitively separated in Christ (cf. vv. 30–31). Even where the concept of ἐλευϑερία (*eleutheria*, freedom) is practically demanded (v. 26) as the antonym to δουλεία (*douleia*, slavery: v. 24), Paul does not go beyond the statement that the free woman is our mother. In parallel to the phrase εἰς δουλείαν γεννῶσα (*eis douleian gennōsa*, bearing children for slavery: v. 24) he does not use the expected formula εἰς ἐλευϑερίαν γεννῶσα (*eis eleutherian gennōsa*, bearing children for freedom). He obviously holds back because he intends not to introduce and develop the concept ἐλευϑερία itself until the last section, to which the story of Hagar and Sarah merely provides a prelude.

We can summarize Paul's interpretation briefly. Initially he cites the story as a whole, with particular reference to Genesis 21 and allusions to Genesis 16 and 17. As in a fresco, he brings out only the points that are important to his purpose, passing over details and distracting subsidiary motifs like the fact that Abraham also had other sons. Only toward the end (v. 30) does he actually quote the text of the Abraham story (Gen. 21:10). Substantially more important is the quotation from Isa. 54:1 interpolated in v. 27. The promise from Deutero-Isaiah for the people of God Paul takes as referring to the descendants of Sarah. When he describes the language of the Genesis text (not, be it noted, his own interpretation!) as allegorical, he adopts a concept common in Hellenistic hermeneutics, which had gained popularity in diaspora Judaism especially through the influence of Philo. In our terminology, he is combining typological exegesis with allegorical interpretation, as illustrated especially by his association of the name "Hagar" with the Sinai covenant. The specific problems raised by v. 25 and the historical aspects of the hermeneutics employed can be looked up in any commentary. We shall merely point out the major stages in Paul's interpretation.

The statement that Abraham had two sons, one by his slave Hagar and one by a free woman, his wife Sarah, is only a kind of peg to hang the discussion on. Paul is already engaged in interpretation, not just quotation: παιδίσκη (*paidiskē*, [female] slave) appears frequently in the Genesis text, but ἐλευθέρα (*eleuthera*, free woman) is added by Paul himself as a correlative, not only in the quotation in v. 30 but also throughout the entire Genesis story of Abraham. He here reveals his exegetical purpose, even though the interpretive term ἐλευθέρα is fully justified by the context. The specifically theological accent, however, does not appear until Paul defines the two modes of birth. The former was κατὰ σάρκα (*kata sarka*, according to the flesh), the latter διὰ τῆς ἐπαγγελίας (*dia tēs epangelias*, through promise). The birth of Isaac was already considered a miracle by Jewish interpreters. Neither they nor Paul, however, interpret it as having anything to do with a virgin birth, which would in fact be contrary to the basic concept of being offspring of Abraham. As the opposite of κατὰ σάρκα (*kata sarka*, according to the flesh) we do not find κατὰ πνεῦμα (*kata pneuma*, according to the Spirit) until v. 29. The initial appearance of the promise in this role here shows that the miracle is not simply a supernatural event but rather the promise that precedes the birth and continues to be associated with it. In this polarity κατὰ σάρκα does not mean something belonging entirely to the natural realm, but rather the absence of the promise.

Now it is conceivable that Paul might be content with this distinction and merely locate his earlier statements about what it means to be children of Abraham within the antithetical schema defined by the two sons of Abraham. But in fact he uses this antithesis merely as a point of departure for the second crucial step. He sees in the two women historico-theological types of two διαθῆκαι (*diathēkai*, covenants, dispensations). From Hagar he traces the line not just to Sinai but to the earthly Jerusalem, and from Sarah to the heavenly Jerusalem, without actually mentioning the logically necessary middle term, the revelation of Christ.

Thus he achieves his real purpose. The Jewish interpretation is turned on its head. The lines of tradition now literally "cross." The Hagar-Ishmael line, leading historically to the Arabs, now leads to the Jews; the Sarah-Isaac line, however, where the Jews have their genealogical locus, leads to the Christians. This reversal is supported with respect to the Jews by the argument that they are in slavery (v. 25) and with respect to those who have faith in Christ by the quotation from Isaiah, which sets up a contrast between spiritual and eschatological genealogy on the one hand and natural birth on the other. The difference between the two modes of birth indicated in v. 23 is in fact heightened: the natural role of the male and the natural process of birth are set in contrast to a totally different type of reproduction—but again having nothing to do with parthenogenesis. Spiritual reproduction is appropriate to the motherhood of the heavenly Jerusalem.

This notion of a heavenly Jerusalem derives from Jewish apocalyptic. For Paul it refers neither to something that will one day replace the earthly Jerusalem nor to something that will come down from heaven at the end of time; it is a radical eschatologizing of the heavenly commonwealth to which Christians already belong on earth (Phil. 3:20). With the statement that it is here that the Galatians have their locus within the two lines of tradition Paul brings his interpretation to a temporary close (v. 28).

The final stage that follows incorporates the persecution motif. It is distantly related to Gen. 21:9. Jewish interpretation already took the "playing" (παίζειν, *paizein*) mentioned there as meaning harassment. The persecution in which Paul had once participated actively and to which he is now himself exposed (5:11; 6:17) is a sign that those who suffer it are among the sons of the free woman. In contrast to what Paul says later in Romans, there is no suggestion that Israel will be reconciled and finally come to share in salvation. The entire section is dominated by antitheses; it ends with proclamation of a definitive separation as God's will (v. 30). This either/or of slavery or freedom is the goal toward which the fundamental theological argument of Galatians has been moving (v. 31).

Galatians 5—6
EXHORTATION

Freedom in Danger

5:1–12

1 For freedom Christ has set us free; stand fast therefore, and do not submit again to a yoke of slavery.

2 Behold I, Paul, say to you: if you receive circumcision, Christ will be of no advantage to you.

3 I testify again to all who receive circumcision that they are bound to keep the whole law.

4 You are severed from Christ, you who would be justified by the law; you have fallen away from grace.

5 For through the Spirit, by faith, we wait for the hope of righteousness.

6 For in Christ Jesus neither circumcision nor uncircumcision is of any avail, but faith working through love.

7 You were running well; who hindered you from obeying the truth?

8 This persuasion is not from him who called you.

9 A little yeast leavens the whole lump.

10 I have confidence in the Lord that you will take no other view than mine; and he who is confusing you will bear his judgment, whoever he is.

11 But if I, brethren, still preach circumcision, why am I still persecuted? In that case the stumbling block of the cross has been removed.

12 I wish those who unsettle you would castrate themselves!

Parenesis is an integral part of Paul's letters. This is a recent term of form criticism, to the best of my knowledge introduced by Martin Dibelius.[42] The noun παραίνεσις (parainesis) does not occur in the New Testament, but the verb παραινεῖν (parainein, address, admonish, exhort) is found, albeit only twice: Acts 27:9, 22. The roughly synonymous verb παρακαλεῖν (parakalein, summon, admonish, exhort, cheer, comfort) along with the noun παράκλησις (paraklēsis, admonishment, exhortation) is much more heavily represented in New Testament usage. The phenomenon is of course not dependent on occurrences of a particular word; neither is it limited to a sharply defined literary genre. Parenesis can appear within doctrinal passages. What is actually characteristic of the form is its tendency to appear as a conclusion, albeit varying greatly in length. Second Corinthians, for example—at least in its present form, which is probably not identical with the original—is concluded in 13:11–12 by a very few exhortations. Romans, on the other hand, provides the classic example. There the doctrinal section (chapters 1—11) is followed by an extensive parenetic section beginning with chapter 12. Galatians, too, includes a substantial parenetic conclusion. In proportion to the entire epistle it is even more important than the parenesis in Romans, since the doctrinal section of Galatians is limited to the instruction in chapters 3 and 4.

Paul's purpose in making this distinction between instruction and exhortation and placing them in this order will be examined later. First, we shall address the question of where our third section begins and ends. The first two sections we designated "Recollection" and "Instruction"; this section we have entitled "Exhortation." Paul's *postscript* in his own handwriting (6:11–18) naturally occupies a special position. In terms of subject matter it could certainly be included with the hortatory section; narrowly defined, however, the latter extends only through 6:10. There is general agreement on this point.

There is no agreement, however, about where the parenesis begins. Many exegetes locate the caesura before 5:13, taking 5:1–12 as the conclusion of the second major section. It is possible to go back even further: certain echoes of 1:6–9 suggest that 5:1–12 concludes both major sections. The fact that 5:1–12 introduces some new accents could be interpreted as evidence for its functioning either as a conclusion or an introduction. In any case, these verses constitute the hinge that links the two major sections: doctrine and parenesis.

Of the new accents that appear in this section I have already mentioned the first: not until this point (v. 1)—but now with full emphasis—is the theme of freedom taken up, with use of the words ἐλευθερία (*eleutheria*, freedom) and ἐλευθεροῦν (*eleutheroun*, set free). This theme has been in the air, as it were, all along, but was explicitly sounded only in 2:4 and given its prelude in 4:21–31. A second new catchword is ἀγάπη (*agapē*, love: v. 6), which is extremely important for the discussion that follows. Once previously (2:20) the verb ἀγαπᾶν (*agapan*, love) appeared, with Christ as its subject in the context of his self-sacrifice (cf. also 1:4). Also new, finally, is the explicit mention of the role played by the question of circumcision for the Galatian communities (vv. 2, 3, 6, 11). Only the account of Paul's second visit to Jerusalem (2:3, 7, 8, 9, 12) used the words περιτέμνειν (*peritemnein*, circumcise) and περιτομή (*peritomē*, circumcision). The burning interest of the Galatians in this topic had to be touched upon constantly in our interpretation, but our knowledge of it is based entirely on its mention in this section and the later reference in 6:12–13, 15.

It is, in fact, primarily this discussion that could suggest treating 5:1–12 not as the beginning of the parenesis but as the conclusion of the doctrinal section. The notion that parenesis deals with ethical questions supports the assignment of vv. 1–12 to what has gone before. Apart from the stylistic form of exhortation and admonition, which now begins with a vengeance, there is a further observation, however, which argues for the alternative of understanding 5:1 — 6:10 as a self-contained unit.

The introductory verse (5:1) exhibits the typical structure of Pauline parenesis: an imperative develops out of an indicative: "For freedom Christ has set us free; stand fast therefore, and do not submit again to a yoke of slavery." Liberation has come through Christ, and we have been set free. It is not limited to a passing event. As something that has taken place once for all, it has made freedom the constitutive element of the life in which we now live. This is the point of the strange pleonasm in τῇ ἐλευθερίᾳ . . . ἠλευθέρωσεν (*tē eleutheria . . . ēleutherōsen*, for freedom . . . he has set free): the freedom is meant to be lived. Therefore, the indicative statement about the gift of freedom is followed by the imperative to live in freedom, not to weaken, not to be fooled, not to give way, not to return to the slavery under the law from which Christ has redeemed us. This structure is repeated twice more.

In v. 13 ("For you were called to freedom, brethren; only do not use your freedom as an opportunity for the flesh. . ."), the indicative states a call to freedom. This call does not mean a task that has just been set, a goal to be attained. The indicative of v. 1 is taken up without any limitation. We have, in fact, shared in the event of liberation through our call to be in the grace of Christ (cf. 1:6). But such a call does not effect a magical transformation, it does not transport us beyond the normal conditions of life and deliver us from life ἐν σαρκί (*en sarki*, in the flesh). Therefore, the indicative leads into an imperative to make the right use of freedom, not to abuse it so that it turns into freedom of the flesh. The result would be loss of freedom and the return of slavery.

In v. 25, finally, freedom is instead represented by the Spirit. In this variation the indicative and imperative are brought into absolute conjunction: "If we live by the Spirit, let us also walk by the Spirit." Living by the Spirit is a fact, something given. But it faces us with the task of accomplishing this life one step at a time. Being is the necessary condition that makes it possible for us to behave and to act. The life we have is not identical with the life we live, but it is the absolute prerequisite for it.

These three formally identical introductions in vv. 1, 13, and 25 give the parenesis its structure: it is an exhortation in three stages. At each stage the appeal evolves from a freedom that is not waiting to be achieved but must be preserved and lived. Everything said by way of exhortation springs from this single source. The parenesis of Galatians is a call to freedom based on freedom. But it has various nuances. The first section (vv. 1–12) is concerned with the danger the Galatians are in by virtue of the Judaizing requirement of circumcision. Here, therefore, the emphasis is on the danger to which freedom is exposed. The second section (vv. 13–24) expands the horizon to include the universal struggle of life as a conflict between flesh and Spirit. Here, therefore, the fundamental theme becomes the life of freedom in the form of freedom to love. The third section (5:25—6:10), finally, addresses specific problems arising from the common life of those who have faith, problems requiring that all must be free from and for themselves. The basic perspective here might be called concrete freedom. The captions "Freedom in Danger," "The Life of Freedom," and "Concrete Freedom" should be considered nothing more than passing emphases. Clearly, there is a danger to freedom implied in the second and third sections, just as each is concerned with how freedom is lived and how it becomes concrete. The extent to which the suggested differentiation is sustained must be determined by detailed exegesis.

This is not the place for a comprehensive discussion of the Pauline concept of freedom and its historical background.[43] As an introduction to what appears in our text, we shall mention only the major points of contact with the historical context. One of the most amazing accomplishments of Pauline theology consists in its successfully claiming the concept of freedom, which derives from Greek philosophy, for the Christian faith with quite unforeseen consequences. There is no immediate equivalent to the concept of freedom in the Old Testament or in Jewish thought. It therefore marks the point at which faith in Jesus Christ goes beyond the Old Testament and breaks its association with Judaism.

Paul's understanding of freedom has certain points of contact with the "freedom" of the Greek *polis* (e.g., the notion of παρρησία *[parrēsia]*, the right to say anything, candor), even more with the Hellenistic notion of freedom (e.g., the concepts of self-knowledge and self-control) and likewise with the incipient Gnostic understanding of freedom (e.g., the notion of liberation from the power of the elemental spirits of the universe). Nevertheless, it is not derivative but in its crucial aspects an original conception.

For him freedom is not primarily an idea but an experience. He saw its implications in an unusual combination of intuition and penetration. The basis of freedom as a new reality in the Christ event, in Jesus' loving sacrifice of himself for humanity in its wickedness, stands in striking contrast to the understanding of freedom current in Paul's world. To the extent that the term "freedom," despite its Greek roots, addresses a fundamental human problem, Greek and Jew are in agreement that freedom is the gift of the νόμος (*nomos*, law)—the νόμος of the *polis* or the Torah of God. Even in the transformation the concept of freedom undergoes in Hellenism, its relationship to the individual and simultaneous expansion to include all humanity, freedom is based on what is now an inner law. When for the Gnostics freedom becomes separation from the world, it loses sight totally of others along with the rest of creation. It turns its back on the call to take life in this world seriously and suffer it to the end. But when Paul sees freedom grounded in the crucified Christ and recognizes it as an experience based on the gift of the Spirit, he distinguishes it from all these approaches. Freedom is found not in the law, not in the individual, not in escape from the world, but in the love of Jesus Christ that we receive, which through faith in him becomes in turn the love we show to others.

Following the basic theme of Galatians, Paul begins his parenesis on freedom with the either/or of Christ as the ground of freedom on the one hand and circumcision as the fatal step backwards into slavery on the other. From our perspective this appears to be a highly specialized and (for us) wholly peripheral example. It is, therefore, not enough to stress how central the question of circumcision was in the situation and in the opinion of Paul. We must push ahead to where an analogous question becomes crucial for us. A hint appears in the extraordinary historical significance, even for us, of the either/or that Paul here displays. In our text the relationship between Judaism and nascent Christianity, at first so blurred, comes to the point of definitive separation. How different history would have been if this separation had not taken place! But that is not all. A second observation is inescapable. Paul's struggle against the opinion that circumcision is necessary for one to be a Christian and that the Christian faith is only an addition to the Torah, in short that Christianity is a Jewish sect—this struggle soon shifted its ground from the rapidly completed process of separation between Judaism and Christianity to Christianity itself. This is attested by confessional divisions to the extent that they are associated with the Christian understanding of freedom.

But we must begin at an even deeper level. The basic problem Paul addresses in the conflict over circumcision is connected with the continual conflict to which the Christian faith is exposed in this life where freedom is lived. Therefore, the theme of circumcision is followed here by a reference to the conflict between flesh and Spirit (vv. 13–24). What is thus shown to affect every Christian has an intimate connection with the question of circumcision, which seems so alien to us. But this connection can be grasped only when it is seen in the larger context of the law as a whole.

For Paul the law is the focus of all the various manifestations of human bondage: not just the need to bear the burden of its demands, but also subjection to the elemental spirits of the universe, imprisonment in sin, captivity to death. The varieties of slavery are many. But for Paul there is only a single contrasting freedom: the freedom for which Christ has set us free. Seen from this perspective, the many varieties of slavery coalesce into a single syndrome. The law is highly appropriate for diagnosing this syndrome because it is precisely in the law, which makes its appeal to human freedom, that our inability to set ourselves free becomes most obvious. Therefore, Paul insists on the totality of the law. His insistence is not based primarily on a polemic against distinguishing ceremonial and moral law. His Judaizing opponents, it is true, attached special importance to the requirement of circumcision. But it is highly improbable that they were not concerned with morality. It is more likely that they proceeded eclectically, riding certain hobby-horses in both areas of the law, as is typical of nomistic thought. This is one reason Paul insists on the totality of the law, so as to bar the escape of those who would evade the problem of how righteousness can be achieved through the law. His primary point, however, is that the law, precisely when it is understood radically and not superficially, through its ultimate demand effects the opposite of righteousness, thus demonstrating the absurdity of a soteriology that is made dependent on human achievement, that is, on flesh and blood.

Here no revision within the framework of the law can help, but only the miracle of the gospel, which Paul now (vv. 4–5) recalls in a compact string of catchwords: Χριστός (*Christos*, Christ), χάρις (*charis*, grace), πνεῦμα (*pneuma*, spirit), πίστις (*pistis*, faith), ἐλπίς (*elpis*, hope), δικαιοσύνη (*dikaiosynē*, righteousness). They all point to ἐλευθερία (*eleutheria*, freedom). It is in a sense the gift of total innocence, liberation from sin, new creation, the pure presence of God. In the face of freedom all such soteriological symbols as περιτομή (*peritomē*, circumcision) and ἀκροβυστία (*akrobystia*, foreskin, uncircumcision)—but not just these, the series could be extended indefinitely—that are valued so highly under the sign of the law lose their value totally at a single stroke, like paper money in an inflation (v. 6). Only the faith that lives through the love of Christ and thus acts in turn through love is of any value here. It is freedom in its fulfillment.

The either/or Paul inculcates here is established by the exclusivity of *solus Christus, sola gratia, sola fide*. The solemn ("Behold, I Paul say to you . . .") warning that those who mistakenly desire more will lose all this (vv. 2–6) Paul connects with an exhortation (vv. 7–12) in which he draws as sharp a line between the Galatians and their seducers (vv. 9–10) as between these latter (his opponents) and himself (vv. 11–12). Friendly, exonerating, even confident words with respect to those Paul is addressing stand in contrast to the harshest of verdicts upon the unnamed agents. The confusion they are causing suggests the διάβολος (*diabolos*, confuser, devil: v. 10b).

The sarcastic conclusion (v. 12) alludes to the Torah's demand that those who are castrated be ejected from the community (Deut. 23:2[1]), already hinted at in more general terms in the story of Hagar (4:30). It was probably far from Paul's intent to deride circumcision as such through association with castration. On the contrary, he wishes to censure the perversion circumcision has undergone at the hands of his opponents, who have turned it for their own advantage into a trap to catch others. On the other side, the notion of extending the protection of the *religio licita* to gentile Christians through circumcision may also have played a part. But Paul insists that the cross and persecution go hand in hand (v. 11; 6:12, 14). That, too, has its place in parenesis.

The Life of Freedom

5:13-24

13 For you were called to freedom, brethren; only do not use your freedom
   as an opportunity for the flesh, but through love be servants of one another.
14 For the whole law is fulfilled in one word: "You shall love your neighbor as yourself."
15 But if you bite and devour one another take heed that you are not consumed by one another.
16 But I say, walk in the Spirit, and you will not gratify the desires of the
   flesh.
17 For the desires of the flesh are against the Spirit, and the desires of the
   Spirit are against the flesh; for these are opposed to each other, to prevent you from doing what you would.
18 But if you are led by the Spirit, you are not under the law.
19 Now the works of the flesh are plain: immorality, impurity, licentiousness,
20 idolatry, sorcery, enmity, strife, jealousy, anger, selfishness, dissension, party spirit,
21 envy, drunkenness, carousing, and the like. I warn you, as I warned
   you before, that those who do such things shall not inherit the kingdom
   of God.
22 But the fruit of the Spirit is love, joy, peace, patience, kindness, good-
   ness, faithfulness,
23 gentleness, self-control; against those who are like this the law brings
   no charges.
24 And those who belong to Christ Jesus have crucified the flesh with its
   passions and desires.

The parenesis now moves on to what is commonly called ethics. The fact
that this section was preceded by what common usage would call religious
parenesis was due to the situation of acute conflict over a question of religious conduct, the correct attitude toward a particular cultic ceremony. This
problem cried out for decision. The vacillating Galatians needed more than
doctrinal instruction; they needed to be shaken up by exhortation. As we
have seen, however, more was involved than a random isolated problem
whose urgency caused it to be dealt with before the ethical exhortations,

even though in itself it is merely on a par with them or perhaps even of lesser importance. No, the question of circumcision represented a danger to freedom and hence to the revolutionary newness of Christian life. The exhortation to persist in freedom therefore concerns the prerequisite for ethical conduct as understood by Christianity. Nowhere else in Paul do we find such a systematic treatment of ethics from the ground up.

Now there is obviously a difficulty in the distinction between religious and ethical parenesis. There is a religious side to ethical questions — elsewhere as well, but certainly in Paul. Restricting ourselves to this new section, we could point to the concept of ἐλευθερία (eleutheria, freedom: v. 13), whose christological background plays a role here. We could also mention the argument based on the πνεῦμα (pneuma, spirit: vv. 16–18, 22–23), the comment on how those who belong to Jesus Christ are related to their flesh (v. 24), and finally the eschatological perspective (v. 21) that includes the concept of judgment. Using scholastic terminology we could characterize this intrusion of religious elements into ethics as formal cause (faith and freedom), efficient cause (Spirit), and final cause (kingdom of God), each of which in its own particular way shapes the material cause, human beings and the conditions under which they live.

On the other hand, we are dealing here with traditional ethical material most of which cannot be claimed to be specifically Christian. The study of so-called catalogs of virtues and vices, of which our text contains an impressive example, in particular shows that they are dependent on popular Hellenistic philosophy and Jewish morality.

But even apart from such evidence, ethics deals in any case with what is correct and honorable, what is just and good; even though it cannot be done by all and is not automatically recognized by all, it can be expected of all. Pauline ethics appears to be open to what can be required of all and what can claim to be a fundamental standard of human conduct. This is especially true in Paul's description of the fruit of the Spirit. The ethics of freedom, which is an ethics of the Spirit, obviously does not lead to moral — or even immoral — extravagance; it does not lead to an elitist in-group ethics or heroic accomplishments but to a surprisingly inconspicuous way of life that for the most part adapts to custom and the existing order. It would, nevertheless, be wrong to give the impression that ethics is merely an unspecific appendix to the Christian faith.

Following the sequence of the text, I began with the relationship between religious and ethical parenesis. Now, however, we must include in our study the larger relationship between the doctrinal section in which the kerygmatic statements were developed and the parenetic section which is concerned primarily with ethical conduct. This organizational principle of Paul's epistles, if we can call it such with a grain of salt, appears analogous to our division of theology into dogmatics and ethics. But we must avoid hasty identifications lest we miss important differences.

The phenomenon can be seen most highly developed in Galatians and Romans. What is presented in their doctrinal sections is quite comparable to what we view as the task of dogmatic theology: intellectual penetration of the statements of the Christian faith. In Paul, of course, the difference between direct kerygmatic statement and theological reflection is not as highly developed as we are accustomed to. Even in his case, however, we seem to be able to distinguish two stages. Kerygmatic language differs from the flexible and variable language of theological reflection primarily in its tendency to be reduced to fixed confessional formulas that can be handed on verbatim. We have already met such traditional elements in Galatians, some of which are pre-Pauline. This tendency toward definitive formulation must not be denigrated as a symptom of ossification. Such formulas exhibit a substantial range of variation. The salvific significance of Christ cannot be reduced to a single statement. Various stages in the early Christian process of understanding can be equally valid. Above all, the indispensable function of such formulas must be kept in mind. Like beacons they provide orientation. Or, to drop the metaphor, they provide strength and comfort in the spiritual assaults that all Christians experience and therefore need to be impressed verbatim on the memory.

The situation is different in the pareneses. As we have already emphasized, they contain much traditional material. Their linguistic shape, however, remains much more fluid. Unlike kerygmatics, ethics does not lead up to confession and liturgy. Its primary locus is not worship. Or to put it another way: it leads up to the worship that takes place in life itself (Rom. 12:1). But it does not come into competition with the worship that takes place as a distinct act. Quite the contrary, life as worship depends on the distinct act of worship if it is to be and remain worship in that extended and derived sense. It is a one-way street. Faith is constitutive for the being of Christians. It gives rise to action. There is a double accent here: faith, which determines one's being before God, comes first, while action, as conduct before and in the world, represents the consequence. But this does not imply any inferiority on the part of ethics. It is essential to faith that it be lived and take effect within life. When 5:6 states that faith works through love, this does not mean an additional demand on faith. The formula πίστις δι' ἀγάπης ἐνεργουμένη (*pistis di'agapēs energoumenē*, faith working through love) is an explicative description of the nature of faith from the perspective of ethics. As such, it does not define what makes faith a justifying faith. Thus, the Pauline distinction between interpretation of the faith and ethical exhortation reveals the distinction between two perspectives that are relevant for what it means to be human: the importance of what God does and the importance of what we do. The full theological significance of both can be grasped only on the basis of their mutual relationship, that is, when they are properly distinguished.

Despite these close ties with ethics, Pauline parenesis differs sharply from what we mean by the discipline of ethics. In Paul, ethics does not find expression in a theory of what is ethical or, more generally, in a theory of action but in an immediate summons to act in a particular way. It does not have the form of reflection on what is and should be required but the form of an imperative. This does not mean that development of the indicative statements of faith takes on the role of a theory on which to base ethical practice. Rather, if I may put it so, in both modes, teaching and exhorting, Paul "practices" the vital language that helps give life with respect to the practice of life itself.

It is, therefore, reasonable to suspect that the concept of ethics actually threatens to conceal the unique characteristic of Pauline parenesis: the direct influence of the word on the life lived by those addressed. We cannot pursue the question of whether this observation might lead to new insights for today's task of moral education, which has almost totally lost the phenomenon of imperative parenesis. From Paul's perspective, of course, speaking in the imperative can be useful only against the background of a strong indicative. Our loss of the Christian parenetic imperative is thus probably due to the impoverishment of the confessional indicative.

Now the derivation of ethical conduct from the proclamation of freedom—freedom from the law, not under the law—appears highly problematic. Paul, however, does nothing to conceal the threatened contradiction between freedom and ethical conduct, between faith and doing what is right. The gospel is the message of something absolutely new that makes all things new; he refuses to add a traditional and prosaic morality to it. Instead he reestablishes ethics on the radically new basis of freedom instead of the law. How is this to be understood?

It does sound as though Paul begins to retreat as soon as the problem of ethics comes up. "For you were called to freedom, brethren; only do not use your freedom as an opportunity for the flesh, but through love be servants of one another. For the whole law is fulfilled in one word: 'You shall love your neighbor as yourself'" (vv. 13–14). That the ethical problem here is not just theoretical but arises out of an egregious occasion is suggested by Paul in the following sentence: "But if you bite and devour one another take heed that you are not consumed by one another" (v. 15). This clearly reflects what is happening in the Galatian communities. There is moral chaos. But what is the reason? Is the message of freedom to blame, so that (as Paul seems to hint) freedom has been abused to gratify the lusts of the flesh, which like a beast of prey paces about its cage waiting for the chance to get loose? Has the enthusiasm that gripped the Galatians been perverted into libertinism?

Caution with respect to such interpretations is suggested by the question in 3:3, which appears to amount to the same thing but demands a very different interpretation: "Are you so foolish? Having begun with the Spirit, are you now ending with the flesh?" Here the retreat from the Spirit to the flesh, far from suggesting an outbreak of antinomianism, represents an escape into Judaizing legalism.

But how is this connected with the moral chaos Paul refers to in 5:15? Here Paul is clearly not thinking of some kind of excess but of the sad state of a community dominated by an absence of love. This may have a double cause: the apostle's preaching of freedom and the Judaizers' preaching of the law. Liberation of the gentile Galatians from bondage to the elemental spirits of the universe brought a deep sense of relief, but it could also bring a no less deep sense of insecurity as to where to find a firm anchor for life, in the face of such totally unaccustomed freedom, after the chains were removed that held the Galatians captive but also provided support. The vertigo that could result from freedom understandably made them vulnerable to an offer to fill the void by means of the Jewish Torah and transform the gospel through the law—soteriologically through circumcision, morally through specific commandments and prohibitions. Both can undermine love: inward insecurity is disturbing and leads to a desperate search for one's own identity; reversion to legalism is anxious for its own legitimation, leading to scrupulosity toward oneself and unscrupulousness toward others. Insecurity and anxiety drive out love. And so it is understandable that the additional conflict within the community as to who was right and who was wrong, Paul or the Judaizers, should lead to the free-for-all that is described mercilessly in v. 15.

In the face of this problem Paul does not make use of specific individual exhortations; these he reserves for the third section of the parenesis, which we have entitled "Concrete Freedom" (5:26—6:10). It is significant that, apart from the brief allusion in v. 15, Paul initially ignores the particular situation of the Galatians completely and goes back to the fundamental ethical problem. But how does he meet it? At first glance he seems himself to be taking the way of the law. Clearly, freedom must now be limited, its scope restricted (μόνον μή, *monon mē*, only do not: v. 13). Even the ominous antonym of freedom, service as a slave (δουλεύειν, *douleuein*: v. 13) is suddenly used in a positive sense. And what is most astonishing—the law itself is clearly called upon as an authority (v. 14), a development taken further in 6:2 by the phrase ὁ νόμος τοῦ Χριστοῦ (*ho nomos tou Christou*, the law of Christ). The concepts become confused after such insistence on antitheses: "But the law does not rest on faith" (3:12); "Christ redeemed us from the curse of the law" (3:13); "But now that faith has come we are no longer under a custodian" (3:25). And just a few verses before: "You are severed from Christ, you who would be justified by the law; you have fallen away from grace" (5:4). But what looks like a self-contradiction, indeed a contradiction of all Paul has said, turns out to embody Paul's crucial ethical realization. It compels us once more to define the Pauline understanding of the law more precisely.

Christian freedom is freedom to love and therefore freedom to serve. According to Paul, this is the Magna Charta of Christian ethics. Here something totally new has taken the field in competition with every previous answer to the question of the nature of morality. The point is the relationship between ἐλευθερία (*eleutheria*, freedom) and δουλεία (*douleia*, slavery). They are not mutually exclusive; they are complementary even in terms of the self-seeking freedom sought by those who transgress the law and the slavery that holds people in bondage to sin and the elemental spirits of the universe and thus also to the law. In Paul's statement freedom and service appear to be contradictory, united only paradoxically in Jesus Christ; in truth, however, they are totally identical in him. For the freedom from those powers attained and given through Jesus Christ is the freedom he himself lived and gave to us, freedom to give ourselves in love to our neighbors even when they seem to stand very far away as our enemies. Rightly understood, the dialectic of freedom and slavery (in a positive sense of the words δοῦλος [*doulos*] and δουλεύειν [*douleuein*]) found with so many variations in Paul is not a dialectic at all, but a simple and clear situation. Freedom is freedom only as love, and love is love only as freedom. To serve one another in love does not limit freedom. It is rather the unfolding and fulfillment of freedom. The very warning not to let freedom become an opportunity for self-emancipation of the flesh does not lead to a demand to rein in freedom and limit it but to encouragement to live the freedom opened through Christ to the uttermost, after the model of Christ. If it needs to be hedged about with reservation and modifications, Christian freedom is misunderstood and fundamentally already lost. Note well: neither the idea of love nor the idea of freedom appears here for the first time as an ethical principle. But their unification in a single whole is something new. This is not the result of intellectual speculation but is grounded in experienced reality: the Christ who gives himself freely in love and the Spirit that sets us free for love.

What, then, is the difference between the ethics of the law and the ethics of freedom? This requires us to ask once more to what extent the freedom referred to here is freedom from the law. Paul never speaks of freedom from the law in the banal sense of abrogating the law. This is not an ethical but a christological question. If one could achieve righteousness simply by ignoring the law, Christ would have died to no purpose every bit as much as if righteousness were attainable through the law (2:21)! Christ is the end of the law (Rom. 10:4), not because he rejected it but because he accepted it and fulfilled it totally, not for his own sake but for ours. He freed us from the curse of the law (3:13), from the unfulfilled law whose dominion is hopeless slavery because those who are in bondage to sin can never redeem themselves from the law and can never be brought to true life by the law.

Although Paul appears to speak here so positively of the law, nothing in his views has changed. Note first that both before and now he says: "If you are led by the Spirit you are not under the law" (v. 18). Second, when he refers to the law here it is the fulfilled law (v. 14). For the statement that the law is fulfilled in a single word, namely the law of love (Lev. 19:18), really does not answer the question of an abbreviated law, a compendium that would reduce the 613 commandments and prohibitions (according to Pharisaic count) to a single sentence. Being unfulfilled, this one commandment involves the same burden and the same curse as the entire law. The expression "fulfill" has associations that go infinitely beyond a mere intellectual summation: a fulfillment that silences the demand and the curse. Therefore, the one implies the other. If true love is present, there is no requirement of the law that is not fulfilled and settled.

This is also the basis on which one must understand Paul's strange expression ὁ νόμος τοῦ Χριστοῦ (*ho nomos tou Christou*, the law of Christ: 6:2). Whether Paul has here borrowed and reinterpreted a slogan of his opponents or formulated the expression himself with polemic intent, the result is the same. In Rom. 8:2 he speaks analogously of the Spirit of life in contrast to the law of sin and death. Paul can certainly express himself thus on occasion, thanks to his sovereign control over his own language. But he is not introducing a terminology that can be systematized, as though one could substitute νόμος (*nomos*, law) for εὐαγγέλιον (*euangelion*, gospel).

It is, therefore, justified to distinguish the ethics of the law and the ethics of freedom as follows. The former is based on unfulfillment, on the driving force of a demand. The latter is based on fulfillment, on the driving force of the Spirit. The former seeks to attain life and righteousness, the latter grows out of gratitude that life and righteousness have been granted by grace. The former must pay laborious heed to infinite detail, never attaining the whole. The latter knows the spontaneity of the Spirit through which the whole is grasped joyfully in the singular detail. The former necessarily concentrates on agents and their actions because they can never be sure of themselves. The latter counts on the self-forgetfulness of agents who enjoy freedom from themselves, concentrating entirely on who needs the agents and their actions.

Such a contrast does not fully grasp the problem of ethics as long as people believe that they can simply make a choice here or presume on their own elect status, so that the ethics of the law can be entirely ignored. Christians also bear responsibility for the non-Christian world and must, therefore, consider how the problem of ethics appears to the non-Christian. In this respect much has changed through the course of church history since the beginnings of Christianity, even though ultimately there has been no fundamental change. Being under the law concerns Christians not only from the perspective of how people are to be set free but also from the perspective of how the function of παιδαγωγός (*paidagōgos*, custodian: 3:24) can be carried out as well as humanly possible. This is important for the sake of non-Christians and for living a common life with them. But it is no less important for Christians themselves. For as long as Christians live in the flesh, the epochal turning-point in sacred history, which Paul speaks of in the same chronological terms he would use for any event of secular history, although already definitively in force, is by no means definitively complete for those who are still in this life of flesh and death. Therefore, the indicative must be followed by an imperative. If we go beyond Paul's Christian parenesis and engage in the business of theoretical ethics, above all in our time, we are faced with the task not merely of contrasting the alternative ethics of freedom and the law, but of relating them to each other so that in the ethics of freedom the ethics of the law is considered, and the ethics of the law is promoted by the ethics of freedom.

This touches on the problem of transposing a chronological sequence of two ages of sacred history into a simultaneous conflict of two ages. This problem already makes itself felt in our text. Christians—Christians above all!—are engaged in the struggle between flesh and Spirit (vv. 16–18). Paul is not referring here to two elements of human nature but to two powers whose battleground is the human self. "Flesh" thus refers to everything that human beings are and accomplish by their own power. It is not limited to corporeality; it includes what is intellectual and spiritual to the extent that it is controlled by sinful human self-centeredness and misused for self-legitimation. The category "flesh," therefore, includes religious striving for justification through the law. "Spirit," on the contrary, is everything wherein God's presence rules in the human sphere and influences it. I am deliberately using this seemingly vague formulation in order to leave open a vexing problem of Pauline exegesis. Verses 16–18 cry out for comparison with Rom. 7:15–23. In the latter passage, modern exegetes are nearly unanimous that Paul is speaking of humanity before Christ; it is indisputable, however, that here Paul has Christians in mind. Such a shift in accent may in fact be important to note, despite the similarity of the statements about those trapped in contradiction who cannot do what they would. I would nevertheless suggest that in Romans 7, too, the so-called Christian interpretation has something to be said for it, just as here in Galatians 5 there is also an element of universal anthropology. But I must let the matter rest with this suggestion.

For the way in which Paul approaches the problem of ethics, the following must be emphasized in the light of the antithesis between flesh and Spirit. He does not base ethics on any desire for or confidence in an uncorrupt human nature. Neither does he base it on good will, which, even if present, turns out to be powerless. Neither, as we have seen, does he base it on the requirements of the law, even though the law is to be taken seriously, precisely because of the power with which it holds us captive coupled with its powerlessness to make us the people it requires us to be. Paul instead approaches ethics from our situation before God, the situation of sinners to whom grace has been shown. This situation is seen correctly only when both are taken seriously: sin and grace, the power of the flesh and the power of the Spirit, described by Paul as the Spirit of the Son of God (4:6).

For Paul, therefore, the ethical realm as such is far from being a realm of triumphs; it is rather a realm of repeated defeats, in which, however, the Spirit cries out "Abba," making this clear: "Those who belong to Christ Jesus have crucified the flesh with its passions and desires" (v. 24). This execution has been commanded and introduced. But the process lasts as long as life ἐν σαρκί (*en sarki*, in the flesh) endures, not in order to subjugate it by violence or even shorten it arbitrarily, but in order to allow the fruit of the Spirit to gain the upper hand over the works of the flesh. From advocates of death we are to be made witnesses on behalf of life.

Paul's inclusion here of a so-called catalog of vices together with a so-called catalog of virtues (vv. 19–23) does not follow directly from the traditional genre. It must be considered both with reference to those addressed and in the context of the ethics of freedom.

Both in particular details and in the stylistic form as a whole, there are many points of contact with traditional morality. Closer examination, however, reveals certain unmistakably Pauline features. In contrast to other similar series of ethical contrasts, Paul does not mention specific kinds of proper conduct or moral behavior, divided into vices and virtues. For this reason the usual designation of these series as catalogs of vices and virtues is misleading. But neither does he speak merely of individual acts as occasions for casuistic interpretation. He describes throughout human conduct that does not fit into the psychological schema of character and act but shines forth to fill the totality of life. Therefore, he is not really concerned with specifics. And how difficult it is to distinguish the twenty-four nouns occurring here with any degree of precision! Paul is, in fact, composing a picture of two sharply antithetical ways of life, thus blunting the point of the moralism that threatens to accompany such lists. Neither list is ultimately a human product; each characterizes human beings themselves as products of the power that drives them, whether the flesh or the Spirit.

If what the two catalogs have in common betrays the characteristics of Pauline thought, this is all the more true of what distinguishes them: a decision, under the sign of the antithesis between flesh and Spirit, as to the nature of being human, not simply a division within the way of being human, a split of the total person into two parts. In the one case Paul uses the concept of works to suggest that this is the outcome when we strive for self-realization on the basis of what we can do on our own. As creatures, above all as fallen creatures, we are flesh and not Spirit, as Paul knows quite well from the sober verdict of Scripture on humanity. In the other case he speaks of fruit, for what the Spirit accomplishes in and through us takes shape as the miracle of growth from the insignificant seed of the Word of God; it is the gift of fruit, not something we manufacture of ourselves. Thus we find a surprising but persuasive contrast between the world of technology, forged by human beings, and the world of nature, created by God. In Pauline thought flesh suggests what is unnatural, Spirit what is natural.

Coupled with this contrast between work and fruit we find a difference between a significant plural ("works of the flesh") and an equally significant singular ("fruit of the Spirit"). This difference is reflected in the structure of the two catalogs.

Just as there is something inherently chaotic about the works of the flesh, there is an element of chaos in the list itself. It does exhibit a certain organization, as we shall see, but it never becomes an organic whole. The series

256

could be continued indefinitely, as Paul himself suggests. If we start to describe humanity as seen from this perspective, we must finally give up in exhaustion, saying only "and the like"—and letting everything repeat all over again. Not, of course, in an eternal cycle, but limited by the coming kingdom of God, which in this context is not looked upon as the desired goal but as something that will finally put an end to such aimless drift. Although Paul uses traditional religious language in his eschatological conclusion (v. 21b), he is not just making a casual remark, but speaking with emphasis. Human history ends with the coming of the kingdom of God, but it does not pass into the kingdom of God.

The fruit of the Spirit, however, is one and indivisible. Although it is described here in three triplets, this harmonious organization (which does not end with "and the like") is meant to symbolize a perfect totality. Everything derives from love, including—and above all—joy. Joy is the seal of the Holy Spirit, although for the most part we experience the Spirit only in the profound cry "Abba, Father!" or in sighs issuing from the heart. Also an expression of love and by no means the antithesis of joy is the ἐγϰράτεια *(enkrateia)* with which Paul concludes the list: the self-control through which we forgo much that is attractive—not out of hatred and resignation, but because and insofar as it is good to do so. "A Christian," Luther remarks, "should not look on others' own rights; he should be a friendly sort whom everyone is happy to be around."[44] This picture of what it is to be a Christian, painted in the colors of a simple, natural, and kindly humanity, can only evoke delighted agreement. When Paul adds: ϰατὰ τῶν τοιούτων οὐϰ ἔστιν νόμος *(kata tōn toioutōn ouk estin nomos,* literally: against such there is no law), he is doing more than making an ironic statement that no law forbids such conduct. He is, rather, stating an eschatological conclusion analogous to the conclusion of the first catalog: the law brings no charges against people like this. Now and for all eternity, they are free from the curse of the law.

A further difference, finally, is suggested by Paul when he says, only of the works of the flesh, that they are plain. And he limits himself to works that come to public attention. This might be considered too restricted a list, making it easy for people to say that it does not apply to them. But Paul is not pursuing sin into its secret hiding place. What needs to be removed, when discovered there, is immediately clear when one applies the second catalog word for word to oneself. What, then, is the point of the first list? In comparison with the much more significant content of the second list does it not present all too coarse a picture, merely a conventional sense of what is required? Why does Paul include it in this letter?

We have almost no direct knowledge of the ethics espoused by Paul's Judaizing opponents or of the moral situation in the Galatian communities. On the basis of certain inferences, however, we can say the following: here Paul is probably in agreement with the Judaizers. The first five terms— immorality, impurity, licentiousness, idolatry, and sorcery—can all be brought under the common heading of religious aberrations typical of that period with its sometimes orgiastic cults. They are an abomination to any devout Jew. It is not by accident that the two major manifestations, πορνεία (*porneia*, [sexual] immorality) and εἰδωλολατρία (*eidōlolatria*, idolatry), are also mentioned in the so-called Apostolic Decree (Acts 15:20, 29) as something the gentile Christians should also consider prohibited. The last two items in the list, drunkenness and carousing, certainly did not have their advocates among the Judaizers either in word or in deed, even though they may not have been rigorous ascetics. There is certainly a happy medium. It is similarly most unlikely that either the first or the last items in the list had caused particular problems in the Galatian communities.

What is striking, however, is the group of eight nouns in the center of the list, all of which refer to disturbances within the community structure. Of course, there would be no one who would not condemn this in principle as well. In this case, however, as we all know, it is easy for a great gulf to exist between words and actions. And all the references to concrete examples among those addressed and the Judaizing agents point in this direction (5:15, 26; 6:1, 3–5, 12, 13). The central section of the so-called catalog of vices is therefore far from vacuous.

And there is a larger point. The expression "works of the flesh" may be meant to echo the expression "works of the law" (2:16; 3:2, 5, 10), although on the surface they refer to contraries: works that are against the law and works that are according to the law. If such an allusion is in fact intended, it would mean this: with the righteousness of the law, which attaches special importance to a ritual act affecting the flesh of the male, the Judaizers are coming perilously near the works of the flesh, which they abhor but are un- consciously close to when one understands the spiritual meaning of the term "flesh." Taken in this way, a hodge-podge of moral truisms becomes a care- ful theological verdict, revealing the interplay of dogmatics and ethics.

Concrete Freedom

5:25—6:10

25 If we live by the Spirit, let us also walk by the Spirit.
26 Let us have no self-conceit, no provoking of one another, no envy of one another.
6:1 Brethren, if anyone is overtaken in any trespass, you who are spiritual should restore that person in a spirit of gentleness. Look to yourself, lest you too be tempted.
2 Bear one another's burdens, and so fulfill the law of Christ.
3 For those who think they are something when they are nothing deceive themselves.
4 But let each test his own work, and then his reason to boast will be found in himself alone and not in others.
5 For each person will have to bear his or her own load.
6 Those who are taught the word should share all good things with those who teach.
7 Do not be deceived; God is not mocked, for what you sow, that you will reap.
8 Those who sow to their own flesh will to their own flesh reap corruption; but those who sow the Spirit will from the Spirit reap eternal life.
9 And let us not grow weary in well-doing, for in due season we shall reap, if we do not lose heart.
10 So then, as we have time and opportunity, let us do good to all, and especially to those who are of the household of faith.

It may seem inappropriate to look for internal structure in such a loose sequence of ethical maxims, most of them stated in the imperative. But if our analysis of the parenesis in 5:1—6:10 is correct, then this third section is unified by its programmatic opening statement in v. 25 (cf. vv. 1 and 13), which again justifies an imperative on the basis of an indicative. Now the "freedom" is replaced by "Spirit," on the basis of what has just been said. "If we live by the Spirit, let us also walk by the Spirit" (5:25). Earthly life is both a gift and a responsibility; so is the life given us by the Spirit.

One common thread that runs through the whole section is the ethical focus on human life in community. Every verse rings changes on this theme. The central ethical focus does not grow out of the nature of the individual personality nor out of the nature of the transpersonal situation. What is crucial is the relationship of one person to another. It is characteristic that the passage repeatedly considers the relationship of individuals to themselves and to others from the perspective of their mutual involvement. Those who would truly see and understand others must first truly see and understand themselves.

Another common thread is the focus not on instances of human solidarity in general but on aspects of life within a Christian community. Judging by the standard of contemporary ethical theory, we may consider this a narrow perspective. But if Paul's purpose is concretely to exemplify and apply the parenesis of an ethics of freedom, he must sharpen his focus and speak of specific examples, which will perforce seem to have been selected casually. Any search for concreteness will lead to specificity. That is its strength but also its weakness. If human life in community is represented by the concrete instance of the Christian community, this special case is highly instructive: there is no other form of human life together conceivable in which human polarities are comparably integrated. This holds true in the first place for the profound human differences of religious background, social class, and sexual orientation, which here simply become irrelevant even though they continue to exist (3:28). And it is also true for the conflict between flesh and Spirit, which continues throughout the lifetime of every Christian, albeit *sub specie aeternitatis*. The concrete form of the Christian community thus brings humanity uniquely together, from both an earthly and an eschatological perspective. When ethics takes concrete shape in this context, it helps visualize an extraordinary range of problems.

Within this framework, the text is organized around three specific concrete problems.

In 5:26—6:1, Paul is dealing with a universal occurrence even within the Christian community: someone not only does something wrong but is discovered, causes a scandal, and thus raises the question of how others are to respond. The concrete ethical problem does not lie in the action but in the response. In questions of faith and doctrine, as we have seen, Paul judges very strictly. Here, however, he displays surprising tolerance. Note well, however: the subject under discussion is not the undefined transgression, which is all too much a topic of discussion among those who are more or less in the know. Those who are on trial are those who have not offended. They would also be led astray if they were to behave unspiritually, displaying pride and indignation instead of helping. It is not the nature of the Spirit to judge others, but rather self-critically to stand by them when they find themselves isolated.

Verses 2–6 appear merely to continue the theme of bearing one another's burdens. But if I am right in thinking that v. 6 is not a separate maxim but belongs to this context, the exhortation is dealing with another concrete case: the relationship between catechumen and catechist. Opinions differ as to what those who are taught are specifically obligated to do. Since they are receiving the benefit, the most immediate answer is remuneration. It is well worth considering, however, whether this fits the circumstances of the contemporary Christian community and whether the expression "share all good things" does not suggest more than material payment. The experience of teachers shows repeatedly how much good they can receive from those who learn from them: through challenging expectations, through responsiveness, through affection, through the reflection of a new experience.

The call to be conscious of such an exchange of roles and enter into it, so that receiver becomes giver, would of course not be the only concrete form taken by the strangely paradoxical admonition to help bear the burdens of others precisely because each is responsible for his or her own load (cf. vv. 2 and 5). But all the associations that arise here have as their central mystery the need to be free from conceit and illusions about oneself if one is to be free for others. For this very reason it is wrong to judge oneself through comparison with others. One must judge oneself by one's own appropriate measure. Such mutual openness, in which each is responsible for himself or herself, makes possible an exchange in which even the burdens each must impose on the other become beneficent gifts.

In vv. 7–10, finally, we find a concluding concrete example: the call to use our time to do good, grasping the opportunity provided by the household in which those who have faith are joined. This does not exclude the universality of being available for others. But instead of stopping at a wide range of vague possibilities, one must respond to the demands where one's life has its concrete locus. The time available must not be wasted. It is limited. Anyone who still has a chance to sow should heed this admonition, not plunging ahead blindly but considering that the decision between flesh and Spirit is always pressing. But only at the harvest will the future decided upon be revealed. To live one's life spiritually through the power of the Spirit in the time remaining gives hope, Paul says; indeed it is the only source of hope. Those who take this course may already look forward to the harvest and are kept from premature weariness and resignation.

The Apostolic Seal

6:11–18

11 See with what large letters I am writing to you with my own hand.

12 It is those who want to make a good showing in the flesh that would compel you to be circumcised, and only in order that they may not be crucified for the cross of Christ.

13 For even those who receive circumcision do not keep the law, but they desire to have you circumcised that they may glory in your flesh.

14 But far be it from me to glory except in the cross of our Lord Jesus Christ, by which the world has been crucified to me, and I to the world.

15 For neither circumcision counts for anything, nor uncircumcision, but a new creation.

16 And all who walk by this rule—peace and mercy be upon them and upon the Israel of God.

17 Henceforth let no one trouble me; for I bear on my body the marks of Jesus.

18 The grace of our Lord Jesus Christ be with your spirit, brethren! Amen.

In the title "The Apostolic Seal" I am attempting to find a common denominator for three major elements of this *postscript:* the fact that it is written by Paul's own hand (v. 11), the summary of the letter's content in a rule (v. 16), and the reference to the stigmata of Jesus that Paul bears (v. 17).

For a letter writer to add a personal *postscript* to the fair copy of what has been dictated is nothing unusual. Nowhere else among the genuine letters of Paul, however, do we find a *postscript* of such size and importance. The desire to authenticate the letter is not a sufficient explanation. Paul's writing down his essential message in his own hand is intended to bring him close to his addressees as personally as possible, through the medium of his own handwriting, thus setting his seal once more on the content of the letter. The use of the aorist (past) tense ("I have written"), although Paul's writing only begins at that point, follows the practice of adapting the tense to the readers' perspective.

Paul is not being apologetic or ironic in mentioning the size of the letters, as though his laborer's hands were awkward or his vision poor. Even if this were the reason, he would still give another interpretation to the astonishing size of his handwriting: the readers cannot miss the impressive letters, which will touch their hearts. The letters become the symbol of the Spirit.

The rule, in which Paul summarizes the conclusion of his argument so as to provide a guiding principle for what it means to be Christian, is a criterion for what we can trust in before God. The discredited alternatives of circumcision and uncircumcision have been replaced by a new creation (v. 15). Paul describes the situation in 2 Cor. 5:17: "If anyone is in Christ, he is a new creation; the old has passed away, behold, the new has come." In effect, the concept of a new creation brings together what has taken place through the cross and resurrection of Jesus Christ, through liberation and through the Spirit: justification by faith alone.

Paul illustrates the polarity of old and new by confronting his opponents once more. There is a difference in reasons for glorying. They glory doubly in the flesh, as Paul sees it. The circumcision to be performed on the flesh of the gentile Galatians only serves the self-glorification of those who are demanding it, requiring others to be under the law while not keeping it themselves. This recalls the scriptural criterion, "Let those who glory glory in the Lord" (Jer. 9:22–23; cf. 1 Cor. 1:31; 2 Cor. 10:17). Paul glories in the Lord as the crucified Christ—a glorying that permits him to share in the cross, so that the world has lost its power over him and no longer holds him in bondage. But those who glory in the flesh shun the cross, which brings persecution. In this refusal of suffering Paul claims to have found the real key to the conduct of the Judaizers. This accounts for their both/and where Paul finds an either/or that cannot be compromised. Of course one must be on one's guard against false dichotomies. But we would show our total ignorance of how we mortals stand before God, we would mock God (cf. v. 7), if we did not see the eschatological relevance of the either/or that confronts us.

The stigmata of Jesus (v. 17) that Paul bears on his body, as slaves or animals have their owner's mark tattooed to them, are the scars of the mistreatment he has suffered for the sake of Christ. Paul reminds the Galatians of this seal of his apostleship in order to bring them truly to their senses. They have only to compare the signs of the crucified Christ found in the appearance of the Judaizers with the signs of Christ with which Paul's very body is marked.

This brings Paul to his conclusion, and this conclusion can only be a blessing. In the formulation of his rule he had already included a blessing for all who walk by it (v. 16). The expression "Israel of God" probably does not look forward to an ultimate conversion of the Jewish people, as in Romans 9—11. Here "Israel of God" means, in opposition to the claims of the Judaizers, the Christians for whom circumcision no longer matters, but only the new creation. At the end, however, Paul speaks directly to his addressees and wishes for their spirit—here meant in the anthropological sense—the presence of the grace of Christ. His last word is to call them brethren. The "Amen" is really the response expected of the Galatians.

NOTES

1. G. Ebeling, "Dogmatik und Exegese," *Zeitschrift fur Theologie und Kirche (ZThK)* 77 (1980): 269–86.

2. For further details, see below, p. 269. Cf. K. Bornkamm, "Luthers Auslegungen des Galaterbriefs von 1519 and 1531: Ein Vergleich," *Arbeiten zur Kirchengeschichte* 35 (Berlin: De Gruyter, 1963).

3. See the list of selected commentaries below, pp. 269–70.

4. Migne's *Patrologia Latina*, vol. 75, col. 515. Often cited by Luther, usually in the form: . . . *in quo agnus peditat et elephas natat* [Martin Luther, Werke. Kritische Gesamtausgabe (Weimarer Ausgabe) = WA] (WA 5,598,3f., 42,2,6f.; cf. also 49,256.8f. and WA.TR [Tischreden] 5,168,18f., No. 5468) of freely rendered as in a sermon of 1534: *Sic Gregorius et miror, wie er zu dem guten spruch: Scriptura sancta est aqua, in qua Elephas erseufft und ovis ghet in durch ut durch einen dunnen bach* (WA 37,366,36–38).

5. Schematically:

$$\overbrace{\qquad\qquad}^{\text{ἀπόστολος}}$$

Corinthians: Χριστοῦ Ἰησοῦ   Galatians: διὰ Ἰησοῦ Χριστοῦ
         διὰ θελήματος θεοῦ   καὶ θεοῦ πατρός

6. The discussion deals with these passages:

Gal. 1:1:   Gal. 1:11–12:
οὐκ ἀπ' ἀνθρώπων   οὐκ ἔστιν κατὰ ἄνθρωπον
οὐδὲ δι' ἀνθρώπου   οὐδὲ . . . παρὰ ἀνθρώπου
      ἀλλὰ κτλ.
           Amos 7:14:
οὐκ ἤμην προφήτης ἐγὼ
οὐδὲ υἱὸς προφήτου
      ἀλλὰ κτλ.

7. This would be the schema:

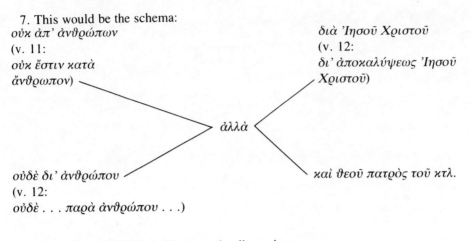

8. This diagram will help illustrate the discussion:

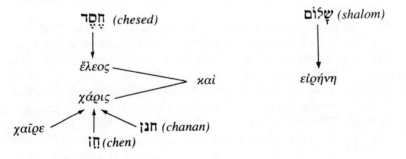

9. A diagram will once again illustrate the situation:

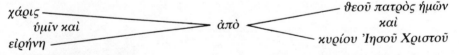

10. WA 40:1; 79:7–9.

11. WA 81:4–6.

12. WA 81:10–82:1.

13. See 28–29 above.

14. A hymn based on the eighth chapter of Romans, verse 16: "If God is for me, nothing/ Against me can arise. . . . "

15. H. Lausberg, *Handbuch der literarischen Rhetorik* (1960), 263.

16. CR 78 (*Calvini opera*, v. 50), 171.

17. See below, 104.

18. WA 40:1; 109:5–6; 110:1–3.

19. *Gnomon Novi Testamenti* on Gal. 1:8.

20. WA 40, 1; 123, 2, 6.

21. WA 40, 1; 123, 7.

22. WA 40, 1; 170, 10–11.

23. WA 40:1; 167:9—168:2: "Si Papa iuberet ein leffel milch essen, nollem, quia res seria de morte filii dei, de immensissimo, quod misit filium in carnem. Si fides credit, tum ista missio et mors est inanis. Si inanis fuisset, sic etiam deus. es gilt maiestatem divinam, vitam aeternam et mortem aeternam et man kans mit eim har versehen: 'veritatem Euangelii.' . . ."

24. See especially: E. Dinkler, "Der Brief an die Galater; zum Kommentar von Heinrich Schlier," *Verkundigung und Forschung* (1953/55), 175–83 = his *Signum crucis: Aufsatze zum Neuen Testament und zur christlichen Archaeologie* (1967), 270–80, with a bibliographical supplement, 281–82; G. Klein, "Galater 2, 6–9 und die Geschichte der Jerusalemer Urgemeinde," *ZThK* 57 (1960): 275–95; *idem*, "Die Verleugnung des Petrus," *ZThK* 58 (1961): 285–328, esp. 317–18.

25. *Widerstand und Ergebung* (1951): 246–47; new edition (1970), 382.

26. WA 2; 495:21—496:34.

27. Cf. I. Lönning, "Gal 2,11 ff als kontroverstheologisches Fundamentalproblem," *Studia theologica*, 24 (1970), 1–69.

28. WA 40:1; 324:6—327:13.

29. This structural analysis of 3:6–14 can be illustrated by the diagram on page 268.

30. Cf. my article "Fides occidit rationem; ein Aspekt der theologia crucis in Luthers Auslegung von Gal. 3:6," in *Theologia crucis—signum crucis* (Festschrift E. Dinkler) (1979), 97–135.

31. WA 40:1; 361:7–8; 362:6, 10–11; 365:4–10; 369:5–10.

32. Ibid., 360:5–6.

33. See above, 125, 137.

34. See above, 137–43.

35. WA 40:1; 471:14–15.

36. Cf. my *Dogmatik des christlichen Glaubens* (1979), 3:280–88.

37. WA 40:1; 526:2–3.

38. WA 40:1; 526:9–10.

39. WA 7; 24:13.

40. WA 19; 207:4; cited with its contents in my *Luther: Einführung in sein Denken* (1964, ⁴1981), 263–64.

41. WA 2: 542:14.

42. M. Dibelius, *Die Formgeschichte des Evangeliums* (1919, ⁵1966), 234–65; idem, *Geschichte der urschristlichen Literatur* (1926), reprinted in *Theologische Bucherei NT* (1975), 58:96, 140–48.

43. Cf. my *Dogmatik des christlichen Glaubens* (1979), 3:171–83.

44. WA 40:2; 119:1–3.

Diagram for note 29

Abraham
v. 6; quotation: Gen. 15:6

v. 7: *conclusio (γινώσκετε ἄρα ὅτι . . .)*:
   οἱ ἐκ πίστεως . . .

v. 8; quotation: Gen. 12:3; 18:18

v. 9: *conclusio (ὥστε . . .)*:
   οἱ ἐκ πίστεως . . .

Nomos

v. 10a: *propositio*:
   . . . ἐξ ἔργων νόμου . . .

v. 10b; quotation: Deut. 27:26
  (γέγραπται γὰρ ὅτι . . .)

v. 11a: *propositio*:
   . . . ἐν νόμῳ . . .

v. 11b; quotation: Hab. 2:4
  (δῆλον, ὅτι . . .)

v. 12a: *propositio*:
   . . . νόμος . . .

v. 12b; quotation: Lev. 18:5
  (ἀλλὰ . . .)

Christos

v. 13a: *causa efficiens*

v. 13b; quotation: Deut. 21:23
  (ὅτι γέγραπται . . .)

v. 14: *causa finalis*

INDEXES

Index of Biblical Passages

Index of Subjects

Abba. *See* God: the Father
Abraham, 93, 164–76, 182, 208, 232–34
Adoption, 208–9, 221
Aeon, 38–39
Anathema, 58–60
Angels, 60, 189–90
Antioch, 80, 86, 111–15, 119, 129–30, 133
Antithesis, 199, 202–3, 210, 256
Apostasy, 43–47, 156–57
Apostle, 9–17, 80, 85–86, 100, 105; false, 18
Apostolic council. *See* Jerusalem
Authority, 13–14, 20, 50, 101–2, 111

Baptism, 93, 141, 145–46, 210–13; of Paul. *See* Paul: baptism of
Barnabas, 85–87, 113
Bengel, Albert, 55
Bible. *See* Scripture
Blessing, 27–30, 56–57, 171
Body of Christ, 21, 215. *See also* Community, Christian; Unity
Bonhoeffer, Dietrich, 117–18
Brethren. *See* Brother
Brother, 20–22, 66. *See also* Child; Sons of God

Call, 19–20, 46–49, 76. *See also* Election
Calvin, John, 48
Cephas, 74, 78–80, 85–86, 100, 103–7, 109, 112–17, 119, 129–30, 135; name, 105–7
Ceremonial law. *See* Law: ceremonial
Change, 44
Chiasmus, 13, 17, 35, 37, 104
Child of God, 21, 209. *See also* Brother; Son
Christ. *See* Jesus Christ
Christ event, 31, 35, 37, 95–97, 99, 141, 172–73, 211, 217, 242
Christianity, 97, 117–18, 243
Christians, Jewish. *See* Jewish Christians
Church. *See* Community, Christian

Circumcision, 87, 89–91, 93–99, 104, 165, 240, 244–45
Clothing, 211–12
Collection, 108
Commandment, 192. *See also* Law
Communion. *See* Unity
Community, Christian, 21–23, 69, 76, 79, 88–89, 103, 113, 260–61. *See also* Unity
Congregation. *See* Community, Christian
Conversion of Paul. *See* Paul: conversion
Covenant, 96, 187, 234
Creation, 172–73
Cross. *See* Jesus Christ: crucifixion
Crucifixion. *See* Jesus Christ: crucifixion
Cursing, 56–60. *See also* Law: curse of

Death, 15–16, 25, 55, 137–48
Discrimination. *See* Antithesis
Dispensation. *See* Covenant
Distinction. *See* Antithesis

Election, 16, 49, 77, 121. *See also* Call
Emperor cult, 96
Epistle. *See* Letter
Equality, 215
Eschatology, 34, 67–68, 172, 257
Eternity, 199, 204
Ethics, 247–50, 254–55
Eucharist. *See* Lord's Supper
Experience, 47, 54, 56, 71, 77–78, 126, 154, 157–60

Faith, 66, 99, 114, 120, 122–28, 134, 143, 149–50, 159–60, 167–68, 170, 175–77, 203, 210–11, 220, 249; of Abraham, 166–67, 175–76
Fall, 45, 173
False Apostle. *See* Apostle: false
Fatherhood of God. *See* God: the Father
Favor. *See* Grace
First Commandment, 47
Flesh, 254–55

Index of Subjects

Freedom, 66, 92–93, 98–99, 113–14, 131, 147, 200–201, 215, 232–34, 240–44, 251–52

Galatia, 22
Gentile Christians, 102–3
Gentiles, 65, 87, 94–96, 117–18, 120, 165, 174, 176, 217–18
God, 46–48, 102; the Father, 28–32, 37, 222; oneness, 190, 195–96; persuasion of, 63; pleasing, 64; relationship to, 34; wrath, 58. *See also* Call; Knowledge of God
Gospel, 18–19, 37, 43–44, 46, 49–50, 54–55, 58–59, 61–62, 66–67, 71, 92–93, 97–98, 115–17, 136, 190, 215, 244
Grace, 26–33, 35–36, 47–49, 77, 108, 150, 188
Greeting, 23–29

Heilsgeschichte. *See* History, Sacred
Heir. *See* Inheritance
Hendiadys, 29
Heresy, 51
History, Sacred, 171–74, 183–84, 193, 195, 204, 207–8, 219–20, 254
Holy, The, 56–57
Holy Spirit. *See* Spirit
Hope, 201–2
Humanity, 33, 62, 66, 99, 125, 173, 186, 212, 254–55
Humility, 200. *See also* Pride

Incarnation, 29
Indifference, 93–98, 101
Inheritance, 182–83
Isaac, 166–67
Israel. *See* Jews; History, Sacred

James, 75, 79, 85, 100, 112, 114, 116
Jerome, 133
Jerusalem, 78–79, 83–88, 92, 100–103, 108, 112, 114, 235
Jesus Christ, 16–17, 28–37, 48–49, 54, 99, 114, 122, 134, 187, 190, 209, 219–20; Abraham and, 165–66, 169–70; baptism and, 213; crucifixion, 31–32, 37, 65, 132, 145, 156, 160, 167, 170, 179, 218; death of, 31, 38, 128, 139, 144; love, 144–45; Paul and, 71–72; resurrection, 15–17, 31; self-sacrifice,

38, 144–45, 179; sonship, 31–32, 208–9; union with, 149–50. *See also* Body of Christ; Christ event; Death; Eschatology; Faith; Life; Revelation
Jewish Christians, 94–97, 109, 112–14, 117, 119, 122–24, 129–31, 136
Jews, 94–96, 118, 120–21, 125, 174; children of Abraham, 164–65
Judaism, 52–53, 75–76, 117, 121, 218, 243
Judaizers, 51–55, 65, 75, 80, 86, 90–93, 96, 98, 100, 120, 135, 258
Justification, 36, 125, 127, 135, 150, 157, 196. *See also* Righteousness

Kerygma, 249
Knowledge of God, 32, 126–27, 223

Language, 57, 65, 84
Law, 36, 49, 52, 54, 57–58, 65, 76, 94, 97–99, 104, 113–14, 117–18, 120–36, 144, 147–48, 159–60, 168–71, 176–78, 182, 187–96, 200–204, 214, 243–44, 252–53, 257; ceremonial, 133–34; curse of, 172–74, 178–79, 185, 218–19. *See also* Commandment; Freedom
Letter (form), 3–8, 263
Life, 137–43, 177, 192, 198–99, 202
Liturgy. *See* Baptism; Lord's Supper
Lord's Supper, 58, 70–71, 113
Love, 93, 98, 240, 251. *See also* Jesus Christ: love
Luther, Martin, 32, 41, 54, 62–63, 84, 98, 132–33, 175, 202, 204, 220, 225

Marcion, 90
Mediation, 190
Mercy, 26
Mission of Paul. *See* Paul: mission
Moses, 189–90
Mysticism. *See* Jesus Christ: union with

Old Testament. *See* Scripture
Oneness of God. *See* God: oneness
Opponents of Paul. *See* Judaizers
Opposites. *See* Antithesis

Paganism, 51, 54, 117, 216
Parenesis, 239, 248–50
Parousia. *See* Eschatology
Paul: baptism of, 70, 78; biography of, 73–81; conversion of, 64, 68–69, 74, 77;